REWARD!

**Stranger: If you find this Diary please return it to me if I know the secret word (which is.........
...............................) and I will give you:**

☐ £1,000,000   ☐ £10,000   ☐ £100
☐ £10   ☐ £1   ☐ 10p   ☐ Nothing

Name...
Address...
....
....
Telephone..
e-mail...

CHEWING GUM PAD
(Place gum here while working on the Diary)

IS THIS DIARY A GIFT?

<u>DONOR:</u> Explore reasons for giving it here
....
....
....
....

<u>RECIPIENT:</u> Explore feelings on receiving it here
....
....
....
....

Important information about the owner of this book in case of emergency:

Blood group..
Allergies..
....
....

Name of closest relative...........................
Telephone..
Mobile..
e-mail...

DRAW YOUR PORTRAIT HERE

Fill in life preferences in case of amnesia

My favourite colour.................................
My favourite food....................................
My lucky number.......................................
My sexual orientation..............................
My best foot..
My best friend...
My most annoying habit..........................
My football team.......................................
My signature...

Fingerprints (right hand): _____

| Thumb | Index Finger | Middle Finger | Ring Finger | Little Finger |

In case of sudden death

Should I die unexpectedly, please tell:

....

(telephone...)

Confession (my worst sin):

I did..

to...

My funeral:

I want to be Buried ☐ Cremated ☐ Other ☐

Song to be played...

Epitaph..

Lasting regret..

My stuff goes to...

Dear............................... (best friend), please go to my room and remove .... from............................... before my poor mother finds it.

HOW TO USE THIS DIARY

The Diary will only help you if you want to be helped. Welcome it into your life and who knows what or who you'll be by this time next year. Ignore it and your life will continue in its current orbit. Now, of course, not everyone will be in a position to follow the instructions to the letter every day, and some are more demanding than others. But make the effort and your reward will be a year to remember, the first of many. Do not underestimate the difficulty of following the Diary. Its dictates may seem arbitrary, but only thus can we counter the arbitrariness of fate.

Life planner

1	Crucial formative influences	13	Puberty (boys)	25	
2		14	First cigarette behind bike shed	26	
3		15		27	
4		16	Exams	28	Marriage and mortgage
5		17		29	
6		18	Drink legally	30	Party
7		19		31	Settle down
8		20		32	
9		21		33	
10		22	End of youthful illusions	34	
11	Puberty (girls)	23		35	Itch (seven year-)
12		24		36	

Other

37	49	61
38	50 Party	62
39	51	63
40 Party	52	64
41	53	65
42	54	66
43	55	67
44 Midlife crisis	56	68
45 Take up golf	57	69
46	58	70 Party
47	59 Pay off mortgage	71
48	60 Retirement party	72

Other

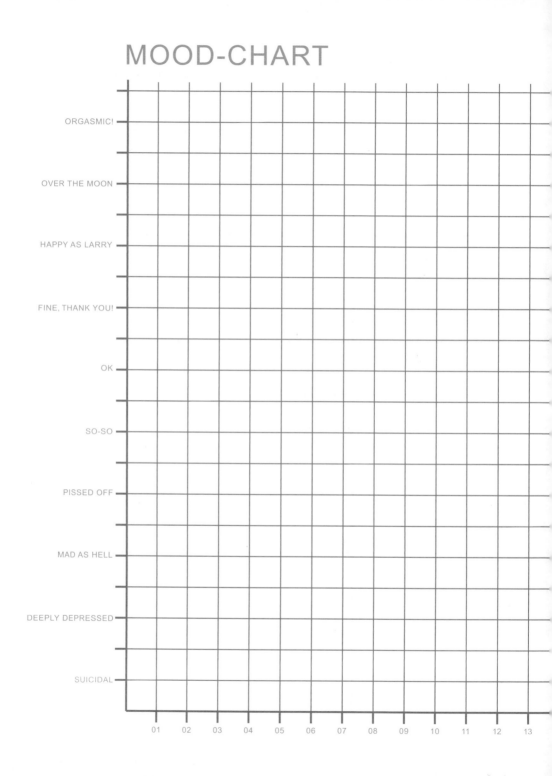

Plot mood level every day of the month against vertical axis. Show one year's results to psychotherapist.

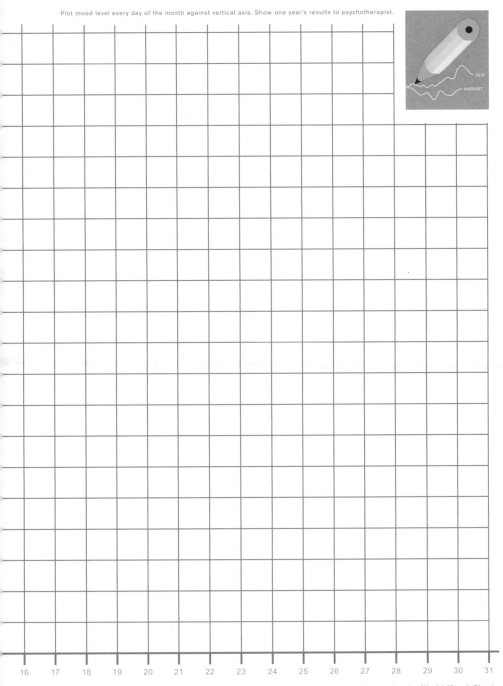

JULY

AUGUST

16   17   18   19   20   21   22   23   24   25   26   27   28   29   30   31

Thursday 1 January
Break Your New Year Resolutions!

New Year resolutions are a poor substitute for an entire year of day-by-day instructions such as you now hold in your hands. So kick off by breaking them.

Resolution..

Broken by..(time)

by doing...

Here are some easy resolutions to break if you don't have any of your own for whatever reason.

Resolution	How to break it
Lose weight.	Eat something that features recognizable animal organs (eg pork pie).
Drink less alcohol.	Vodka looks just like mineral water and doesn't smell either.
Stop smoking.	Start smoking.
Save money.	Give £20 to a tramp, it's New Year after all.
Give more to charity.	Grab that £20 back, are you mad.

8

9

10

11

12

13

14

15

16

17

18

19

happy
new year!

Friday 2 January

»It is a truth universally acknowledged, that a single man in possession of a good fortune, must be in want of a wife.« Pride and Prejudice, Jane Austen

»1801– I have just returned from a visit to my landlord – the solitary neighbour that I shall be troubled with.« Wuthering Heights, Emily Brontë

»Mother died today.« L'ÉTRANGER, ALBERT CAMUS

»You are about to begin reading Italo Calvino's new novel, If on a winter's night a traveller.« If On A Winter's Night A Traveller, Italo Calvino

»Longtemps je me suis couché de bonne heure.« A la recherche du temps perdu, Marcel Proust

»I have carefully collected all I could possibly find out about the history of poor Werther and I lay it before you here, knowing that you will thank me for doing so.« The Sorrows of Young Werther, Johan Wolfgang von Goethe

»All happy families resemble each other; each unhappy family is unhappy in its own way.« Anna Karenina, Tolstoy

»The past is a foreign country: they do things differently there.« The Go-Between, L.P.Hartley

»…the first thing you'll probably want to know is where I was born, and what my lousy childhood was like, and how my parents were occupied and all before they had me, and all that David Copperfield kind of crap, but I don't feel like going into it.« THE CATCHER IN THE RYE, J.D.SALINGER

»Call me Ishmael.« Moby Dick, Herman Melville

Today write the opening sentence of your début novel:

»Hale knew they meant to murder him before he had been in Brighton three hours.« Brighton Rock, Graham Greene

»And this also, has been one of the dark places of the earth.« Heart of Darkness, Joseph Conrad

»Riverrun, past Eve and Adam's, from swerve of shore to bend of bay, brings us by a commodius vicus of recirculation back to Howth Castle and Environs.« Finnegans Wake, James Joyce

»In the beginning God created the heavens and the earth.« Old Testament, Anonymous

»Someone must have been telling lies about Joseph K., for without having done anything wrong he was arrested one fine morning.« The Trial, Franz Kafka

»It was a bright cold day in April, and the clocks were striking thirteen.« 1984, GEORGE ORWELL

»Now, what I want is, Facts.« Hard Times, Charles Dickens

»You don't know about me, without you have read a book by the name of The Adventures of Tom Sawyer, but that ain't no matter.« Huckleberry Finn, Mark Twain

»LOLITA, light of my life, fire of my loins.« Lolita, Vladimir Nabokov

»The snow in the mountains was melting and Bunny had been dead for several weeks before we came to understand the gravity of our situation.« The Secret History, Donna Tartt

»Stately, plump Buck Milligan came from the stairhead, bearing a bowl of lather on which a mirror and a razor lay crossed.« Ulysses, James Joyce

8	12	16
9	13	17
10	14	18
11	15	19

8		14	
9		15	
10		16	
11		17	
12		18	
13		19	

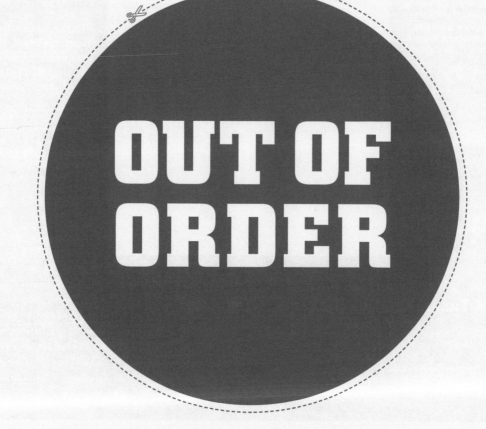

Mass social experiment. Cut out and stick this sign on any item of public infrastructure you might encounter today, including, but not limited to: lifts, rubbish trucks, cranes, phone booths, toilets, ventilation units, escalators, entrances to underground stations. The aim is to achieve comprehensive social breakdown across the UK.

THE LOVE OF YOUR LIFE

Today, gaze at everyone wondering whether they might be the one true love of your life, the one destined for you and you alone, and whether you might be passing them by forever... Act in consequence.

Sunday 4 January

8

9

10

11

12

13

14

15

16

17

18

Today throw something away that you like.

WORLD COLOURING-IN DAY

Today, work out your globetrotting plans for the rest of your time on earth, and get on the phone to an accredited travel agent. NB: the Foreign Office currently discourages travel to the following countries: Afghanistan, Iraq, North Korea, Turkmenistan, Zimbabwe, North Yemen. **Fill in country by country:** ● Been there done that ● Intend to go there this year ● Intend to go there sometime before I die ● Happy never to set foot there in my whole life.

RUSSIA

AUSTRALIA

KAZAKHSTAN

CHINA

BRAZIL

GREENLAND

UNITED STATES OF AMERICA

CANADA

MEXICO

U.S.A

Tuesday 6 January

8
9
10
11
12
13
14
15
16
17
18

WOMEN:

Dark storm clouds were gathering over the Alpine mountain top as Emma finally reached the refuge. Where were the others? Where was her husband Edward? Perhaps they had fallen behind and taken the safe track back towards *St-Paul-des-Clercs* and civilization, she wondered. Well there was no point in panicking now. Night was falling fast, and she would have to spend it up here all alone at the mercy of these peaks. Exhausted, she entered the deserted cabin and barely had time to strip off her drenched clothes and slip into the thermal sleeping bag that Edward had thoughtfully given her for their sixth anniversary, before a deep slumber overtook her naked body.

As even the moon retreated from the inhospitable horizon, strange and fitful dreams came upon her. She tossed and turned in the night, her feverish brow victim to wild imaginings, full of visions of werewolf-like creatures creeping around the cabin, circling, surrounding her with deep-breathing low whistles that seemed to hiss and crackle like FIRE?!!! Emma opened her eyes and shrieked in the empty night. There, across the room, stood the tall, dark stranger. She held her breath in terror as he looked up from the fire he had lit in the wide hearth and stared at her inscrutably. His eyes seemed to contain worlds beyond her ken.

»Who - who are you? What do you want?« she cried. The man made no reply, but simply tossed another log onto the fire with barely a flicker of his powerful deep-veined forearm. He breathed in deeply, closing his eyes. Emma's voice was trembling.

»Look, now, I don't know what is going on but...«

He silenced her with a look from his piercing green eyes that seemed to cut right through her. Before she even realized what she was doing, Emma raced through the door in a mad dash for freedom, through the door and out into a thick curtain of rain lashing down over her exposed skin. He caught up with her easily, his strong arms grabbing her by the waist and hauling her back into the cabin. She writhed desperately in his grip until she could no more. He held her still, stared into her eyes and finally spoke in halting English, in the manner of one who seemed above words.

»Don't. It is too dangerous out there for you. You are safe here with me.«

And somehow she knew that this was so.

The fire dispensed a warm glow to the room. Before she had even recovered from the onslaught of the elements, she was trapped in an embrace as powerful as any of Nature's Furies. As the storm raged on outside, she stared into the infinite depth of his eyes. And then he was upon her, touching her deep within, roughly of course but with infinite tenderness. Suddenly lightning struck a tree nearby, while its thunder covered her animal moans. He held her tight for what seemed an eternity, until the first light of dawn broke the enchanting spell the mountain Gods had woven around them. And he was gone, as swiftly as he had come. Was it but a dream? Emma wondered wistfully, as she drifted off back to sleep smiling, her brow no longer troubled.

MEN:

Two blondes. Doing it. Together.

8	14	
9	15	
10	16	
11	17	
12	18	
13	19	

Addiction-Free Day

Your body is your temple. Cut out addictive substances for the day and see how much purer you feel.

8		14	
9		15	
10		16	
11		17	
12		18	
13		19	

SPECIAL TIP FOR ANY DIARY OWNERS ADDICTED TO CRACK COCAINE: You may not feel purer immediately. Stick at this one for at least a couple of months to see the full lifestyle benefits.

DO SOMETHING BEFORE BREAKFAST TODAY

GO FOR A FIVE-MILE RUN

CALL A FRIEND AND EXPRESS SURPRISE THEY'RE NOT UP YET

FIND OUT WHAT'S ON TV AT THIS HOUR

LICK MORNING DEW OFF A LEAF

HAVE SLEEPY SEX

MILK A COW

GOSSIP ABOUT YOUR NEIGHBOURS WITH THE RUBBISH COLLECTORS

WATCH THE SUN RISE

As any peasant worth his salt will tell you, the early morning is the best part of the day, so set the alarm for 5 o'clock and rise and shine.

5 (GET UP)

6

7

8

9

10

11

12

13

14

15 (BEDTIME)

FRIDAY 9 JANUARY

MEET JONAS DAY!

This is Jonas Jansson, a courageous young fellow who has agreed to follow the Diary's injunctions to the letter. In this, his first week, he has already been arrested once and lost his girlfriend. Go Jonas!

Jonas was born in 1982, in the small village of Gävle in Sweden. He grew up, went to school, made some friends, studied a bit, got drunk a couple of times, got a job – but something was still lacking in his otherwise eventful life. One day last year, the authors of the Diary spotted him playing pinball in his local mall. Something about his style

and look caught their eye. They approached him and asked Mr Jansson if he would play the guinea pig for their venture. He said he'd think about it, and before he knew it, his life was totally and utterly transformed. It's only been a few days since Jonas has been following the Diary but already it's pepped up his life no end. On January 4th, he read the »love of your life« page, and followed it a bit too far. First he chucked his girlfriend Magda, even though nothing was said about getting rid of current loves. Then he thought he spotted the love of his life, 59-year-old Canadian tourist Bibi Jeanmaire, busy enjoying a coffee in

downtown Stockholm with ex-Mountie husband Pierre-Louis. Jonas approached her, showed her the relevant Diary page, and proceeded to woo her with a passionate kiss. That's the spirit Jonas! Local police agreed to drop all charges the next day, but not without fining him a substantial 1000 crowns. Better luck next time!

Jonas will be discussing his adventures during the year on www.thiswebsitewillchangeyourlife.com; be sure to compare his experiences to yours.

SATURDAY 10 JANUARY		14
9		15
10		16
11		17
12		18
13		19

VISIT US ON WWW.THISWEBSITEWILLCHANGEYOURLIFE.COM!
FULL OF ALL THE GOOD STUFF WE COULDN'T GET AWAY WITH PUBLISHING IN THIS FAMILY-FRIENDLY EDITION!

Today introduce yourself to someone you know but never speak to.

A NEIGHBOUR!
TALK ABOUT:
THE WEATHER
THE FENCE
OTHER NEIGHBOURS

A LOCAL HOOKER!
TALK ABOUT:
PRICES
POSSIBLE DISCOUNTS
OTHER HOOKERS

A SHOPKEEPER!
TALK ABOUT:
THE LOCAL AREA NEWS
FRESHNESS OF PRODUCE
OTHER SHOPKEEPERS

A COLLEAGUE!
TALK ABOUT:
THE COFFEE MACHINE
THE BOSS
OTHER COLLEAGUES

OFF LICENCE

Sunday 11 January

8	12	16
9	13	17
10	14	18
11	15	19

WHAT's YOUR TYPE?

Tick it here today as reminder at drunken parties

- ☐ **Dumb blonde**
- ☐ **Clever brunette**
- ☐ **Wild redhead**
- ☐ **Lesbian**
- ☐ **Nag**
- ☐ **Cold Fish**

Beefcake ☐
Mr Nice Guy ☐
Loaded ☐
Married with kids ☐
Sleazeball ☐
Handsome prince ☐

Monday 12 January	
8	
9	
10	
11	
12	
13	

14	
15	
16	
17	
18	
19	

SEND A LETTER TO A MASS MURDERER

Richard Ramirez (USA, 1960–)
16 victims+
Nickname: »The Night Stalker«
Death Row, San Quentin Penitentiary,
San Quentin, CA 94974, USA

David Berkowitz (USA, 1953–)
6 victims
Nickname: »Son of Sam«
King's County Hospital,
Brooklyn, NY 11212, USA

Peter Sutcliffe (UK, 1945–)
13 victims
Nickname: »The Yorkshire Ripper«
Broadmoor Special Hospital,
Crowthorne, RG45 7EG Berkshire, UK

Dennis Nilsen (UK, 1945–)
15 victims
Nickname: -----
1X Parkhurst Rd,
Holloway, London N7 9TK, UK

Edmund Kemper (USA, 1948–)
10 victims
Nickname: »The Co-Ed Killer«
California Medical Facility, PO BOX 2000,
Vacaville, CA 95696–2000, USA

Charles Manson (USA, 1934–)
6+ victims
Nickname: -----
California State Prison, B–33920, 4A 4R–23,
PO BOX 3476, Corcora, CA 93212, USA

Angel Resendez (MEXICO, 1960–)
9 victims
Nickname: »The Railroad Killer«
Death Row, Polunski Unit, 12002 FM,
350 South Livingston, TX 77351, USA

Theodore Kaczynski (USA, 1942–)
3 victims
Nickname: »The Unabomber«
Florence Admax USP, P.O. BOX 8500,
5880 HWY 673, Florence, CO 81226, USA

Robert Lee Yates Jr (USA, 1943–)
14+ victims
Nickname: »The Spokane Serial Killer«
Death Row, Washington State Penitentiary,
1313 N. 13th, Walla Walla, WA 99362, USA

A DAY OF COMPLIMENTS

Flatter someone today and see if it does indeed get you anywhere.

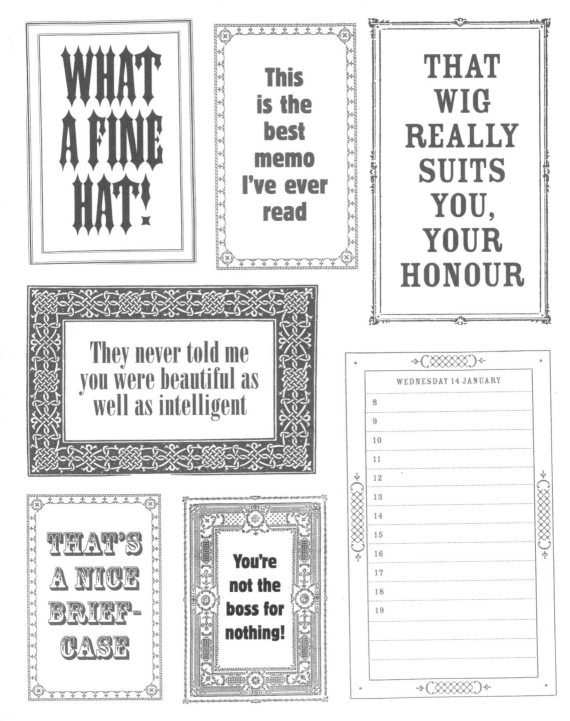

WHAT A FINE HAT!

This is the best memo I've ever read

THAT WIG REALLY SUITS YOU, YOUR HONOUR

They never told me you were beautiful as well as intelligent

THAT'S A NICE BRIEF-CASE

You're not the boss for nothing!

WEDNESDAY 14 JANUARY

8
9
10
11
12
13
14
15
16
17
18
19

SATURDAY 17 JANUARY
Eat nothing but asparagus all day long to ascertain just how noxious your pee can get.

Been there done that? Try one of the lesser urine-affecting vegetables: fennel, eggplant, okra, turnip, ginger.

8
9
10
11
12
13

14
15
16
17
18
19

KILL
SOMETHING DAY

So-called »Western civilization« suppresses our legitimate aggressive impulses. Cast off the chains of narrow morality and stamp out the sad life of a member of some inferior species today: an ant, or perhaps a gnat of some kind. Indulge your dark urges before they overwhelm you. After all, as top Russian anarchist Mikhail Bakunin declared: *the passion for destruction is also a creative passion...*

PATRIOTISM DAY!

It is the duty of every citizen to be patriotic. A country is one's soil, one's blood, one's tears, one's roots. Here is a list of countries along with their strong points, so you can choose which one to feel patriotic about today.

FRANCE — /5

LANGUAGE: French.
ANTHEM: La Marseillaise.
MILITARY RECORD: Prone to invasion.
PATRIOTIC POTENTIAL: Gung-ho anthem, easy to get worked up about.

UNITED KINGDOM — /5

LANGUAGE: English.
ANTHEM: God Save The Queen.
MILITARY RECORD: Good, though the English Channel has undoubtedly helped.
PATRIOTIC POTENTIAL: Wide choice of tones, from Churchill to football hooliganism.

CHINA — /5

LANGUAGE: Mandarin.
ANTHEM: March of the Volunteers.
MILITARY RECORD: Strength in numbers.
PATRIOTIC POTENTIAL: If you like your patriotism tinged with ideology, this could be for you.

NIGERIA — /5

LANGUAGE: English/Yoruba/Hausa.
ANTHEM: Arise O Compatriots!
MILITARY RECORD: Very good at fighting each other.
PATRIOTIC POTENTIAL: Limited except during football World Cups.

MOLDOVA — /5

LANGUAGE: Moldovan.
ANTHEM: Awaken Thee Romania!
MILITARY RECORD: Nothing yet, but evidence of anti-Russian rowdiness.
PATRIOTIC POTENTIAL: Still all to play for!

RUSSIA — /5

LANGUAGE: Russian.
ANTHEM: The Patriotic Song (no words).
MILITARY RECORD: Defeated Hitler, but lost cold war.
PATRIOTIC POTENTIAL: Never a dull moment.

8
9
10
11
12
13
14
15
16
17
18

THURSDAY 22 JANUARY

Today agree to meet someone in 10 years' time. Fill in this coupon and hand it to a stranger or someone you hardly know.

8	
9	
10	
11	
12	
13	
14	
15	
16	
17	
18	

We, the undersigned, may only know each other casually, but we hereby agree to meet up in exactly ten years' time at.......(hour) on the 22nd of January 2014 at...................(place). In case we have changed beyond recognition, we agree to wear the following identifying features:..

In case we have nothing to say to each other, here is a list of »hot« 2004 topics to reminisce about:

....

....

....

....

Signed

....

See you in ten years' time.

1 stone
= 2 sticks

BARTER DAY

Bartering provides fun for all the family, bypasses the taxman, and is a useful skill to acquire in the event civilization should suddenly revert to the Stone Age. Here are some useful equivalencies to get you started.

1 mud hut
= 4 donkeys

1 leaf
= 5 dead ants

1 giraffe
= 1 bicycle

2 apples
= 1 loaf bread

12 french fries
= 1 pencil

1 cow
= 2 dogs

110 fresh eggs
= 1 DVD

17 seatbelts
= 1 year's cable TV subscription

1 motor-bike
= 1 front garden

2 bottles vodka + 1 scarf
= 1 guitar

1 mobile phone
= 1 big rock

Saturday 24 January

8
9
10
11
12
13
14
15
16
17
18

3 articulated lorries
= 1 small house with no window

1 skyscraper + 4 pears
= 2 remote villages

Column 1

Read Proust................................□
Climb Everest..............................□
Swim with dolphins........................□
Learn Italian..............................□
Visit Bhutan...............................□
Write that novel/screenplay...............□
Become world chess champion...............□
Rob a bank................................□
Run away..................................□
Have a sex change (just for a day)........□
Become a queen............................□
Become a king.............................□
Wear coloured lenses......................□
Donate your liver.........................□
Compromise................................□
Become a millionaire......................□
Go to heaven..............................□
Parachute.................................□
Walk to the North Pole ....□
Learn Russian.............................□
Live off charity..........................□
Contract an STD...........................□
Swallow a coin............................□
Spend a night in prison...................□
Start a revolution........................□
Pretend everything is all right...........□
Follow this diary rigorously..............□
Learn how to drive........................□
Hurt a friend.............................□
Celebrate Xmas in May.....................□
Call your father »Pa«.....................□
Call your mother »Ma«.....................□
Learn the Periodic Table by heart.........□
Go to a drive-in cinema...................□
Become an artist..........................□
Collect stamps............................□
Work in a coalmine........................□
Be late for a date........................□
Watch all of Bergman......................□
Follow Mao's teachings....................□
Bite the dust.............................□
Kiss a stranger...........................□
Move to Japan.............................□
Visit space...............................□
Invent a biscuit..........................□
Become grumpy when old....................□
Wear a rucksack...........................□
Ride a camel..............................□
Use a semi-colon..........................□
Inject heroin.............................□
Wear loafers..............................□
Speak in tongues..........................□
Become a fanatic..........................□
Dress like a hip-hopper...................□
Faint with love...........................□
Save the world............................□
Become insensitive to suffering...........□
Be gay....................................□
Be heterosexual...........................□
Start a cult..............................□
Stand and speak up for your rights........□
Talk to strangers.........................□
Start a fire..............................□
Drink yourself silly in New Zealand.......□
Order tap water...........................□
Grow a beard..............................□
Master the yoyo...........................□
Become a fitness instructor...............□
Be on TV..................................□
Laugh at a bad joke.......................□
Feel like Batman..........................□
Apply for a patent........................□
Become a rockstar.........................□
Fall for advertising......................□
Live for a year on a desert island........□
Stop worrying.............................□
Use the term »solutionize«................□
Confess to a priest.......................□
Confess to a whore........................□
Eat leaves from a tree....................□
Graffiti a motorway bridge................□
Be drunk during office hours..............□

Column 2

Own an owl................................□
Contemplate suicide.......................□
Ride a Harley.............................□
Take NO for an answer.....................□
Say a prayer..............................□
Gamble your shirt.........................□
Break a promise...........................□
Learn to fly..............................□
Get a tattoo..............................□
Learn to live with gnats..................□
Go on a field trip........................□
Take part in a brain storming.............□
Invade a small country....................□
Be the fifth wheel........................□
Ride a donkey.............................□
Demand a ransom...........................□
Proclaim yourself emperor.................□
Disinherit your heirs.....................□
Say NO when you mean YES..................□
Adopt a Romanian..........................□
Seduce the prom queen.....................□
Paint someone in tar and feathers.........□
Run for your life.........................□
Witness a miracle.........................□
Light a fart..............................□
Shave off your pubic hair.................□
Smoke a cat...............................□
Make the front page.......................□
Cross-dress...............................□
Win the Nobel Peace Prize.................□
Make love in front of a stranger..........□
Volunteer for a dangerous mission.........□
Overdose..................................□
Give birth to a goatboy...................□
Win the rat race..........................□
Make like a tree..........................□
Overthrow a regime........................□
Bake a soufflé............................□
Organize an orgy..........................□
Understand Hitler.........................□
Race at Monaco............................□
Live within your means....................□
Marry someone you've just met.............□
Marry someone you've never met............□
Star in a Hollywood blockbuster...........□
Shovel manure.............................□
Discover the lost city of Atlantis........□
Dream in black and white..................□
See your face on a banknote...............□
Be eaten by cannibals.....................□
Own a grotto..............................□
Solve a crime.............................□
Host a gameshow...........................□
Sue the government........................□
Win the lottery...........................□
Sleep with your best friend's partner.....□
Start your own religion...................□
Experience an earthquake..................□
Meet Santa................................□
Shoot the last buffalo....................□
Bump'n'grind..............................□
Hibernate.................................□
Burn your bra (women).....................□
Burn your Y-fronts (men)..................□
Find a guru...............................□
Turn 117 years old........................□
Update the Kamasutra......................□
Marry a prince or princess................□
Settle in Pittsburgh......................□
Run with the wolves.......................□
Become pope...............................□
Inherit the crown jewels..................□
Be used as a manga character..............□
Grow a tail...............................□
Crash a helicopter in the jungle..........□
Take a vow of silence.....................□
Take a vow of chastity....................□
Jump bail.................................□
Move someone to tears.....................□
Fake a multiple orgasm....................□
Become employee of the month..............□
Go live with a hermit.....................□

Column 3

Greet the extraterrestrial delegation.....□
Become a Muslim...........................□
Become a Buddhist.........................□
Become a Christian........................□
Tie the perfect shoelace knot.............□
Eradicate hepatitis C.....................□
Kiss your own lips........................□
Shoot the pianist.........................□
Ride off into the sunset..................□
Invent a typeface.........................□
Reject society............................□
Beat Bjorn Borg at tennis.................□
Fulfill your true potential...............□
Be in the eye of the storm................□
Break the bank in Vegas...................□
Have a park bench named after you.........□
Risk your life............................□
Refuse a new technology...................□
Meet your great-great-grandchildren.......□
Suffer a fool gladly......................□
Sway a jury...............................□
Sweep a chimney...........................□
Fight the power...........................□
Be the 78th person on the moon............□
Collect coins.............................□
Be called upon by your president..........□
Win best-looking baby of the year.........□
Smoke a Cuban cigar.......................□
Think up a new swear word.................□
Fight a duel..............................□
Jump the gun..............................□
Escape your past..........................□
Suck on 12 lollipops at once..............□
Have your own brand of olive oil..........□
Become immortal...........................□
Learn pole dancing........................□
Play the lead in Swan Lake................□
Master the remote control.................□
Catch that bird that pooped on you........□
Loop the loop.............................□
Make a pact with the devil................□
Wish upon a star..........................□
Tell your deepest secret..................□
Witness the mating of flamingoes..........□
Feel ugly.................................□
Feel pretty...............................□
Confess under duress......................□
Walk down the yellow brick road...........□
Travel at warp speed......................□
Stab someone in the back..................□
Implode...................................□
Swim in Lake Titicaca.....................□
Jump on a real bandwagon..................□
Run an arms dealership....................□
Shit in the woods.........................□
Exterminate a zombie......................□
Sniff supreglue...........................□
Whistle while you work....................□
Become a superhero........................□
Memorize an encyclopedia..................□
Floss twice a day.........................□
Go on a rampage...........................□
Make your bank manager beg................□
Lick an electric eel......................□
Broker a ceasefire........................□
Conduct an orchestra......................□
Jump ship.................................□
Make a leap of faith......................□
Get drunk on meths........................□
Sacrifice a goat..........................□
Live to tell the tale.....................□
Inaugurate a building.....................□
Forgive and forget........................□
Sleep with a whore of Babylon.............□
Reach nirvana.............................□
Find out what it's all about..............□
Crush grapes with your bare feet..........□
Ride a yak................................□
Sup with Satan............................□
Bite the hand that feeds you..............□
Track down Lord Lucan.....................□
Cause an intergalactic rift...............□

Column 4

Get away with murder......................□
Travel back in time.......................□
Apologize for existing....................□
Think the unthinkable.....................□
Appease a dictator........................□
Lose your mojo............................□
Face a firing squad.......................□
Become an object of worship...............□
Gatecrash the White House.................□
Burn a banknote...........................□
Have the Midas touch......................□
Trigger an avalanche......................□
Cure the common cold......................□
Own an oilfield...........................□
Save the whale............................□
Discover a new continent..................□
Serenade a lover..........................□
Come out of a black hole alive............□
Precipitate the decline of the west.......□
Jump for joy..............................□
Suck your little toe in public............□
Mate with another species.................□
Become possessed..........................□
Surpass Einstein..........................□
Understand Einstein.......................□
Look like Einstein........................□
Predict an eclipse........................□
Participate in the Olympics...............□
Catch a shark.............................□
Meet your maker...........................□
Commit arson..............................□
Wear a cape...............................□
Talk dirty to a flower....................□
Spot the Invisible Man....................□
Head a posse..............................□
Undergo emergency liposuction.............□
Do the Rubik's Cube.......................□
Blame God for everything..................□
Acquire a hard-ass nickname...............□
Betray your country.......................□
Regain your virginity.....................□
Change astrological signs.................□
Bring back Bambi..........................□
Write in cuneiform........................□
Get fired for being truculent.............□
Become like your father...................□
Become like your mother...................□
Join the French Foreign Legion............□
Achieve perfection........................□
Spell »egg« differently...................□
Win top prize for your verruca............□
Beg in the street.........................□
Channel lava away from a village..........□
Grow a third nipple.......................□
Spend all your salary on payday...........□
Witness the Big Bang......................□
Gerrymander...............................□
Generate controversy......................□
Meet a bolshevik..........................□
Ooze charm................................□
Moult.....................................□
Have too much of a good thing.............□
Die of hard work..........................□
Run amok..................................□
Discover your ancestor is Napoleon........□
Make it to the top........................□
Successfully crashland a jumbo jet........□
Fiddle while Rome burns...................□
Design the perfect crouton................□
Run out of tears..........................□
Howl at the full moon.....................□
Win an Oscar..............................□
Unbreak a taboo...........................□
Give rise to a cause célèbre..............□
Part the Red Sea..........................□
Have sex with your clone..................□
Know the truth about JFK..................□
Wave a red rag to a bull..................□
Get high on life..........................□
Find your self............................□
Rule the world............................□
Other.....................................□

7	11	15	
8	12	16	
9	13	17	
10	14	18	

today choose what you'd prefer to be reincarnated as

Circle your first choice and send off with a $5 donation to the Dalai Lama, Lhassa, Tibet.

Monday 26 January

8

9

10

11

12

13

14

15

16

17

18

19

Today dial a phone number at random and read this script with an all-American accent.

You know, without Christ, without Jesus, we have no hope. Why? Well, because we know that the standard of God's righteousness is Law, a law of the Ten Commandments, a law of statutes and judgments. And which God gave unto Moses on Sinai, saying this is thy righteousness, O Israel. But you know, God also gave another law. A law revolving around a system of shedding a poor and innocent lamb's blood. So that all who would break the Law of God, who would seek God for forgiveness and pardon, had to bring a lamb, something innocent, and slay it – although, Israel themselves never really knew the real meaning of this. Nonetheless, they were commanded to do it. Also there were other sacrifices, such as: turtle-doves, goats, oxen, red heifers.

But, it was a very sophisticated and very prolific type system of worship. Of course, God had to give these people their own country. He had to give them blessings and things, to be able to perform these, rituals. And naturally of course, having to slay a lamb for your sins or such sacrifices, it would definitely keep a man on guard, not to sin too much, because otherwise he could lose the livestock pretty quick, couldn't he? Well anyway, (thanks be unto God), from as far back as Deuteronomy 32, all the way through to Malachi, there has been other writings, writings of the Prophets. Writings who do not usurp the authority of Moses, but actually exalt The Law of Moses. But yet there's an additional testimony. For the same God of Heaven – Who's rich in mercy – has not only given to men a Law, but also a way of escape, for those Repentant Souls who might fall short of the glory of God's law. Which some scholars will agree, that the glory of God's law is that it's a divine precept of His own character. God's character is revealed in The Law. Now, Christ is the only hope for a world that sins. Now, how do we know? Well – The Prophets – have prophesied? But what if we're not familiar with the prophets? Well, were the Jews familiar with the prophets when this Word-of-God was made flesh? When Mary, The Virgin, had a baby boy, did everyone believe, that she was really a virgin when Christ was conceived? If we search the Scriptures,

we'll find in certain arguments the Pharisees confronted Christ – and said to him, »We be not sons born of fornication.« So obviously, not everyone believed that he was a child of a virgin birth! If they hadn't looked back to Isaiah chapter 8, and learned the mystery of Immanuel – that a virgin would conceive and bear a son – then they might not really put too much ahhm… consistency into the fact that Christ at that day claimed to be born of a virgin. I mean, if Isaiah the prophet was a false prophet, well then naturally they would conclude that anyone claiming to have these things fulfilled would be false, too.

But of course, Christ, he did something much more, than to just fulfill prophecy. He did miracles. Miracles of mercy such as: healing the sick, feeding the hungry, raising the dead. And if we study we'll see that »Matthew, Mark, Luke, and John« gives us in somewhat, a full view of the oppositions, and also, the confidements, that he had in doing these miracles. He gathered many unto him through the means of these miracles.

But sad to say, even though he had done so many miracles, Scripture says, yet when it came right down to it, they didn't believe in him. It's amazing that even his own disciples forsook him – except Mary Magdalene. She stayed with him to the end, didn't she? Last to leave The Cross, first to come to the sepulchre. Now, we need to sit here, and we need to ask the question, »how come the men of that generation didn't believe in Christ?«

In Matthew 23, Christ had to say to the Jews »O Jerusalem, Jerusalem« how often I would have gathered you, but you would not. Why? He tells them that they have forsaken The Prophets. »Thou that killest the prophets,« how often I would have gathered you. How does the subject of ›gathering Israel‹ and ›the prophets‹ combine together? He tells them that their houses, their temple, is left to them desolate.

And that in Matthew 24, as Christ said on the Mount of Olives, his disciples came to him to ask him, concerning these things. What should be the sign of thy coming and of the end of the world? Well, Christ begins to tell them, let no man deceive you, »For many shall come in my name, saying, I am Christ; and shall deceive many.«

Thursday 29 January
8
9
10
11
12
13
14
15
16
17
18

If you dial an answering machine, try to fit it all in the time allocated. If you can't, call back later to complete the message.

SATURDAY 31 JANUARY

Celebrate Nauru National Day by sending His Excellency the President a congratulatory letter at Office of the President, c/o Ministry of Works, Yaren Nauru.

NAURU
NATIONAL DAY!

Political update: Nauru became independent as a republic in 1968 and joined the Commonwealth as a special member, which means they make a voluntary contribution towards the running of the Secretariat.

8
9
10
11
12
13
14
15
16
17
18
19

Six-time President of Nauru Bernard Dowiyogi (1946–2003)

How the rest of the world is celebrating Nauru National Day: events will be taking place in most major cities, with fireworks over the Eiffel Tower, the Thames, Times Square and the Vatican. Start time: 9pm GMT (midday in Nauru itself). Make sure to try the Naurean national dish if you haven't already: roast Nauru pig.

Tonight control your dreams

Freud postulated that our dreams are essentially the recombined elements of things that had affected us during the day. Today think very hard about these three things and see if they crop up in your dreams tonight.

Hedgehog

Aeroplane

Midget

8	12	16
9	13	17
10	14	18
11	15	19

TODAY, BE ON THE LOOKOUT FOR THE PARANORMAL

There is more to the world than meets the eye.
Today try to be especially receptive to paranormal manifestations and determine for yourself whether there is indeed a world beyond the veil. Here is a list of clues to look out for in ascending order of conclusiveness.

Odd feeling
Strange wind-like whisper
Flutey sounds in the distance
Scratching noises
Unexplained smells
Unexplained footsteps
Fleeting shadows
Feelings of being watched
Dogs barking
Cats barking

DON'T JUMP TO CONCLUSIONS, THERE'S PROBABLY A PERFECTLY INNOCENT EXPLANATION.

Voices
Voices of people dead for months
Voices of people dead for years
Doors opening
Cupboard doors opening
Keys disappearing
Keys reappearing
Lights turning on and off
Mist appearing out of nowhere
Being touched by an invisible hand

CURIOUSER AND CURIOUSER! CONTACT YOUR LOCAL PARANORMAL INVESTIGATOR, AND PROBE FURTHER.

Being slapped by invisible hand
Furniture moving
Dinner plates flying across the room
Spouse speaking in tongues
Apparition (ghost)
Apparition (zombie)
Apparition (hungry zombie)
Blood sluicing down walls
Head of daughter spinning
Being strangled by own intestines

YOU'VE PROBED TOO FAR. GET THE HELL OUT IF IT'S NOT TOO LATE.

MONDAY 2 FEBRUARY

8	12	16
9	13	17
10	14	18
11	15	19

Today write to a dictator to stop torture

Sample letter:

Dear General/Minister/Grand Leader,

I have been greatly disturbed to hear of the arrests of _____ (check Amnesty International for recent names). I am writing to request that their whereabouts be disclosed and that they be granted immediate access to their families and lawyers. I also request that they be immediately released unless charged and brought before an ordinary court of law.

Yours sincerely,

Official forms of address

Your Majesty... to Kings, Queens & other monarchs
Your Excellency... for Presidents & other Heads of State

Dear Sir/Madam,... for Prime Ministers & Ministers

Dear Ambassador/High Commissioner...
for Ambassadors & High Commissioners

Dear Sir/Madam... for other Embassy staff such as Chargé d'Affaires

Dear Admiral/General/Captain etc... for military officials

Your Grace... for Archbishops

Your Eminence... for Cardinals

Dear Bishop... for Bishops

Dear Mr/Father/Reverend... for other Clergy

Tuesday 3 February

8

9

10

11

12

13

14

15

16

17

18

19

FRIDAY 6 FEBRUARY

READY, STEADY...

TODAY DO A RUNNER

RUNNER ETIQUETTE:

1) Wait until the coffee course, particularly if there is a set menu.

2) Do not leave your date behind, unless you are sure it is the last time you wish to see them.

3) Do not start actually »running« until you are outside the restaurant.

4) Do not select the heaviest items on the menu. Running on a bouillabaisse is medically inadvisable.

5) Beginners and the shy: do a practice »runner« before ordering any food.

8	14	
9	15	
10	16	
11	17	
12	18	
13	19	

Saturday 7 February
Spend some time in a church today

Even the irreligious amongst us can appreciate the sanctuary that churches provide, away from the hyperkinetic madness of modern life.

Breathe in the air of centuries.

Let the shadows envelop you.

Light a candle for a long-lost friend.

Contemplate the silence.

Perhaps even find God.

What to say to God if you find him

God is fed up with being quizzed about the same old chestnuts like evil and creation all the time.

Make Him notice you with a cheeky question, like what's his favourite breakfast cereal, or did Adam and Eve have belly buttons.

8	14
9	15
10	16
11	17
12	18
13	19

Today apply for a knighthood

Don't remain plain old Mr or Mrs all your life. To become a Knight or a Dame, simply write to the British Prime Minister c/o the Prime Minister's Office, 10 Downing St, London SW1A 2AA. Explain what exceptional achievement or service you feel merits the award of a knighthood. Previous successful applicants have used the following, just to give you an idea: »been head nurse for 60 years«, »Nobel Peace Prize winner«, »raised millions for obscure charity«, »served in minor government position for whole life«, »won World War 2«, »saved cat from extra-tall tree«. Even better, get someone to recommend you.

The honours ceremony takes place on the Queen's Official Birthday on June 9th. So make sure you keep it free!

(Foreigners: write to the Secretary of State for Foreign and Commonwealth Affairs, King Charles St, London, SW1A 2AH. Note that nationals of countries of which the Queen is not head of state may not style themselves Sir or Dame, though they may place the appropriate letters after their name.)

8

9

10

11

12

13

14

15

16

17

18

19

TODAY WALK BAREFOOT ON GRASS.

Grass was well-known amongst Indian shamans for its soothing anti-ulcerative properties. When a papoose was sickly, the shaman would lie him down on a grass bank and sprinkle him with dew from the bark of a Great Conifer Tree, for 5 days and 5 nights (at least). Today grass is widely available of course in parks, gardens and the like. The current theory is that the leaves contain herbacinium, a derivative of morphine, which »rubs off« on the fibrous nerves of our bare feet, gets into the bloodstream and slows down our heart rate by up to 14%, thus »relaxing« us. Indeed, poets have long known this, as is conclusively demonstrated by the following:

LEAVES OF GRASS

A child said, What is the grass? fetching it to me with full hands;
How could I answer the child? I do not know what it is, any more than he.

I guess it must be the flag of my disposition, out of hopeful green stuff woven.

Or I guess it is the handkerchief of the Lord,
A scented gift and remembrancer, designedly dropped,
Bearing the owner's name someway in the corners, that we may see and remark, and say Whose?
Or I guess the grass is itself a child, the produced babe of the vegetation.
Or I guess it is a uniform hieroglyphic,
And it means, Sprouting alike in broad zones and narrow zones,
Growing among black folks as among white,
Kanuck, Tuckahoe, Congressman, Cuff, I give them the same, I receive them the same.
And now it seems to me the beautiful uncut hair of graves.
(Walt Whitman)

Wednesday 11 February				
8		14		
9		15		
10		16		
11		17		
12		18		
13		19		

8
9
10
11
12
13
14
15
16
17
18
19

Open your umbrella inside

Walk under a ladder

Whistle inside the house

Put keys on the table

8
9
10
11
12
13
14
15
16
17
18
19 DEAD YET?

Break a mirror

Step on a crack in the sidewalk

Let milk boil over

Cross paths with a black cat

Saturday 14 February

Valentine's Day:

*Come up with a compliment
that has never been made before.*

Top male compliment clichés
Do you work out?
Nice driving!
*Boy, you sure can handle
your drink.*
*Look at those hands – are
you a lumberjack?*

Top female compliment clichés:
*You are the woman
of my dreams.*
Your eyes are like two stars.
*It must have hurt, when you
fell from heaven.*
*You're not like any girl
I've ever met.*

8
9
10
11
12
13

OOPS! Did you forget about Valentine's Day?

Here is a list of convincing excuses:

I couldn't remember where you lived

I knocked my head on the pavement and suffered 24-hour amnesia

We're married now, so what's the point?

It's only a corporate marketing conspiracy

With me every day is Valentine's Day

They'd sold out of red roses so I thought I'd ignore it

You didn't remind me

I gave you some flowers last year

Wht're u tlkng bout? I snt u a txt msge, d'nt u gt it?

MY Valentine's Day is on the 12th of May

I'm going to leave you soon anyway

My ultra-rare roses are stuck in the Spanish customs

I spent time with my mother

I only follow the Chinese calendar

I went through a very quick gay phase yesterday

A rose pricked me and I nearly bled to death

I'm only with you for your money anyway

I didn't forget! You must have an evil double

8	(SHAME ON YOU)	14	(SHAME ON YOU)		(SHAME ON YOU)
9	(SHAME ON YOU)	15	(SHAME ON YOU)		(SHAME ON YOU)
10	(SHAME ON YOU)	16	(SHAME ON YOU)		(SHAME ON YOU)
11	(SHAME ON YOU)	17	(SHAME ON YOU)		(SHAME ON YOU)
12	(SHAME ON YOU)	18	(SHAME ON YOU)		(SHAME ON YOU)
13	(SHAME ON YOU)	19	(SHAME ON YOU)		(SHAME ON YOU)

WEDNESDAY 18 FEBRUARY

MAKE A CITIZEN'S ARREST! When a crime is committed and no police officer is in the vicinity, you have the right and responsibility to make a Citizen's Arrest. Such crimes include: murder, manslaughter, armed assault, conspiracy to defraud, littering.

CITIZEN'S ARREST ⬤ PW56CJFb 00087 /

ARRESTOR DETAILS

Full name...
Home address...
City..Postcode...

ARRESTEE DETAILS

Full name...
Nickname (if any) ....
Home address ....
City...
Postcode..
Height.............................Weight..................
Eyes..
Hair.....................Race.....................Gender......
Identifying scars/tattoos (if able to draw please attach drawing)..
Fingerprints:

CRIME:..
Plea: Guilty ☐ Not guilty ☐
Other...
Motive: Drugs ☐ Alcohol ☐ Money ☐
Blackmail ☐ Revenge ☐ Insanity ☐
Other...
Statement/confession...........................
....
....
....
....
....

Signatures:
CITIZEN...
CRIMINAL...

THAT'S RIGHT BUDDY! JUST CUT IT OUT AND HANG IT AROUND SOMEONE'S NECK!

8	14
9	15
10	16
11	17
12	18
13	19

MAKE PEOPLE NOTICE YOU TODAY!

KEEP ONE EYE
SHUT ALL DAY

HAVE MONEY STICKING
OUT OF YOUR POCKETS

TALK RUBBISH NON-STOP

DON'T
SHAVE

SPREAD
MONEY
AROUND

WEAR A
CROWN

WEAR A
HIGH HAT

DRESS IN
COLOURFUL
CLOTHES

CARRY A
MIDGET UNDER
YOUR LEFT ARM

WALK SIDEWAYS
CRAB-LIKE

WHISTLE
OUT OF
TUNE

READ THE
NEWSPAPER
UPSIDE DOWN

THURSDAY 19 FEBRUARY

GLUE A SPATULA
TO YOUR ARM

8	14
9	15
10	16
11	17
12	18
13	19

Sense-less Day GO THROUGH TODAY WITHOUT USING YOUR SENSE OF: SIGHT

How to: Very dark glasses and white cane.

True story: There is an extraordinary study by Marius Von Senden, called »Space and Sight«. In it he examines the experiences of those born blind whose sight has recently been restored by cataract surgery. For them, vision is a radical new experience. They see the world as a field of colours. One girl was so moved by its dazzling brilliance that she kept her eyes shut for two weeks, only opening them briefly now and again, to repeat »Oh God! How beautiful«. Alas, she found it impossible to understand space, and kept bumping into these colours. She was only ever happy with her eyes closed, pretending to be blind again.

FRIDAY 20 FEBRUARY		
8	14	Write down the pros and cons of this sense as you discover them.
9	15	Pros:
10	16	Cons:
11	17	
12	18	End of day assessment: How crucial is
13	19	my sense of sight to me ..../10

WHAT IS THE MEANING OF LIFE? TODAY SOLVE THAT ETERNAL PROBLEM BY LOOKING IT UP IN THE DICTIONARY.

SATURDAY 21 FEBRUARY

8
9
10
11
12
13

14
15
16
17
18
19

IT'S MARDI GRAS!
Pancake Day

TODAY, A TEST OF PATIENCE: FLIP THE PERFECT PANCAKE.

1) The pancake mixture must be very smooth. Start with 100g of flour and a pinch of salt in large bowl. Whisk in two eggs. Mix 200ml of milk and 80ml of water, and add them in gradually, whisking until the batter is creamily smooth.

2) Lubricate your frying pan with butter and put it on medium-high heat. Spoon in roughly one ladleful of mixture per pancake, tipping it around the pan so it spreads evenly. As soon as the underside is golden, it's time for the tricky bit.

3) Flipping (or »tossing«) is all in the forearm. Lift the pan away from the heat, then slide the pancake around slightly to avoid stickiness, and whip the pan up in a forceful yet precise movement. The pancake should rotate 180 degrees vertically and land back in the same spot it became airborne. (Beginners, children under 12 and the elderly: you are free to adjust the pan slightly to catch it though.)

This highly unusual rock formation known as »Pancake Rocks« is situated at Punakaiki, on the West Coast of the South Island, New Zealand. It received its name in May 1832 from the white settlers, as the indigenous Maoris were not familiar with the concept of pancake.

What makes the perfect pancake? 10% technique, 10% instinct, 80% patience.

Take care »tossing« your pancakes. Firefighter Stuart Mitchell says: »Cooking and flipping pancakes is great fun but people should take care with hot oil. You hardly need any oil and people should be very wary that they flip their pancakes away from the cooker so that if the tossed pancake isn't caught it can be cleared up.«

Tuesday 24 February	12	17
8	13	18
9	14	19
10	15	
11	16	

ROCK'N'ROLL

Today, live the Heavy Metal lifestyle at its most decadent...

WEDNESDAY 25 FEBRUARY

4pm wake up to the gentle bobbing motion of fellatio from some nameless groupie **5pm** snort two industrial-sized lines of coke to help you out of bed **6pm** at least leave the **7pm** threaten manager and take a swig of J. Daniels or, if too wrecked, nameless hotel room, or, if too wrecked, and take a swig out the window trash hotel room, doing a convincing imitation of television set out the window, doing a convincing imitation of with loaded gun, **5th**

someone who doesn't know or care if the safety is on **8pm** time for refreshments: pills washed down with vodka and a spliff **9pm** copulate with two Dallas Cowboys cheerleaders in full view of Dallas Cowboy **10pm** convince them to tattoo your name on their ass, misspelling it for them **11pm** the night is young and so are the girls around here, so time to hit the town

12am Meet your current dealer in bar with bag full of loose banknotes **1am** Shoot up in bar toilet, standing up to avoid the unhygienic **2am** OD in limo, but not before trying to wrestle steering **3am** get arrested trying to throttle nurse wheel from driver and stealing your precious blood **5am** seat for stabbing, you and stealing your precious blood **7am** set fire to OD again, this time in prison hospital

prison sheets, trying to light concealed emergency coma-like sleep in pool of own vomit, ensuring plenty of personal space in otherwise crowded cell **10am** throw up again on lawyer, who should know better than to wear best suit to these occasions **11am** restorative sleep in tour van **4pm** repeat until early death and instant immortality

8	14
9	15
10	16
11	17
12	18
13	19

Today, try food that scares you

8	14
9	15
10	16
11	17
12	18
13	19

TRIPE · SNAILS · BRUSSELS SPROUTS · DOG · FROG'S LEGS · HORSE · OYSTERS · TIGER TESTICLE · JELLIED EEL · HAGGIS

Families are the nuclei of society, cells of history and knowledge through which wisdom and morals are transmitted from generation to generation and beyond. What age-old traditions and skills define your family? Make a conscious effort to inculcate them to your children and grandchildren today. Here is a case study to inspire you.

WHITTLING

The Medvak family of Cloverdale, Oregon, (Robert, Annie, Gabriele, Sammy and animal companion Pooch) have long enjoyed whittling as a hobby. But it's something more too. Let's hear it from Rob Medvak: »Whittling's not just an inexpensive and fun pastime, it's a way of life. I learnt to whittle from my grandfather Bobbie Medvak, a bear of a man, who could turn a 10-by-10 chunk of good solid basswood into, say, a cowboy boot or a love spoon in ten minutes flat... Now that's whittling!« The Medvaks went through a rough patch in their marriage a few years ago when Annie entered a

Friday 27 February	
8	
9	
10	
11	
12	
13	
14	
15	
16	
17	
18	

lesbian »phase«, and Rob reckons whittling not only helped him and the kids through it, but made them stronger as a family. »Me and the kids we used to carve little pictures of Ann when she was gone, which was a really quite difficult thing, very elaborate because you've got to get the expression right, and of course after she shaved her hair they

didn't look much like her anymore so we moved on to carving bottle stoppers instead. Sam even carved these beautiful wooden horses all on his own.« Rob Medvak is proud to have passed the tradition on to his children. »I reckon Gaby and Sam will be whittling for life. It's a good character-building discipline. Anyway, they can't wait to show Mummy all their work as soon as she comes back.«

ARE YOU PSYCHIC?

TODAY TRY LIFTING AN OBJECT WITH YOUR MIND.

BEGINNERS	INTERMEDIATE	FREAKS
TWIG	CHAIR	WEIGHTS
STAMP	BICYCLE	FAT LADY
PEN	CHILD	BUILDING

URI GELLER	URI STARTED BENDING SPOONS AT THE AGE OF FOUR. HE USED TO THRILL HIS CLASSMATES AT SCHOOL BY MAKING THE CLOCK HANDS MOVE FORWARD SO LESSONS WOULD END EARLY. HE IS NOW A MULTI-MILLIONAIRE SEVERAL TIMES OVER. SO YOU SEE IT'S WELL WORTH CULTIVATING THOSE HIDDEN POWERS.

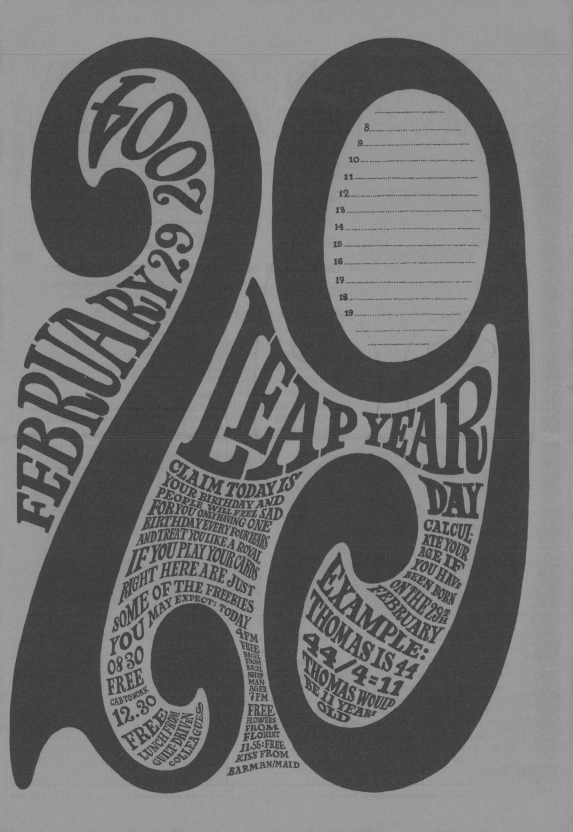

DIFFICULT
- Fastest man on earth (C. Lewis, 26.95mph)
- Longest manned space flight (V. Poliyakov, 437 days, 17hr, 58 min, 16 sec)
- Hottest Planet in the solar system (864°F, Venus)

AVERAGE
- Largest pumpkin (481kg, Nathan and Paula Zehr, USA)
- Longest letter to an editor (25,513 words, J. Sultzbaugh in »the Upper Dauphin Sentinel of Pennsylvania,« 1979)
- Longest paper plane flight (20.9 seconds, Chris Edge and Andy Currey, UK 1996)
- Most mosquitos killed in 5 minutes (21, Henry Pellonpaa, Finland, 1995)

EASY (no record officially established)
- Most spots on face (Teenager/Adult)
- Longest time holding up an umbrella
- Quickest recitation of the alphabet
- Longest occupation of attic

How to register your world record: contact
THE GUINNESS BOOK OF RECORDS
+44 891 517 607 or write to
Guinness Publishing Ltd, 338 Euston Rd,
London, NW1 3BD, UK.

WEDNESDAY 3 MARCH

8	12	16
9	13	17
10	14	18
11	15	19

TODAY SEND A LETTER TO SOMEONE AT RANDOM WITH A PHOTO OF YOUR SELF, A £5 NOTE, NO EXPLANATION AND NO SENDER ADDRESS. SEE WHAT COMES OF IT.

Friday 5 March
Today learn a poem by heart.

Hope is a Thing With Feathers
by Emily Dickinson

Hope is a thing with feathers
That perches in the soul,
And sings a tune without words,
And never stops at all,

And sweetest, in the gale, is heard;
And sore must be the storm
That could abash the little bird
That keeps so many warm.

I've heard it in the chilliest land,
And on the strangest sea;
Yet, never, in extremity,
It ask a crumb of me.

8	14
9	15
10	16
11	17
12	18
13	19 *Now recite it to a friend or colleague.*

Saturday 6 March. *Today save water.* The battle-ground of the 21st century will be water supply. Due to global warming and demographic trends, huge swathes of Africa and Asia will find their water demand drastically overrun their supply. Inevitably this will result in migratory pressure towards the more temperate regions. Do your bit to prevent this by safeguarding water. Hold off going to the WC as far as physically possible (one flush per five people is enough). Don't shower or bathe quite so often: once a week is quite sufficient. And why water the lawn? Concrete is a much more contemporary look. Remember: water is life.

ONE-DAY DETOX

AIM: today, your goal is to try and expel some of the toxins that are building up and gradually poisoning your body. Only consume cleansing food and drink. By tonight, your internal organs will have begun to purge all the drugs, preservatives, additives and excess bile that you've been lugging around for years. This is the first step towards the new you!

WHAT TO EAT
»Nothing« is the short answer! Because we are following an intensive one-day-only programme, an essentially liquid diet is necessary. But that doesn't mean you won't enjoy it! Start off with a yummy breakf[o] of lemon juice in warm water: go on, squeeze a wh[] lemon in there and treat yourself. (Citrus juice is a po[] ful bowel-purging agent.) Drink mineral water throug[] the day, and again, don't stint on quantity, the mor[e] better. For lunch, a treat: an apple to keep the doc[] away, washed down with two cups of camomile te[] you are feeling desperately hungry, you may eat[] teaspoonful of sesame seeds towards 5pm, thoug[] strictly speaking you shouldn't! For dinner, a nice[] clear soup of hot water, flavoured with some fennel. And before going to bed, a cup of peppermint tea, to aid the digestion.

POSSIBLE SIDE EFFECTS
As is often said, »no pain, no gain«! Your one-day detox may produce some »unwanted« side effects. Indeed, if it doesn't, you're probably doing something wrong. You may in fact wish to take the day off work before attempting it. Now, what should you expect? You will certainly experience headaches, starting before lunch. This is partly due to the brain's cravings for its usual stimulant, caffeine. As the day progresses, your tissues will also be eliminating noxious substances through the bloodstream, and thus through the brain, causing irritation. By lunchtime, you will feel weak, weak and hungry. This is no excuse to eat. Mid-afternoon, your detoxing skin may erupt in local rashes. As the day draws to a close, frequent urination, diarrhoea and gas are often observed, along with negative, anti-social feelings. Bravo! Cherish these side effects, for they mean you have successfully completed the »one-day detox«!

Well done! if you've followed this diet today, you will live longer by: {age x 4.5} – {weight/maternal great-grand-mother's age at death} minutes.

SUNDAY 7 MARCH

8
9
10
11
12
13
14
15
16
17
18

Today choose one hair on your body that you will let grow 1 metre long. Most hair grows at approximately 1cm a month, so within 8 years your chosen hair should be reaching optimum length. Remember to keep it clean, using shampoo and conditioner every day, and avoiding any tangling. Special note for pubic hair: tape it to your inside leg during sexual congress so as not to ruffle it.

Monday 8 March

8 ....

9 ....

10 ....

11 ....

12 ....

13 ....

14 ....

15 ....

16 ....

17 ....

18 ....

You'll never get bored of your special hair. Here for instance, we've used ours to recreate the Mona Lisa, only better.

Downsizing Day

In the current economic climate, we must all cut costs. Today fire someone from your entourage.

This advice comes to you courtesy of Shailesh Gor, accountant to the stars. Besides accountancy, Shailesh loves cricket and pizza, and is available for your downsizing needs for a reasonable fee. Contact him via www.thiswebsitewillchangeyourlife.com.

HAIRDRESSER? **-£10** Cut your own hair or get a handy friend to do it.	**CLEANER?** **-£30** Cleaners cost money and nick stuff. Plus it's good exercise for you.	**BUTCHER?** **-£9** Become a vegetarian, it's cheaper!	**BROKER?** **-£75** If they're any good, why haven't they retired rich by now?
BANKER? **-£50** Keep your money under your mattress, the new generation of thieves aren't trained to look there.	**TRAINER?** **-£25** With all that cleaning (see above), you won't need this one anymore.	**PARTNER?** **-£900** All that romantic tête-a-tête stuff costs a bomb. Ditch the bitch (or bastard).	**CABLE GUY?** **-£10** You watch too much TV.
DENTIST? **-£110** Original teeth are over-rated. There are very life-like prosthetics on the market these days.	**LIBRARIAN?** **-£2** Can you afford those swingeing fines? Reread your old books.	**GARDENER?** **-£15** You'll learn to love gardening when you retire. Why not start now?	**BODYGUARD?** **-£870** No one's going to kidnap you if you're worth nothing.
OLD FRIENDS? **-£100** Old friends expect birth-day gifts and other such luxuries you can ill afford. Lose'em.	**PET?** **-£25** Save money twice by not only downsizing your pet, but eating it (if is edible).	**ACCOUNTANT?** **-£15000** This one's a no-no. They know too much about you. Keep'em.	**THERAPIST?** **-£150** They also know too much about you, but nothing truly interesting. End it.
TUESDAY 9 MARCH	11	15	
8	12	16	
9	13	17	
10	14	18	

GET A HOBBY!

Today is the first day of your new hobby.
Choose one or several of the following and look
them up on the web for a comprehensive
introduction to your new life-long passion.

Count other
people's teeth.

Build a houseboat.

Teach dogs to
stand on one leg.

Cultivate pimples
around your mouth

Set out to see a
films with Morg
Freeman.

Search for subliminal
messages on heavy
metal albums. Report
your findings.

SATURDAY 13 MARCH

8	14
9	15
10	16
11	17
12	18
13	19

Set fire to all
brown shoes.

Topple a dictator
using only the
internet.

Attempt to mak
gold out of cotto
and raisins.

Try to grow
another toe.

Read the Bible in
all languages.

Make the perfect
tax return.

Record birds singing
and edit into hit songs.

Drink one glass
of every wine
ever bottled.

Organize fires.

Try to forget every-
thing you ever
learnt in school.

Watch the moon
complete its circle
from new to full.

Invent a pair of
sunglasses that
see very small
animals.

Play Russian
roulette.

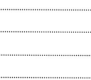

MACY

EXPRESS YOUR VIEWS TODAY
One month from now, posters will
go up across the world. They could
showcase your views. What do you want
to say? Let us know by the end of
today (11.59pm). The Diary user with
the most original views will see them
up in print by the end of the year.

8	14	
9	15	
10	16	
11	17	
12	18	
13	19	www.thiswebsitewillchangeyourlife.com

TUESDAY 16 MARCH

Wear shoes that are one size too small. That way you will experience huge relief when you come home and take them off tonight.

There is no more certain tonic!

ROYAL

Make yourself a nice footbath to celebrate.

Females! Cures diseases of womankind too!

A boon to the temperament, indispensable in curing all manner of affliction, from softening of the brain to biliousness.

HIGHLY UNUSUAL!

No Pain
↓
No Pleasure

Pronounced a miracle remedy by many eminent doctors from the universities and elsewhere

8			14
9			15
10			16
11			17
12			18
13			19

BECOME AN EXPERT ON TODAY

Read all the newspapers from A to Z and watch all the news bulletins so that by midnight tonight no one in the world knows more about the events of **FRIDAY 19 MARCH** 2004 than you. Here is a quick test to check your knowledge before you use it to attain unheard-of riches and power:

Weather in Zambia today:

Number of wars in progress today:

World population today:

Result of main sporting event today:

First topic on Jerry Springer today:

Middle East oil reserves today:

Number of astronauts in space today:

Lottery results in Colorado today:

Percentage of faked orgasms today:

Time spent waiting for phones to be picked up:

Moon-Earth distance at midday:

Horoscope of Leos with Scorpio ascendant:

Number of birthdays worldwide:

8	13	18
9	14	19
10	15	Congratulations: you are now the world's leading expert on today's news. Tomorrow morning be sure to get a business card printed and send it to everyone you know.
11	16	
12	17	

Saturday 20 March

TODAY START TO EAT A
PIECE OF FURNITURE

You will need: A piece of wooden furniture (wardrobe, bookshelf, table, chair), a nail file. Shave off a small amount of wood from your piece of furniture. Sprinkle it on your lunch. Enjoy! Persevere every day, and you should be able to eat the entire piece of furniture within 20 years.

8	14
9	15
10	16
11	17
12	18
13	19

WELCOME SPRING!

LURE A FLY ONTO THIS PAGE AND SWAT IT HERE

FOLLOW THIS ARROW TO A BOX

21 MARCH

7
8
9
10
11
12
13
14
15
16
17
18
19

Monday 22 March: Sit in the lotus position for 30 minutes today. *Lotus Position (Padmasana)* Sit on the floor with spine erect and legs stretched out in front of you, slightly apart. Place right foot on left thigh with the sole of foot turned up. Rest right knee on the ground. Take left foot and place it high on right thigh with sole facing up and left knee resting on the ground. Let feet rest on the pressure points at the top of the groin.

8
9
10
11
12
13

16
17
18
19
20
21

TODAY RELEASE
A RED BALLOON

Look! There it goes, soaring into the blue skies, a tiny beacon of friendship and hope, up, up, up and away, scattering the sparrows, inspiring the eagles, and perhaps eventually causing a major commercial airliner disaster.

THURSDAY 25 MARCH
8
9
10
11
12
13
14
15
16
17
18
19

TODAY, GO TO THE WRONG SIDE OF THE TRACKS

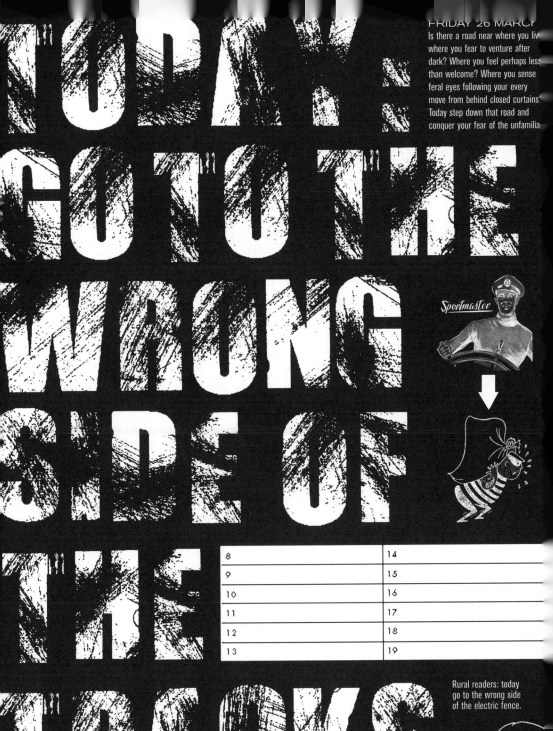

Is there a road near where you live where you fear to venture after dark? Where you feel perhaps less than welcome? Where you sense feral eyes following your every move from behind closed curtains? Today step down that road and conquer your fear of the unfamiliar.

Sportmaster

8		14	
9		15	
10		16	
11		17	
12		18	
13		19	

Rural readers: today go to the wrong side of the electric fence.

Tonight send a message in Morse from your window and see if anyone responds

JUST TESTING
.--- .-- ... - / - . ... - . .. -. --.

GOOD EVENING
--. --- --- -.. / . ...- . -. .. -. --.

SORRY TO DISTURB YOU
... --- .-. .-. -.-- / - --- / -.. .. ... - ..- .-. -... / -.-- --- ..-

I'M FEELING LONELY
.. -- .-- -. / .-. . . .-.. .. -. --. / .-.. --- -. . .-.. -.--

AND RANDY
.- -. -.. / .-. .- -. -.. -.--

FANCY SOME FUN?
.-. .- -. -.-. -.-- / ... --- -- . / ..-. ..- -. ..--..

ONLY KIDDING
--- -. .-.. -.-- / -.- .. -.. -.. .. -. --.

IS THAT A RIFLE?
.. ... / - .... .- - / .- / .-. .. ..-. .-.. . ..--..

AAARRGGH
.- .- .- .-. .-. --. --. ....

SOS
...---...

Sunday 28 March

8
9
10
11
12
13
14
15
16
17
18
19

oday measure your biceps. Get a tape measure and measure your biceps, while flexed, at its widest point.

ound off to the nearest inch. (If you can't find a tape measure, use a piece of string, then measure the string with a straight ruler).

Under 9 inches: we kick sand in your face, weasel-boy.

Between 10 and 20 inches: average to good.

Over 20 inches: pretty damn impressive (unless you're a woman).

30 inches: you have the biggest biceps in the world, but probably also the smallest penis.

PRIMAL SCREAM DAY

your system,
go on, let loose
baby oh yeah.

MONDAY 29 MARCH

The Four Types of...
1) YEEEEAAARRRRRGGGGHH!!!!!!
2) RAAAAAAAAAAHHHHHHHRGH!!!!!
3) WHOOOOOOOOAAAAARRRRR!!!!!!
4) EEEEEEEEEKKK!!!!!!(women only)

8
9
10
11
12
13
14
15
16
17
18
19

Tuesday 30 March

Today help collapse a currency! The Bangladeshi Taka is currently a bargain at 58.40tk to the US dollar. If every Diary owner buys a mere 100 takas today and then sells them at 4.55pm Bangladeshi time, the Taka shouldn't be worth the recycled paper it's printed on. To participate, simply call the DFE, Dhaka Foreign Exchange with your credit card details on: (88 02) 9667712-3.

8		14	
9		15	
10		16	
11		17	
12		18	
13		19	

DON'T WORRY! The IMF and the World Bank will step in to restore financial and economic stability. In the process, they'll probably get rid of a couple of unnecessary social programs as well, so you'll be doing Bangladesh a good turn.

Wednesday 31 March. Today invent a new way of peeling potatoes.

No one is happy with the current situation. That's why potato peeling is the province of the jailbird or the disgruntled housewife. Think laterally – perhaps peeling isn't the real problem here… Anyhow: come up with a novel solution and your fortune is assured!

08		14	
09		15	
10		16	
11		17	
12		18	
13		19	

Write your will here

Too many people leave their will until literally the last moment.
As a result, greedy relatives end up filing lawsuits and lawyers
fill their pockets. Spare your loved ones this fate by using this
readymade form to apportion your worldly goods.

I, ... (name), being of sound body
and mind, do declare this my last will and testament.

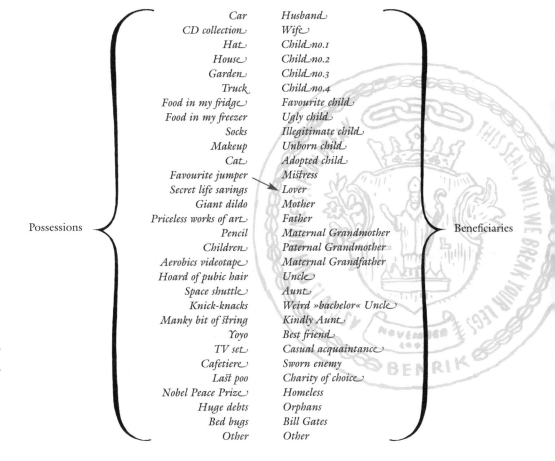

Possessions

Possessions	Beneficiaries
Car	Husband
CD collection	Wife
Hat	Child no.1
House	Child no.2
Garden	Child no.3
Truck	Child no.4
Food in my fridge	Favourite child
Food in my freezer	Ugly child
Socks	Illegitimate child
Makeup	Unborn child
Cat	Adopted child
Favourite jumper	Mistress
Secret life savings	Lover
Giant dildo	Mother
Priceless works of art	Father
Pencil	Maternal Grandmother
Children	Paternal Grandmother
Aerobics videotape	Maternal Grandfather
Hoard of pubic hair	Uncle
Space shuttle	Aunt
Knick-knacks	Weird »bachelor« Uncle
Manky bit of string	Kindly Aunt
Yoyo	Best friend
TV set	Casual acquaintance
Cafetiere	Sworn enemy
Last poo	Charity of choice
Nobel Peace Prize	Homeless
Huge debts	Orphans
Bed bugs	Bill Gates
Other	Other

Beneficiaries

Dated:...

Signature:...

Witnessed by: ....

Send to your lawyer with instructions to open upon death.

8	12	16
9	13	17
10	14	18
11	15	19

TODAY AVOID ALL SOURCES OF ELECTROMAGNETIC ENERGY
Clinical studies have conclusively established that continued exposure to man-made electromagnetic energy is associated with higher mortality and morbidity rates in the exposed population. Epidemiological studies have also demonstrated links to cancer and suicide.

STAY AWAY FROM:
High voltage powerlines
(2-200 Milligauss)

STAY AWAY FROM:
Mobile Phone Base stations
(2-60 Milligauss)

STAY AWAY FROM:
Microwave ovens
(2-50 Milligauss)

STAY AWAY FROM:
Electric blankets
(5-30 Milligauss)

STAY AWAY FROM:
Radio/TV towers
(2-20 Milligauss)

STAY AWAY FROM:
Pacemakers
(10-5000 Milligauss)

8	14
9	15
10	16
11	17
12	18
13	19

Only a complete booby would deny that extraterrestrial visitors are here already, and here to stay, despite government lies to the contrary. Many have taken human shape, all the better to study us. Today, learn how to spot them

Dead Eyes

The alien has glazed expression-less eyes. This is because these are only a front for his extrasensory perceptual apparatus.

Closed Mouth

Think about it. The aliens don't need to speak, as they communicate telepathetically. When they do speak to genuine humans, their speech is stilted, like they are stoned or something.

Ears Oozing Green Goo

Sometimes green goo will escape through the ears, if the alien cannot keep its head straight. This is a clear sign that something is seriously amiss.

Flaring nostrils

Nostrils are the only facial openings the aliens truly find useful. They use them to move from one human body to another. If a suspected alien comes near you with flaring nostrils, run for your life.

What to do if you find an alien

Try not to let on that you're onto the alien, as they can read your thoughts. Think of something innocuous instead, like a nice summer picnic for instance. Then quickly kill the alien by beheading it with a big axe, and burn the body. Report the incident to your local police station.

Monday 5 April

8	
9	
10	
11	
12	
13	
14	
15	
16	
17	
18	
19	

What are the alien intentions? The latest theory is that the aliens are waiting for the Rapture of the Church, when it happens. They will attempt to pass off the Day of the return of Jesus Christ Our Lord as some kind of mass abduction, or to say they took us somewhere to save us from something (God's wrath). We'll soon see anyway.

STOCKPILE AS MUCH FREE SUGAR AS POSSIBLE IN ONE DAY

Crazy but true: lots of people give out their hard-earned sugar entirely free such as in cafés, restaurants, the workplace kitchen, and so on. A person who collected it all and resold it at street value could make a small fortune. And that could be you!

COMMON SUGAR FORMATS

SUGAR IS FREE!

WHITE ANGLED LUMP	WHITE CUBIC LUMP	BROWN ANGLED LUMP
BROWN CUBIC LUMP	»HOMEMADE« LUMP	WHITE POWDER

8	14	
9	15	
10	16	
11	17	
12	18	
13	19	

BROWN POWDER	WHITE SUGAR SACHET	BROWN SUGAR SACHET

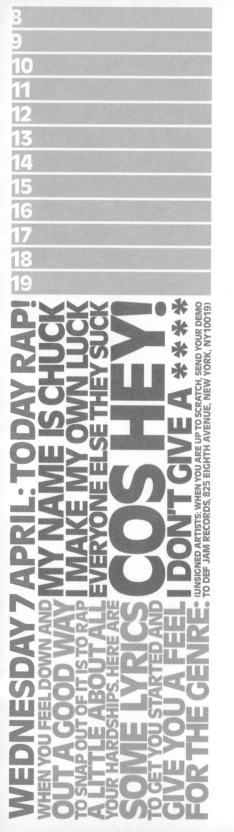

8
9
10
11
12
13
14
15
16
17
18
19

WEDNESDAY 7 APRIL: TODAY RAP! WHEN YOU FEEL DOWN AND OUT A GOOD WAY TO SNAP OUT OF IT IS TO RAP. A LITTLE ABOUT ALL YOUR HARDSHIPS. HERE ARE SOME LYRICS TO GET YOU STARTED AND GIVE YOU A FEEL FOR THE GENRE.* MY NAME IS CHUCK I MAKE MY OWN LUCK EVERYONE ELSE THEY SUCK COS HEY! I DON'T GIVE A ***** *(UNSIGNED ARTISTS: WHEN YOU ARE UP TO SCRATCH, SEND YOUR DEMO TO DEF JAM RECORDS, 825 EIGHTH AVENUE, NEW YORK, NY10019)

No swea-ring day

Send us one pound sterling for every swear word that escapes your uncouth lips

UP DATE The following are no longer considered effective swear words: **Damn Bloody Rot Bugger Imbecile Hell Sod Tart Strewth**

Thursday 8 April

7

8

9

10

11

12

13

14

15

16

17

18

19

GOOD FRIDAY: EXPERIENCE THE LORD'S PLIGHT FOR YOURSELF WITH OUR DIY CRUCIFIXION KIT.

1. THIS IS WHAT YOU NEED:

2. CUT OUT AS FOLLOWS:

3. GLUE THE TWO PIECES TOGETHER:

4. TAPE YOUR HANDS TO YOUR CROSS:
(IT COULD BE HELPFUL TO ASK FOR ASSISTANCE.)

5. SUFFER!

NOTES

A.

B.

SATURDAY 10 APRIL: COUNTERFEITING DAY: 1. Cut this fake banknote out. 2. Stick A & B back-to-back. 3. Crumple it up a few times. 4. Convince someone to accept it as legal tender

8	14
9	15
10	16
11	17
12	18
13	19

Today become a chocolate junkie

Chocolate is the only legal psychoactive drug, a veritable cocktail of mind-interfering chemicals. It's a unique source of theobromine, an addictive xanthine alkaloid. It contains anandamide, which binds to the same receptors in the brain as the psychoactive elements in marijuana (cannabinoids). And it boosts levels of serotonin in the brain, much as anti-depressants do.

Now: mild doses of serotonin act as a sedative on the brain, but higher doses can cause an addictive high followed by crash followed by craving response. You're looking at a good 12kg to get high, which may seem a lot, but is actually much better value than illegal drugs, and won't get you in trouble with the law. So get munching!

The confection of perfection!

Danger! Chocolate is good for you, but not for your pet. Cats and dogs can't metabolize or excrete the theobromine in chocolate and may end up having a seizure as a result. If you suspect your pet has eaten chocolate in any form, call a vet immediately.

8	Easter Sunday 11 April	14
9		15
10		16
11		17
12		18
13		19

Today, break one or several of the

The Ten Commandments

1. You shall have no other Gods besides Me.
2. You shall not make for yourself an idol.
3. You shall not take the name of
   the Lord your God in vain.
4. Remember the sabbath day, to keep it holy.
5. Honor your father and your mother.
6. You shall not murder.
7. You shall not commit adultery.
8. You shall not steal.
9. You shall not bear false witness
   against your neighbour.
10. You shall not covet.

Easter Monday 12 April	
8	14
9	15
10	16
11	17
12	18
13	19

(If you are struck by a bolt of lightning, you will have solid grounds on which to base your faith.)

TODAY LIE TO SOMEONE ABOUT YOUR PAST

There are four main types of lie about one's past, all designed to enhance one's reputation: *1. White lies:* My first word was »symposium«. *2. Blatant lies:* I'm descended through my mother's side from Attila the Hun. *3. Lies no one can check:* I used to work for MI5, but the bureaucracy was too stifling. *4. Lies no one wants to check:* They really bungled my sex change operation.

	THURSDAY	
8	15 APRIL	14
9		15
10		16
11		17
12		18
13		19

GLOBALIZATION DAY

Today surf internet chat rooms and make friends with someone on the other side of the world. Eventually you could gain a new best chum, an invitation to visit a distant land, and a better understanding of what makes us all human. Alternatively, you might befriend some nutter who will turn up on your doorstep with a pickaxe. Anyway here's where to begin.

SATURDAY 17 APRIL
9
10
11
12
13
14
15
16
17
18

towerchat.com
thepalace.com
parachat.com
bbackdoors.com
a1chat-rooms.com
excite.com
chatbox.com
worlds.net
looksmart.com
yahoo.com
theglobe.com
talkcity.com
classmates.com
babylon.com
hearme.com
topica.com
network54.com
travlang.com
mirc.com
tucows.com
inreach.com
crossdaily.com

chathouse.com
peoplelink.com
teenchat.com
absolutechat.com
800predict.com
freerepublic.com
thegrid.net
smartbotpro.net
icqgreetings.com
undernet.org
chatway.com
christiancafe.com
the-park.com
4-lane.com
activeworlds.com
developer.com
irchelp.org
netdive.com
cuseemeworld.com
arabchat.com
cuseeme.com
tribal.com

chattopia.com
chatseek.com
chat.fashion.net
austnet.org
hyperchat.com
chatweb.net
chattown.com
knowpost.com
chatlist.com
quilttalk.com
pirch.com
coolchat.com
peopleweb.com
go.com
chatfreak.com
sixdegrees.com
rememory.com
veggiedate.com
xworld.org
hotelchat.com
webchatting.com
thepark.com

Sunday 18 April

LONDON MARATHON
Win it by taking a surprise shortcut!

8					
9					
10					
11					
12					
13					
14					
15					
16					
17					
18					
19					

After Mile 8, take a left into Southwark Park. Not only do you avoid Rotherhithe entirely, thereby gaining a good 30 minutes on the others, but it's also a much more pleasant run. You emerge after Mile 11 on Jamaica Rd. Just be sure to act nonchalant as you slip back into the race. Top prize: $55, 000. Runner-up: $30,000. 3rd: $22,500.

Or why not simply take a taxi and avoid all that running? Nothing in the rules expressly forbids it.

Today and tomorrow, note w

8	14
9	15
10	16
11	17
12	18
13	19

Has your day been lucky or unlucky?

LUCKY ☐

UNLUCKY ☐

foot you get out of bed on.

DAY 2 TUESDAY 20 APRIL

	14		8	Has your day
	15		9	been lucky or
	16		10	unlucky?
	17		11	
	18		12	LUCKY ☐
	19		13	UNLUCKY ☐

there a difference? Which works best for you? LEFT ☐   RIGHT ☐
om now on, only ever get out of bed on your lucky foot.

TREAT'EM MEAN KEEP'EM KEEN

Test this relationship theory today on your significant other.

8	14
9	15
10	16
11	17
12	18
13	19

•Tell them you'll call and don't. •Turn up half an hour late for a rendezvous. •When they say »I love you«, just answer »thanks«. •Accidentally call them by the name of your ex. •Pick the part of their body they're most sensitive about and gaze at it cryptically. •Suddenly laugh out loud during intercourse.

How to measure success: Have you managed to inject a welcome frisson into your stale relationship? Or have they packed their bags and advised you to seek psychiatric help? Relationship guru Dr Kirk Frampton says: »you can't turn a humdrum suburban relationship into a Hollywood romance overnight. You need to keep your loved one on his or her toes constantly. Only six months down the line would I normally expect to see results, one way or another.«

Thursday 22 April
TODAY TRACE YOUR ROOTS
Fill in your family tree as far
back as you can.

HANDY HINTS:
- Start close to home. Everyone has a distant cousin who's got the genealogy bug!
- Interview elderly relatives. Give Aunt Mae a call before she passes on and grill her.
- Check out census/land/probate records; boy, you're getting keen now.

WHAT TO DO IF YOU FIND OUT YOU'RE DESCENDED FROM THE KING
All depends on whether you're legitimate or illegitimate. If you're legitimate (»legit«), call up your government and make them aware of your claim. They have 21 days to respond, upon which you may ascend the throne. If you are illegitimate (»bastard«), you run the risk of being sent to the Tower where you will spend the rest of your life hung up against a mossy wall with rats chewing away at your genitalia.

8	14	
9	15	
10	16	
11	17	
12	18	
13	19	

F

F IS FOR FAKE
F.I.S.T.
F/X
FABULOUS BAKER BOYS, THE
FABULOUS DORSEYS, THE
FABULOUS FLEISCHER, THE
FACE IN THE CROWD
FACE/OFF
FACES
FACULTY, THE
FADE TO BLACK
FAERIES
FAHRENHEIT 451
FAIL SAFE
FAIRYTALE- A TRUE STORY
FAKE
FALCON & THE SNOWMAN, THE
FALL OF THE HOUSE OF USHER
FALL OF THE ROMAN EMPIRE, THE
FALLEN
FALLING DOWN
FALLING IN LOVE
FALSTAFF: CHIMES AT MIDNIGHT
FAME
FAMILY BUSINESS
FAMILY PLOT
FAMILY THING, A
FANCY PANTS
FANDANGO
FANNY
FANNY & ALEXANDER
FANTASIA
FANTASTIC PLANET
FANTASTIC VOYAGE
FANTASY MISSION FORCE
FAR AND AWAY
FAR AWAY, SO CLOSE
FAR COUNTRY, THE
FAR FROM THE MADDING
CROWD
FAR OFF PLACE, A
FAR PAVILIONS,THE
FAREWELL MY CONCUBINE
FAREWELL TO ARMS, A
FAREWELL TO THE KING
FARGO
FARINELLI
FARMER'S DAUGHTER, A
FAST TIMES AT RIDGEMONT HIGH
FASTER PUSSYCAT, KILL! KILL!
FAT MAN & LITTLE BOY
FATAL ATTRACTION
FATAL FLYING GUILLOTINE
FATAL INVERSION, A
FATAL VISION
FATHER GOOSE
FATHER OF THE BRIDE
FATHERLAND
FATHER'S LITTLE DIVIDEND

FATS DOMINO & FRIENDS
FAUST
FAUST (SILENT)
FEAR & LOATHING IN LAS VEGAS
FEAR
FEARLESS
FEARLESS HYENA
FEARLESS HYENA 2
FEARLESS VAMPIRE KILLERS
FEDERAL HILL (BLACK & WHITE)
FEELING MINNESOTA
FELIX THE CAT (ADVENTURES OF)
FELLINI'S SATYRICON
FEMALE PERVERSIONS
FEMALE TROUBLE
FERN GULLY
FERRIS BUELLER'S DAY OFF
FETISHES
FEW GOOD MEN, A
FIDDLER ON THE ROOF
FIELD OF DREAMS, A
FIELD, THE
FIEND WITHOUT A FACE
FIERCE CREATURES
FIFTH ELEMENT, THE
FIFTH MUSKETEER, THE
FIFTY FOUR (54 - STUDIO)
FIGHT CLUB
FIGHTING 69TH, THE
FIGHTING SEABEES
FIGHTING SULLIVANS, THE
FILTH AND THE FURY, THE
FINAL ASCENT: CHIEFS YEARBOOK
FINAL COUNTDOWN
FINAL DESTINATION
FINAL FOUR – THE MOVIE
FINDERS KEEPERS. LOVERS
WEEPER.
FINGERS
FINIAN'S RAINBOW
FIORILE
FIRE
FIRE & ICE
FIRE IN THE SKY
FIRE ON THE AMAZON
FIRE ON THE MOUNTAIN
FIREFOX
FIRESTARTER
FIREWORKS
FIRM, THE
FIRST BLOOD
FIRST KNIGHT
FIRST MEN ON THE MOON
FIRST NUDIE MUSICAL
FIRST STRIKE
FIRST WIVES CLUB
FISH CALLED WANDA, A
FISH THAT SAVED PITTSBURGH
FISHER KING, THE

FIST OF FEAR, TOUCH OF DEATH
FIST OF THE NORTH STAR
FISTFUL OF DOLLARS
FISTFUL OF DYNAMITE
FISTS OF FURY
FITZCARRALDO
FIVE CORNERS
FIVE EASY PIECES
FIVE FINGERS
FIVE PENNIES
FIVE SENSES
FIVE THOUSAND
FINGERS OF DR. T
FLAMING STAR
FLAMINGO KID, THE
FLASH GORDON
FLASHBACK
FLASHDANCE
FLATLINERS
FLAWLESS
FLESH
FLESH & BONE
FLESH AND BLOOD
FLESH GORDON
FLETCH
FLETCH LIVES
FLICKERS
FLIGHT OF THE NAVIGATOR, THE
FLIGHT OF THE PHOENIX, THE
FLIGHT TO MARS
FLIM-FLAM MAN
FLINTSTONES IN VIVA ROCK
VEGAS
FLINTSTONES-THE MOVIE
FLIPPER
FLIRTING WITH DISASTER
FLORENTINE, THE
FLOWER DRUM SONG
FLOWERS IN THE ATTIC
FLOYDS HAIR-RAISING ADVENTURE
FLUBBER
FLUSHED
FLY AWAY HOME
FLY, THE (1958)
FLY, THE (1986)
FLYING DOWN TO RIO
FLYING LEATHERNECKS
FLYING TIGERS
FOG, THE
FOGHORN LEGHORN FRACTURED
FUNN
FOLLOW ME BOYS
FOLLOW THAT DREAM
FOLLOW THE FLEET
FOOTLITE PARADE
FOOTLOOSE
FOR A LOST SOLDIER
FOR ART'S SAKE
FOR FEW DOLLARS MORE

FOR LOVE OF THE GAME
FOR ME AND MY GAL
FOR THE BOYS
FOR WHOM THE BELL TOLLS
FOR YOUR EYES ONLY
FORBIDDEN CHOICES
FORBIDDEN PLANET
FORCE OF EVIL
FORCE OF ONE
FORCE TEN FROM NAVARONE
FORCED VENGEANCE
FORCES OF NATURE
FOREVER YOUNG
FORGET PARIS
FORREST GUMP
FORT APACHE
FORT APACHE: THE BRONX
FORT SAGANNE
FORTUNE COOKIE
FORTY EIGHT (48) HOURS
FORTY SECOND STREET
FORTY YEARS OF MJQ
FOUL PLAY
FOUNTAINHEAD, THE
FOUR DAYS IN NOVEMBER
FOUR DAYS IN SEPTEMBER
FOUR HUNDRED BLOWS
FOUR MUSKETEERS
FOUR ROOMS
FOUR SEASONS
FOUR WEDDINGS & A FUNERAL
FOURTEEN NINETY-TWO (1492):
CONQUEST OF PARADISE
FOURTH FLOOR, THE
FOURTH MAN, THE
FOX & THE HOUND
FOZZIE'S SCRAPBOOK
FRACTAL UNIVERSE
FRANCIS IN THE
HAUNTED HOUSE
FRANCIS THE TALKING MULE
FRANK CAPRA'S BATTLE OF
BRITAIN
FRANK SINATRA HIS LIFE & TIMES
FRANK,LIZA,AND SAMMY
FRANKENSTEIN (ORIG)
FRANKENSTEIN MEETS
THE WOLF MAN
FRANKENSTEIN-MARY SHELLEY'S
FRANKENWEENIE
FRANKIE & JOHNNIE
FRANTIC
FREAKED
FREAKS
FREAKS UNCENSORED
FREAKY FRIDAY
FREDDYS DEAD:
FINAL NIGHTMARE
FREE TO BE YOU AND ME

FREE WILLY
FREE WILLY 2
FREEBIE AND THE BEAN
FREEWAY
FRENCH CONNECTION
FRENCH CONNECTION II
FRENCH KISS
FRENCH LIEUTENANT'S WOMAN
FRENCH TWIST
FRENZY
FREQUENCY
FRESH (DRAMA)
FRESHMAN, THE
FREUD LEAVING HOME
FRIDAY
FRIDAY THE 13TH
FRIDAY THE 13TH PART 2
FRIDAY THE 13TH PART 3
FRIDAY THE 13TH PART 4
FRIDAY THE 13TH PART 5
FRIDAY THE 13TH PART 6
FRIDAY THE 13TH PART 7
FRIDAY THE 13TH PART 8
FRIDAY THE 13TH PART 9
FRIDAY THE 13TH PART 10
FRIED GREEN TOMATOES
FRIENDLY PERSUASION
FRIGHT NIGHT
FRIGHTENERS, THE
FRISCO KID
FROM BEYOND
FROM DUSK TILL DAWN
FROM DUSK TO DAWN 2
FROM HERE TO ETERNITY
FROM PLUTO WITH LOVE
FROM RUSSIA WITH LOVE
FROM STAR WARS TO JEDI
FROM THE MANGER TO THE
CROSS
FRONT PAGE, THE FRONT, THE
FUGITIVE, THE
FULL METAL JACKET
FULL MONTY, THE
FULLER BRUSH GIRL
FULLER BRUSH MAN
FULL-TILT BOOGIE
FUN
FUN & FANCY FREE
FUN IN ACAPULCO
FUN WITH DICK AND JANE
FUNERAL, THE
FUNNY BONES
FUNNY FACE
FUNNY GIRL
FUNNY LADY
FUNNY THING HAPPENED ON
THE WAY
FURY, THE
FUTUREWORLD

FRIDAY 23 APRIL. Today see a film beginning with F. If there is none on in your neighbourhood, you may see one beginning with Z.

8	12	16
9	13	17
10	14	18
11	15	19

Saturday 24 April
Today: tattoo a banana and display it on your windowsill. (Scrape its skin with a sharp implement and watch it go black in minutes!)

8	14	
9	15	
10	16	
11	17	
12	18	
13	19	

SUNDAY 25 APRIL:
Today use this exclusive pass to violate a law of your choice.

ABOVE THE LAW PASS

BY UNITED NATIONS RESOLUTION 34

The carrier is hereby declared immune to arrest and prosecution for violation of any civil and/or criminal laws in countries signatory to the Bamako Protocol 1973.
To all officers of the law: please ensure freedom of movement and provide assistance.
Any damage to goods&property should be notified to UNPDR (5643-09) for eventual compensation.

Resolution des Nations-Unies numero 34: Le porteur n'est pas assujetti aux lois civiles ni criminelles des pays signataires du protocole de Bamako 1973.
Authorites policieres: veuillez le (ou la) laisser passer et lui porter toute assistance.

ABOVE THE LAW PASS

BY UNITED NATIONS RESOLUTION 34

PHOTO HERE

The carrier is hereby declared immune to arrest and prosecution for violation of any civil and/or criminal laws in countries signatory to the Bamako Protocol 1973.
To all officers of the law: please ensure freedom of movement and provide assistance.
Any damage to goods&property should be notified to UNPDR (5643-09) for eventual compensation.

Resolution des Nations-Unies numero 34: Le porteur n'est pas assujetti aux lois civiles ni criminelles des pays signataires du protocole de Bamako 1973.
Authorites policieres: veuillez le (ou la) laisser passer et lui porter toute assistance.

8

9

10

11

12

13

14

15

16

17

18

19

HI! I am currently experimenting with the concept of siesta. Therefore any issues, no matter how important, will have to wait to be brought before me between the hours of 11am and 3pm. If I like this I will start doing it every day. PS: A light lunch would be great when I wake up.

DIARY SIESTA CLUB

ZZ ZZ
ZZ ZZ
ZZ ZZ

Today place this sign on your door handle.

8
9
10
11
12
13
14
15
16
17
18
19

ATTENTION! Forward planning: Book your summer holiday now for the week of July 24. This year, you are going to France. Mais oui!

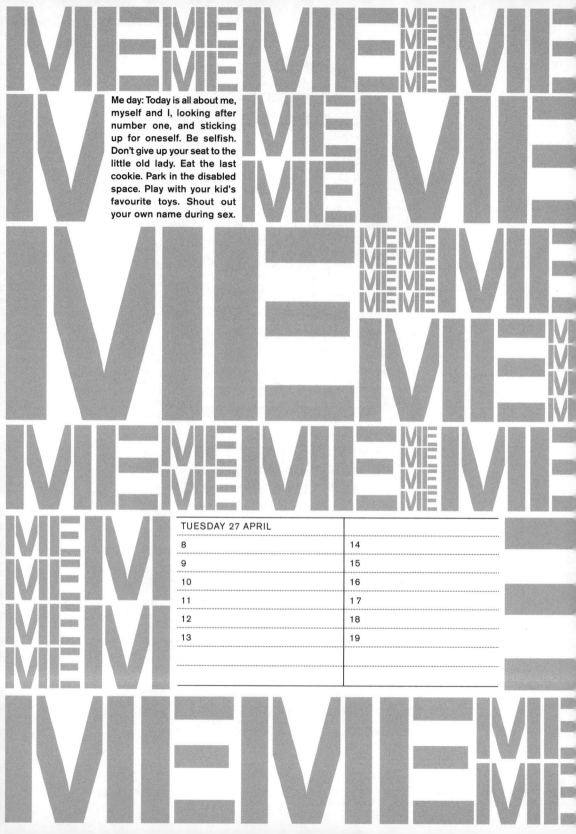

Me day: Today is all about me, myself and I, looking after number one, and sticking up for oneself. Be selfish. Don't give up your seat to the little old lady. Eat the last cookie. Park in the disabled space. Play with your kid's favourite toys. Shout out your own name during sex.

TUESDAY 27 APRIL	
8	14
9	15
10	16
11	17
12	18
13	19

SNOOPER ALERT!

Dear..

I know you are snooping in my diary, you have had guilt written all over your stupid face for the last few weeks, this is what I think of you if you really must know:

....

....

....

....

....

....

....

WEDNESDAY 28 APRIL		
8	12	16
9	13	17
10	14	18
11	15	19

Now get your nose out of it and mind your own sorry business in the future.

How to: Wax ear plugs, available at any chemist.

True story: Beethoven's descent into deafness is part and parcel of his myth. Less well-known is the extent to which his other senses overcompensated. At a rehearsal of one of his later quartets in 1825, lead violinist Joseph Bohm took it upon himself to ignore a change in tempo (Meno vivace) without telling Beethoven, who by now was pretty thoroughly deaf. Bohm related what happened: »Beethoven, crouched in a corner, heard nothing, but watched with strained attention. After the last stroke of the bows, he said laconically, »Let it remain so«, went to the desks and crossed out the Meno vivace in the four parts.«

THURSDAY 29 APRIL		
8	14	Write down the pros and cons of this sense as you discover them.
9	15	Pros: ....
10	16	Cons: ....
11	17	
12	18	End of day assessment: How crucial is
13	19	my sense of hearing to me ..../10

DON'T SPEND ANY MONEY DAY

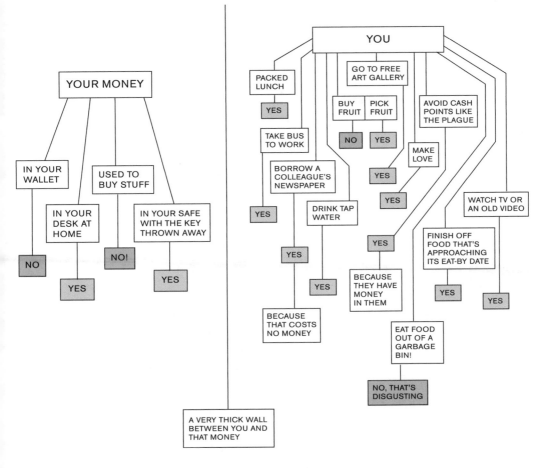

8			14
9			15
10			16
11			17
12			18
13			19

NO TV W

The publishers of the Diary have arranged a deal with news organizations and world leaders whereby nothing of real importance will happen this weekend, so you can feel at ease giving your remote a break. Instead, here are some pre-TV era activities that will feel a lot more wholesome.

WALKING

Walking is a fun activity that can be enjoyed at any age, and what's more, it's free! You can walk on your own or with someone, in the street or in the park. The possibilities are endless.

CHATTING BY THE FIRE

Everyone loves a good fire. »Round the fire« is a traditional place to chat, as everyone is gathered together. Starter topics include how well the fire is going, size of logs, how cold it must be outside.

PLAYING GAMES

There are literally dozens of games, from chess to hide-and-seek. Some of these are more advanced than others, so if you're new to games, start with something easy, like popular card game SNAP.

BIRDWATCHING

Fun AND educational. The British Isles are rich in birdlife. Look out for the yellow-tailed sparrow for instance, so named after his yellow-coloured tail. To make the most of this one, binoculars are a must.

CROQUET

Not just for elderly aunts! The game of croquet is in fact a vicious sport where the most amiable-seeming individuals soon battle it out for supremacy. »Uncle Jo« Stalin's favourite pastime.

STARING AT THE CLOUDS

Anyone can enjoy this: all you need is a patch of sky... Clouds can assume many familiar shapes: cows, faces, goldfish, wheelbarrows. Names of clouds are fun too: »cumulo-nimbus«, for instance.

WHISTLING

The great advantage of whistling is that it can be done anywhere, even while you work, as the song goes. Everyone likes a good tune, so brighten up their day as well.

SKIPPING

Beloved by schoolgirls and boxers alike, so there must be something to it. You'll need a rope and a bit of practice, but once you get the hang of it, there's no turning back!

KNITTING

One for the ladies: knitting jumpers, socks and hats is one of the most stress-relieving activities imaginable, and it's a useful skill to acquire in times of economic uncertainty.

READING

Once upon

You're doing this as we speak, so you must know the basics. Hundreds of books on all sorts of topics await your perusal. Join your local library and the world of reading is your oyster.

WRESTLING

Not as difficult as it's made out to be, though you will need a partner. Grapple each other and try to push the other one to the ground. Hours of entertainment guaranteed.

CHURCHGOING (SUNDAY)

After a wrestling bout early on Sunday, why not settle body, mind and spirit with some church? Churchgoing has a long and proud history. This one has it all: singing, thinking, clapping.

EEKEND!

	9
	10
	11
	12
	13
	14
	15
	16
	17
	18

ACUTE APPENDICITIS

Symptoms: pain in the lower right abdomen, nausea, loss of appetite, vomiting

PROCEDURE: 1. Anaesthesize the patient

2. Make an incision in the lower right abdomen

3. Pull appendix out and tie it at its base

4. Remove appendix (taking care to avoid spillage)

5. Suture the incision

OPEN APPENDECTOMY COMPLICATIONS: if the appendix has ruptured, clean out with a warm saline solution, insert drain through incision to allow pus to drain out of abdomen, leave skin open but pack with sterile gauze and leave in place until pus is drained and there is no sign of infection. If abdomen is too infected to locate appendix, treat with antibiotics before removing. Do not attempt this procedure unless you are a qualified surgeon, and even then think twice about it.

8	12	16
9	13	17
10	14	18
11	15	19

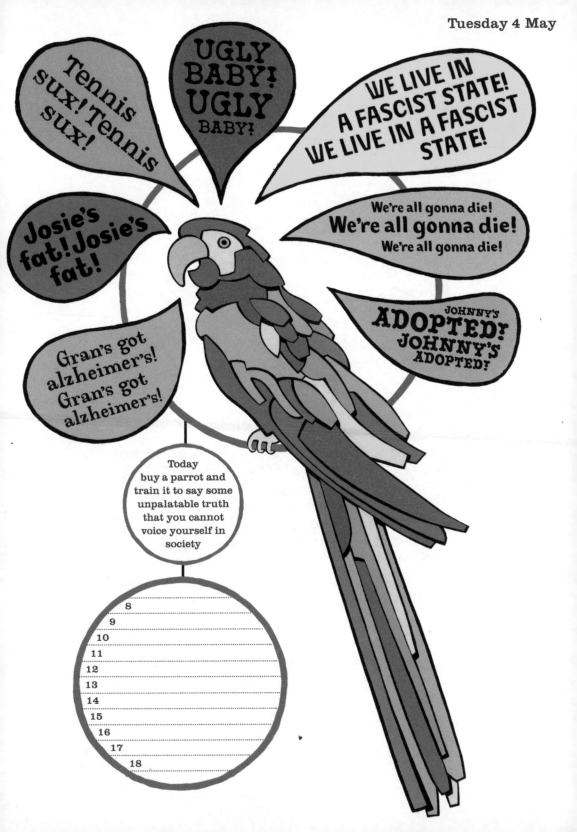

8	14	
9	15	
10	16	
11	17	
12	18	
13	19	

YOUR STARS TODAY:
For once, take your horoscope seriously. To help, we've had this one
designed scientifically, by the world's leading expert. Follow it to the letter.

Thursday 6 May

Today exercise your full rights as a consumer.

You are legally entitled to buy a lot of prepackaged material by the unit.

Buy one beer out of a sixpack. Buy two biscuits out of a packet of 20.

Buy five pistachios, a dollop of face cream, or one sock,

and experiment with shopkeepers' knowledge of the law.

8
9
10
11
12
13
14
15
16
17
18
19

REDUNDANCIES (draft)/ HR/009-6753
CC: Clermont Srees Solicitors

Possibles? (circulate management)

ANDY
TOM B.
SARAH ?

P. W.

Anyone else?

8	12	16
9	13	17
10	14	18
11	15	19

Saturday 8 May

8
9
10
11
12
13
14
15
16
17
18
19

Try a
new fruit
today

Count your blessings

In the great hubbub of life, we often forget to pause and consider how lucky we are. Today, assess this scientifically.

Blessing	Score	Total
Are you alive?	10 points	
Are you in good health?	9 points	
Do you have a partner?	7 points	
Do you have regular sex?	6 points	
Do you have children?	3 points/child (-3 POINTS PER NAUGHTY CHILD)	
Do you have a roof over your head?	5 points	
Can you feed yourself and your family?	5 points	
Do you have a steady job?	3 points	
Are you free from racial or sexual discrimination?	5 points	
Is your country currently at peace?	6 points	
Is your country well away from any geological fault lines?	6 points	
Are your parents still alive?	4 points	
Are you still on speaking terms with them?	4 points	
Have you found God?	3 points	
Have you found yourself?	2 points	
Are your bowel movements regular?	8 points	
Were you born into one of the richer social classes?	5 points	
Are you a born optimist?	6 points	
Are you a born pessimist?	−6 points	
Do you have a sense of humour?	(+1 points if you replied yes +4 points if you replied no)	
Total		

If you have scored more than *40* points, you are luckier than 90% of the human race.

CONGRATULATIONS.

Sunday 9 May	12	16
08	13	17
09	14	18
10	15	19
11		

Today write a letter to your local newspaper to achieve a high profile in your community. Before you know it, you'll be the spokesperson for a local campaign. You could be elected mayor on the back of a wave of popular support, and next step it's the White House (especially if you're American). US President Dwight Eisenhower started off in politics by complaining in the *DesMoines Digest* that corncobs were just too darned pricey these days. Popular inflammatory topics: Dog poo everywhere, Broken pavement, Pesky kids, Rubbish men never pick up boxes, Town Hall corrupt.

LOCAL NEWS

THE MODEL CITIZEN!!!

MAYOR CONGRATULATES HAVE-A-GO HERO

KEYS OF THE CITY ARE ONLY MODEST TOKEN OF APPRE- CIATION FOR ACHIEVEMENT

VIGILANT CITIZEN SAVES MILLIONS OF CHILDREN FROM CERTAIN DEATH

TOWN COUNCIL SAYS THANKS BY RENAMING TALLEST SKYSCRAPER

NO MORE ROOM FOR MEDALS ON JUMPER!

MONDAY 10 MAY

8

9

10

11

12

13

14

15

16

17

18

19

DEFY HIERARCHY TODAY

DON'T JUST ACCEPT SOCIETY'S RULES. TALK BACK. STAND UP. BE THE COG THAT CLOGS UP THE MACHINE.

NO THANX!

AUTHORITY FIGURE No1: THE BOSS

DO NOT SAY: CERTAINLY MR JOHNSON, YOU'LL HAVE THAT REPORT ON YOUR DESK FIRST THING IN THE MORNING SIR.

INSTEAD, SAY: HEY MR BOSSMAN PIECE-OF-SHIT CAPITALIST EXPLOITER, I'M TIRED OF FOLLOWING YOUR WHIMS SO TAKE YOUR JOB AND STICK IT UP YOUR FAT CAT ARSE.

AUTHORITY FIGURE No2: THE LAW

DO NOT SAY: I'M SORRY OFFICER, I'LL MOVE ALONG STRAIGHT AWAY, I DON'T WANT TO CAUSE AN AFFRAY.

INSTEAD, SAY: FUCK YOU, PIG. IF YOU THINK I'M GOING TO MOVE AN INCH YOU'VE GOT ANOTHER THING COMING, YOU UNDERSIZED-PENIS SCUM, IT'S A FREE COUNTRY, NOW MIND YOUR OWN BUSINESS AND PISS RIGHT OFF.

AUTHORITY FIGURE No3: THE TEACHER

DO NOT SAY: YOU'RE ABSOLUTELY CORRECT, I DO NOT IN FACT KNOW WHAT I AM TALKING ABOUT, I'LL JUST LISTEN TO YOUR EXPERTISE AND TAKE NOTES FROM NOW ON.

INSTEAD, SAY: I DON'T KNOW WHICH IS MORE PITIFUL, THE ROLE YOU PLAY IN PERPETUATING THE POST-CAPITALIST PATRIARCHAL ORDER, OR THE PITTANCE YOU GET PAID TO DO SO. EVER HEARD OF PINK FLOYD? NO I DIDN'T THINK SO. ANYWAY, I'M TAKING MY KIDS OUT OF SCHOOL AND THAT'S FINAL, DAMMIT.

AUTHORITY FIGURE No4: THE FAMILY

DO NOT SAY: YES FATHER, I'M SURE YOU'RE RIGHT, I'LL GO FOR THAT INSURANCE SALESMAN JOB, IT DOES LOOK PROMISING.

INSTEAD, SAY: LOOK MAN, JUST COS I CAME OUT OF YOUR BALLS DOESN'T MEAN I HAVE TO LISTEN TO YOUR STUPID ADVICE. I'M GONNA BE A HEAVY METAL DRUMMER, EARN TEN TIMES MORE THAN YOU, AND THAT'S FINAL, SO GET OFF MY CASE OR I'LL LIE AND HAVE YOU DONE FOR ABUSE.

TUESDAY 11 MAY		
8	14	
9	15	
10	16	
11	17	
12	18	
13	19	

Today we can reveal that your lucky number is:

12

PLAY THE LOT-TERY

BET ON A HORSE (No 12 IN THE 12th RACE)

TAKE THE NO 12 BUS

BET ON THE 12 AT ROULETTE

BUY A HOUSE AT NO 12

Incredible but true: Marsha Vranitsky's lucky number is three. She has triplets, all born on the third of March 2003, from her third husband Rick. And: soon she will be 23! Luck is a beautiful and mysterious lady.

WEDNESDAY
12
MAY

8

9

10

11

12

13

14

15

16

17

18

19

Invent a new colour
In 1957, French painter Yves Klein invented and patented an especially intense ultramarine blue pigment, »International Klein Blue,« shown here. Today, dream up a new colour of your own, and contact your lawyers.

Thursday 13 May

8
9
10
11
12
13
14
15
16
17
18
19

Today hack into a computer network

Hacking is a useful and potentially lucrative hobby. All you need is a computer connected to the internet and a few hours to spare. Here are some popular sites to hack into:

www.pentagon.com
www.mi5.gsi.org.uk
www.federalreserve.gov.org
www.microsoft.com
www.starbucks.com

Friday 14 May

Starter tips: Since the early days of intruders breaking into computers, they have tried to develop backdoors techniques that allow them to get into the system. Here are some common backdoors, concentrating on Unix backdoors and some discussion on future Windows NT backdoors. This will show you the difficulties in how to choose the right methods, both for beginners and advanced intruders. This will not cover every possible way to create a backdoor as the possibilities to hack are limitless. The backdoor for most intruders provide two or three main functions:
– Be able to get back into a computer even if the administrator tries to secure it, e.g., changing all the passwords.
– Be able to get back into the computer with the least amount of detectability. Most backdoors provide a way to avoid being logged and many times the machine can appear to have no one online even while an intruder is using it.
– Be able to get back into the computer with the least amount of time. Most intruders want to easily get back into the machine without having to do all the work of exploiting a hole to gain access.
In some cases, if the intruder may think the administrator may detect any installed backdoor, they will resort to using the vulnerability repeatedly to get on a machine as the only backdoor. Thus not touching anything that may tip off the administrator. Therefore in some cases, the vulnerabilities on a machine remain the only unnoticed backdoor.

Password Cracking Backdoor. One of the first and oldest methods of intruders used to gain not only access to a Unix machine but backdoors was to run a password cracker. This uncovers weak passworded accounts. All these new accounts are now possible backdoors into a machine even if the system administrator locks out the intruder's current account. Many times, the intruder will look for unused accounts with easy passwords and change the password to something difficult. When the administrator looked for all the weak passworded accounts, the accounts with modified passwords will not appear. Thus the administrator will not be able to easily determine which accounts to lock out.

Rhosts + + Backdoor. On networked Unix machines, services like Rsh and Rlogin used a simple authentication method based on hostnames that appear in rhosts. A user could easily configure which machines not to require a password to log into. An intruder that gained access to someone's rhosts file could put a »+ ++ in the file and that would allow anyone from anywhere to log into that account without a password. Many intruders use this method especially when NFS is exporting home directories to the world. These accounts become backdoors for intruders to get back into the system. Many intruders prefer using Rsh over Rlogin because it is many times lacking any logging capability. Many administrators check for »+ ++ therefore an intruder may actually put in a hostname and username from another compromised account on the network, making it less obvious to spot.

Checksum and Timestamp Backdoors. Early on, many intruders replaced binaries with their own trojan versions. Many system administrators relied on time-stamping and the system checksum programs, e.g., Unix's sum program, to try to determine when a binary file has been modified. Intruders have developed technology that will recreate the same time-stamp for the trojan file as the original file. This is accomplished by setting the system clock time back to the original file's time and then adjusting the trojan file's time to the system clock. Once the binary trojan file has the exact same time as the original, the system clock is reset to the current time. The sum program relies on a CRC checksum and is easily spoofed. Intruders have developed programs that would modify the trojan binary to have the nec-

essary original checksum, thus fooling the administrators. MD5 checksums is the recommended choice to use today by most vendors. MD5 is based on an algorithm that no one has yet to date proven can be spoofed.

Login Backdoor. On Unix, the login program is the software that usually does the password authentication when someone telnets to the machine. Intruders grabbed the source code to login.c and modified it that when login compared the user's password with the stored password, it would first check for a backdoor password. If the user typed in the backdoor password, it would allow you to log in regardless of what the administrator sets the passwords to. Thus this allowed the intruder to log into any account, even root. The password backdoor would spawn access before the user actually logged in and appeared in utmp and wtmp. Therefore an intruder could be logged in and have shell access without it appearing anyone is on that machine as that account. Administrators started noticing these backdoors especially if they did a »strings« command to find what text was in the login program. Many times the backdoor password would show up. The intruders then encrypted or hid the backdoor password better so it would not appear by just doing strings. Many of the administrators can detect these backdoors with MD5 checksums.

Telnetd Backdoor. When a user telnets to the machine, inetd service listens on the port and receive the connection and then passes it to in.telnetd, that then runs login. Some intruders knew the administrator was checking the login program for tampering, so they modified in.telnetd. Within in.telnetd, it does several checks from the user for things like what kind of terminal the user was using. Typically, the terminal setting might be Xterm or VT100. An intruder could backdoor it so that when the terminal was set to »let-mein«, it would spawn a shell without requiring any authentication. Intruders have backdoored some services so that any connection from a specific source port can spawn a shell.

Services Backdoor. Almost every network service has at one time been backdoored by an intruder. Backdoored versions of finger, rsh, rexec, rlogin, ftp, even inetd, etc., have been floating around forever. There are programs that are nothing more than a shell connected to a TCP port with maybe a backdoor password to gain access. These programs sometimes replace a service like uucp that never gets used or they get added to the inetd.conf file as a new service. Administrators should be very wary of what services are running and analyze the original services by MD5 checksums.

Cronjob backdoor. Cronjob on Unix schedules when certain programs should be run. An intruder could add a backdoor shell program to run between 1 AM and 2 AM. So for 1 hour every night, the intruder could gain access. Intruders have also looked at legitimate programs that typically run in cronjob and built backdoors into those programs as well.

Library backdoors. Almost every UNIX system uses shared libraries. The shared libraries are intended to reuse many of the same routines thus cutting down on the size of programs. Some intruders have backdoored some of the routines like crypt.c and _crypt.c. Programs like login.c would use the crypt() routine and if a backdoor password was used it would spawn a shell. Therefore, even if the administrator was checking the MD5 of the login program, it was still spawning a backdoor routine and many administrators were not checking the libraries as a possible source of backdoors. One problem for many intruders was that some administrators started MD5 checksums of almost everything. One method intruders used to get around that is to backdoor the open() and file access rou-

tines. The backdoor routines were configured to read the original files, but execute the trojan backdoors. Therefore, when the MD5 checksum program was reading these files, the checksums always looked good. But when the system ran the program, it executed the trojan version. Even the trojan library itself, could be hidden from the MD5 checksums. One way to an administrator could get around this backdoor was to statically link the MD5 checksum checker and run on the system. The statically linked program does not use the trojan shared libraries.

Kernel backdoors. The kernel on Unix is the core of how Unix works. The same method used for libraries for bypassing MD5 checksum could be used at the kernel level, except even a statically linked program could not tell the difference. A good backdoored kernel is probably one of the hardest to find by administrators, fortunately kernel backdoor scripts have not yet been widely made available and no one knows how widespread they really are.

File system backdoors. An intruder may want to store their loot or data on a server somewhere without the administrator finding the files. The intruder's files can typically contain their toolbox of exploit scripts, backdoors, sniffer logs, copied data like email messages, source code, etc. To hide these sometimes large files from an administrator, an intruder may patch the files system commands like »ls«, »du«, and »fsck« to hide the existence of certain directories or files. At a very low level, one intruder's backdoor created a section on the hard drive to have a proprietary format that was designated as »bad« sectors on the hard drive. Thus an intruder could access those hidden files with only special tools, but to the regular administrator, it is very difficult to determine that the marked »bad« sectors were indeed storage area for the hidden file system.

Bootblock backdoors. In the PC world, many viruses have hid themselves within the bootblock section and most antivirus software will check to see if the bootblock has been altered. On Unix, most administrators do not have any software that checks the bootblock, therefore some intruders have hidden some backdoors in the bootblock area.

Process hiding backdoors. An intruder many times wants to hide the programs they are running. The programs they want to hide are commonly a password cracker or a sniffer. There are quite a few methods and here are some of the more common: An intruder may write the program to modify its own argv[] to make it look like another process name. An intruder could rename the sniffer program to a legitimate service like in.syslog and run it. Thus when an administrator does a »ps« or looks at what is running, the standard service names appear. An intruder could modify the library routines so that »ps« does not show all the processes. An intruder could patch a backdoor or program into an interrupt driven routine so it does not appear in the process table. An example backdoor using this technique is amod.tar.gz available on http://star.nmmpiimm.spb.su/~maillist/bugtraq.1/0777.html. An intruder could modify the kernel to hide certain processes as well.

Rootkit. One of the most popular packages to install backdoors is rootkit. It can easily be located using Web search engines. From the Rootkit README, here are the typical files that get installed: z2 – removes entries from utmp, wtmp, and lastlog.
Fix – try to fake checksums, install with same dates/perms/u/g.
SI – become root via a magic password sent to login. Ic – modified ifconfig to remove PROMISC flag from output. ps: – hides the processes.
Ns – modified netstat to hide connections to certain machines. Ls – hides certain directories and

files from being listed. du5 – hides how much space is being used on your hard drive. ls5 – hides certain files and directories from being listed.

Network traffic backdoors. Not only do intruders want to hide their tracks on the machine, but also they want to hide their network traffic as much as possible. These network traffic backdoors sometimes allow an intruder to gain access through a firewall. There are many network backdoor programs that allow an intruder to set up on a certain port number on a machine that will allow access without ever going through the normal services. Because the traffic is going to a non-standard network port, the administrator can overlook the intruder's traffic. These network traffic backdoors are typically using TCP, UDP, and ICMP, but it could be many other kinds of packets.

TCP Shell Backdoors. The intruder can set up these TCP Shell backdoors on some high port number possibly where the firewall is not blocking that TCP port. Many times, they will be protected with a password just so that an administrator that connects to it, will not immediately see shell access. An administrator can look for these connections with netstat to see what ports are listening and where current connections are going to and from. Many times, these backdoors allow an intruder to get past TCP Wrapper technology. These backdoors could be run on the SMTP port, which many firewalls allow traffic to pass for e-mail.

UDP Shell Backdoors. Administrator many times can spot a TCP connection and notice the odd behavior, while UDP shell backdoors lack any connection so netstat would not show an intruder accessing the Unix machine. Many firewalls have been configured to allow UDP packets for services like DNS through. Many times, intruders will place the UDP Shell backdoor on that port and it will be allowed to by-pass the firewall.

ICMP Shell Backdoors. Ping is one of the most common ways to find out if a machine is alive by sending and receiving ICMP packets. Many firewalls allow outsiders to ping internal machines. An intruder can put data in the Ping ICMP packets and tunnel a shell between the pinging machines. An administrator may notice a flurry of Ping packets, but unless the administrator looks at the data in the packets, an intruder can be unnoticed.

Encrypted Link. An administrator can set up a sniffer trying to see data appears as someone accessing a shell, but an intruder can add encryption to the Network traffic backdoors and it becomes almost impossible to determine what is actually being transmitted between two machines.

Windows NT. Because Windows NT does not easily allow multiple users on a single machine and remote access similar as Unix, it becomes harder for the intruder to break into Windows NT, install a backdoor, and launch an attack from it. Thus you will find more frequently network attacks that are spring boarded from a Unix box than Windows NT. As Windows NT advances in multi-user technologies, this may give a higher frequency of intruders who use Windows NT to their advantage. And if this does happen, many of the concepts from Unix backdoors can be ported to Windows NT and administrators can be ready for the intruder. Today, there are already telnet daemons available for Windows NT. With Network Traffic backdoors, they are very feasible for intruders to install on Windows NT.

As backdoor technology advances, it becomes even harder for administrators to determine if an intruder has gotten in or if they have been successfully locked out.

8		14	
9		15	
10		16	
11		17	
12		18	
13		19	

Subtext Day. Today read between the lines as people talk to you.

–Hi!
–Shit!

–How are you?
–Who are you?

–Long time no see!
–Where do I know you from?

–Goodness how you've changed.
–Was it long ago?

–How's you know whatsisname?
–What's your name again?

–I'm very well thanks, very well indeed.
–Ask me how my career's going.

–Fine, yeah, they made me account director actually.
–Yes yes yes! I'm better than you.

–And how's your job going?
–Still unemployed?

–It's this recession, isn't it?
–What a loser.

–How about the love life?
–Still going out with fatso?

–I'm sorry to hear that, it must have been difficult.
–I wonder who dumped who?

–Anyway, we must get together for a drink!
–Another second of this and I'll implode.

–Here's my number.
–Here's the number of a dry-cleaner in Croydon.

–See you soon!
–Drop dead.

SATURDAY 15 MAY
8
9
10
11
12
13
14
15
16
17
18
19

Sunday 16 May
Today make sure your
parents know you love them.
It may seem impossible to say.
But don't wait until it is.

8	14
9	15
10	16
11	17
12	18
13	19

DOES CHEESE REALLY GIVE YOU NIGHTMARES?
Find out by eating 100g of one of following and recording your dreams.

DANISH BLUE
(zombies)

GORGONZOLA
(vampires)

GRUYERE
(castration anxiety)

PARMESAN
(friends deserting you)

STILTON
(loss of loved one)

BRIE
(falling from great height)

EMMENTAL
(going to hell)

ROCQUEFORT
(general sweatiness)

MONDAY 17 MAY	
8	14
9	15
10	16
11	17
12	18
13	19

Today learn a new knot.
It could save your life.

USE IT TO: Escape from a fire.
Escape from a kidnapping.
Tie up a maniac until the police arrive.
Tie yourself to a tree during a tornado.

SINGLE WALL KNOT
Unlay the end of a rope, and form a bight with the strand. Take strand b round the end of a. Cross a over the end of b. Take b through the bight made by c. Haul the ends taut.

Tuesday 18 May	
	8
	9
	10
	11
	12
	13
	14
	15
	16
	17
	18
	19

TODAY, BLEED HERE:

In a million years' time with advanced technology they'll be able to reconstitute you from your DNA. How to extract blood:

Name:..................................

Address: .... Postcode: ....

Why I'm worth reconstituting from my DNA a million years hence...

Wednesday 19 May		
8	14	
9	15	
10	16	
11	17	
12	18	
13	19	

THURSDAY
20 MAY

JAM THE LINE!

Everyone call the national Ku Klux Klan Head-
quarters, Harrison, Arkansas (001) 870–427
3414 at precisely 4pm today and jam the line.

8
9
10
11
12
13
14
15
16
17
18
19

Friday 21 May
Today build a nest and see if a bird comes...

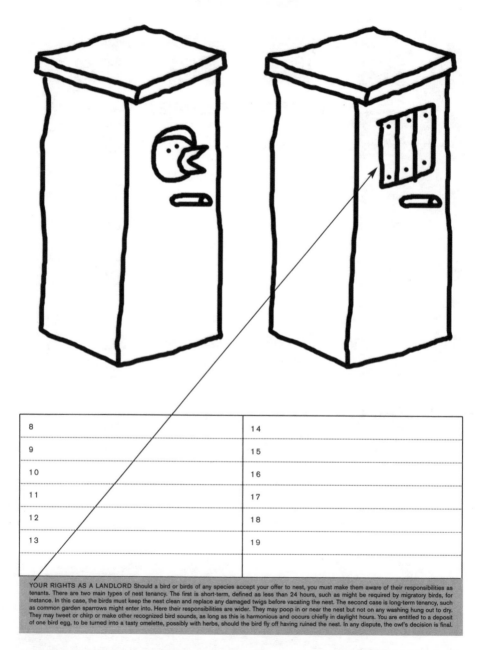

8	14
9	15
10	16
11	17
12	18
13	19

YOUR RIGHTS AS A LANDLORD Should a bird or birds of any species accept your offer to nest, you must make them aware of their responsibilities as tenants. There are two main types of nest tenancy. The first is short-term, defined as less than 24 hours, such as might be required by migratory birds, for instance. In this case, the birds must keep the nest clean and replace any damaged twigs before vacating the nest. The second case is long-term tenancy, such as common garden sparrows might enter into. Here their responsibilities are wider. They may poop in or near the nest but not on any washing hung out to dry. They may tweet or chirp or make other recognized bird sounds, as long as this is harmonious and occurs chiefly in daylight hours. You are entitled to a deposit of one bird egg, to be turned into a tasty omelette, possibly with herbs, should the bird fly off having ruined the nest. In any dispute, the owl's decision is final.

Sense-less Day

How to: Gargle with sore throat topical anaesthetic (containing phenol or benzocaine) to numb your tongue before eating.

True story: Michael F., 45, lost his sense of taste at the age of 8 following a viral infection that damaged the cranial nerve fibres that carry information from the taste buds to the brain. His condition is known as »ageusia«, meaning full loss of taste, which is a very rare disorder. At the time, his main gripe concerned inability to distinguish between ice cream flavours. He did however develop a reputation for being able to ingest insects and some of the smaller lizards without batting an eyelid. He now lives in Denver with his wife and 2 children, and is reconciled to his loss.

SATURDAY 22 MAY		
8	14	Write down the pros and cons of this sense as you discover them.
9	15	Pros: ....
10	16	Cons: ....
11	17	....
12	18	End of day assessment: How crucial is
13	19	my sense of taste to me ..../10

Start an urban myth

See how fast a rumour can spread. To be successful, an urban myth must include two or more of the following elements: • Imaginative revenge by jilted lover • Pet's life ending in gruesome circumstances (preferably sexual) • Hidden deadly flaw in consumer product.

Example: »a man in Chicago decided to take revenge on his ex-wife by poisoning her cat by mixing a huge dose of popular painkiller Xylenol into the catfood. Xylenol, however, in large quantities is an aphrodisiac to cats. So the cat didn't die but instead raped the ex-husband's favorite gerbil to death.«

WHAT TO DO IF YOU LIVE IN A NON-URBAN AREA
Don't worry: the historical ancestor to the urban myth is the fisherman's tale. Be aware that it spreads less rapidly however, and that subject matter is slightly more restrictive: tales must be based mainly around catching a very big fish.

8
9
10
11
12
13
14
15
16
17
18
19

famous last words: prepare yours ahead of time

"I've had eighteen straight whiskies, I think that's a record"
— Dylan Thomas

8	
9	
10	
11	
12	
13	
14	
15	
16	
17	
18	
19	

Change someone's mind today

Only fools never change their mind. Help save someone from such folly by arguing them out of their deeply held views on a controversial subject, like cannibalism. Now, most reasonable people are in favour of cannibalism, but a tenacious minority cling to outdated views about its health risks. Tell them no independent clinical study has ever been able to establish that lifelong cannibalism is bad for your health. That's a fact. And here's the clincher: have they ever tried it? No? THEN HOW DO THEY KNOW? The great Socrates himself could not win an argument more easily.

Thursday 27 May

8

9

10

11

12

13

14

15

16

17

18

Friday 28 May: Leave a note on someone's car windshield

I'm a traffic warden but today I feel lenient. Don't do it again though.

I'm the engineer who made this vehicle. The brakes aren't very good cos I was hungover that day. Watch out.

We've discovered your car is the one responsible for all the damage to the ozone layer; please bike to work in future.

I've left someone in your boot. I'll pick him up next week if that's OK.

8	14
9	15
10	16
11	17
12	18
13	19

TODAY HELP RESOLVE AN INTRACTABLE GLOBAL GEOPOLITICAL CRISIS!

Some bright spark out there must be able to come up with an answer to the world's various problems. Could it be you? Put your mind to it for a couple of minutes. Redraw maps using coloured crayons and explain your plan in no more than 80 words. Send to: Secretary-General, UNITED NATIONS, S-378, New York, NY 10017, USA.

Saturday 29 May	14
8	15
9	16
10	17
11	18
12	19
13	

Reconnect with your aquatic origins by spending all of today underwater. It is common knowledge that the old theory about man evolving from apes on the dry plains of Africa is wrong. Rather, scientists now believe that man got caught in flooded swamp land and was thus forced to rise from a four-legged posture to a two-legged one, so as to avoid drowning. Hence the various features that distinguish us from apes: our hairlessness, our capacity to control our breathing, our relatively large proportions of subcutaneous fat. Spend today underwater, and feel the fish within.

MONDAY 31 MAY: EVERYONE HAS A FAVOURITE DINOSAUR. Go to your local natural history museum and make sure yours is properly displ

8	14	
9	15	
10	16	
11	17	
12	18	
13	19	

Write a message to the future

Mark the envelope »DO NOT OPEN UNTIL JUNE 1, 2104«. Begin the letter with today's date and To Whom It May Concern. Suitable topics: world peace, evolutionary trends, suggestions on how to deal with living on other planets, predictions, anecdotes from 2004 that might interest future generations (sport, »hot news«, society, dress trends, etc). Hide the envelope so that it won't be found for a hundred years.

8	14	
9	15	
10	16	
11	17	
12	18	
13	19	

TALK TO A PLANT

FOR AT LEAST ONE HOUR

Good things to say to a plant:
"Grow, you plants are the best"
"Try to touch the sky"
"You're the best plant in the world"
"Try your best at growing"
"You're so pretty with your light green,
 dark green and green colours"

Bad things to say to a plant:
"Die you nasty plants, die"
"You are the worst plants in the world"
"Die you worthless pieces of green seeds"
"You are so ugly when you are standing
 up, so fall over and don't get up"
"You are so ugly when you're green,
 and you wouldn't be ugly if you were
 brown and falling over"

A house
is not a
home.

8
9
10
11

12
13
14
15

16
17
18
19

HARD WORK DAY

Hard work is good for the soul, besides being the basis of Western society's economic dominance. Follow these instructions to make sure you earn your money today.

| CLOCK IN TIME: | | STATEMENT OF PURPOSE | Today I will work harder than |
| CLOCK OUT TIME: | | ever and make it happen. Signature:.. | |

LIST OF TASKS	PRIORITY:	ACTION:	DEADLINE:	RESULTS:
Sales report	Urgent	Write and circulate	11am	☐ Approved by JD
				☐
				☐
				☐
				☐
				☐
				☐
				☐
				☐
				☐
				☐
				☐
				☐
				☐
				☐

MOTIVATION CORNER

WINNERS MAKE IT HAPPEN, LOSERS WATCH IT HAPPEN!

Sell Sell Sell!

Be you, only more so.

Prepare for tomorrow: do your best today.

The only place success comes before work is in the dictionary.

EMPLOYER CONFIRMATION

I,.., employer of this Diary owner, confirm that he/she has completed these tasks and has worked hard for me today and fully deserves the.................. I've paid them for their labour. Well done and keep it up. Signature:...

8	14	20
9	15	21
10	16	22
11	17	23
12	18	24
13	19	25

CONFESS TO A PRIEST

Even if you are not religious, the act of confession is rich in therapeutic value, not to mention a damn sight cheaper. So head for your nearest church and book a convenient time. Count on 1 minute per trivial sin (stealing from cookie jar as a child), 5 minutes per major sin (stealing cookie from child), and at least 20 minutes per heinous sin (killing child and stuffing it in cookie jar).

Friday 4 June	
8	
9	
10	
11	
12	
13	
14	
15	
16	
17	
18	
19	

Confession dos

DO: sound contrite, even if you
actually enjoyed the sinning
DO: at least feign belief in
a supreme being
DO: accept your penance, this
is no time for haggling

Confession don'ts

DON'T: ask if they're recording this
DON'T: confess sins on behalf of other
people, like your two-timing neighbour
DON'T: confess you've broken wind
DON'T: end by saying
»your turn now«

Today, redesign an everyday product

James Dyson redesigned the humble vacuum cleaner and made millions. Pick an everyday object that everyone in the world uses and find a way of improving it. Then patent it, and make a mint.

The Double-Toothpick™
Saves valuable time by picking two teeth at once!

His'n'Hers Toothbrush™
Leaves couples more room around the sink!

The Talking Umbrella™
Lets you know when it's stopped raining!

The Foldable Coat Hanger™
Take it with you!

The Mystic Mug™
Electronically reads your tea leaves!

HIS HERS

8	14
9	15
10	16
11	17
12	18
13	19

The Remote Control Belt Leash™
You'll never lose it again!

Human Chess Day

TODAY BEHAVE AS IF YOU WERE PLAYING CHESS.

PRINCIPLES: Assess the powers and intentions of people around you. Are they friend or foe? Think ahead. Always plan your next move. Be prepared to lose your pawns to win the match. But beware: In real life, there is no such thing as a draw.

Which piece do you think you are?

KING: YOU LIKE TO DOMINATE OTHERS FROM A DISTANCE, LETTING MINIONS DO YOUR DIRTY WORK.

QUEEN: ARE YOU A POWER-CRAZED ENFORCER FIGURE, BENT ON INFLICTING YOUR WILL ACROSS THE BOARD?

BISHOP: ARE YOU INTELLIGENT BUT SLIGHTLY DEVIOUS, APPROACHING CONFLICT FROM AN ANGLE?

ROOK: ARE YOU THE STRONG TRUSTWORTHY TYPE? ESSENTIALLY STRAIGHT BUT RELIABLE IN A CRISIS?

KNIGHT: ARE YOU A FREE SPIRIT, REFUSING TO LET PRACTICAL OBSTACLES STAND IN YOUR WAY?

PAWN: YOU MAY HAVE DRAWN THE SHORT STRAW IN LIFE, BUT LO! SURVIVE, AND YOU MIGHT BECOME QUEEN...

Sunday 6 June

08
09
10
11
12
13
14
15
16
17
18
19

day 7 June. So far this year, you have been working purely for the government. Each year the Adam Smith Institute ulates the Tax Freedom Day: the day on which you have earned enough to pay all your taxes (41.7% of GDP) and can to work for yourself. Write and complain to the Taxman for this gross imposition on your time and liberty.

13

14

15

16

17

18

19

Find a way of making a £10 note grow into £100 in one day

Buy all the town's umbrellas, wait for heavy rain and resell them at huge profit

Add a zero on the bill in the same writing style

Bet it on a horse at 10-1

Start a lemonade stand and spike the lemonade with an addictive substance

Photocopy it nine times

Try claiming there's been a mix-up at the bank

Tuesday 8 June

8	14
9	15
10	16
11	17
12	18
13	19

A cautionary tale: the story of Narcissus, first victim of vanity

»Young Greek boy Narcissus was hunting in a forest one day when he came upon a calm stream. He was thirsty and so he bent over to drink. As he leaned over, he caught sight of his reflection in the water. He was taken by its beauty and immediately spoke »I love you.« He became so engrossed with himself that he failed to notice the nymph Echo nearby. His self-love became an obsession and he would not leave the stream to eat, nor disturb his image to drink and so he died of thirst and hunger and unrequited self-love. Where he had lain a flower grew, the Narcissus, the same flower that lured the innocent Persephone into the snares of Pluto.«

WEDNESDAY 9 JUNE

8
9
10
11
12
13
14
15
16
17
18
19

Compose a poem and leave it in a public place to brighten up someone's day.

POEM

THE CAT SAT ON THE MAT

8
9
10
11
12
13
14
15
16
17
18
19

8
9
10
11
12
13
14
15
16
17
18
19

Make prolonged eye contact with everyone you meet

Eye contact: communication before words. Monkeys stare each other down. Be the alpha male. Who dares stand up to you? Bite their head off, that'll learn them. Grrrr.

SHOPLIFT TODAY

Average custodial sentences for stealing:

A sweet:..police caution
A car:...4 years
A handbag:...2 years
A little old granny's handbag:.............................5 years
A house:...N/A

CAUTION: in the state of California, shoplifting three times will automatically result in a 25 years-to-life sentence (»three strikes and you're out« legislation).

Saturday 12 June

8	14
9	15
10	16
11	17
12	18
13	19

Share someone's pain today.

A burden shared is a burden halved. Find a friend in distress and bear some of their grief.

Sunday 13 June

8
9
10
11
12
13
14
15
16
17
18

Tuesday 15 June. Today get someone famous to autograph this page

Tips for autograph hunters: Hang out outside celebrity haunts, like trendy new discos. Be polite: say please and thank you, and get their name right. Have pen and Diary at the ready! »Cheeky« alternative: get female celebrity to kiss this page! (with lipstick on, obviously)

Category of celebrity (tick):

A-list ☐

B-list ☐

C-list ☐

D-list ☐

Use these 11 boxes if you meet an entire football team.

8

9

10

11

12

13

14

15

16

17

18

19

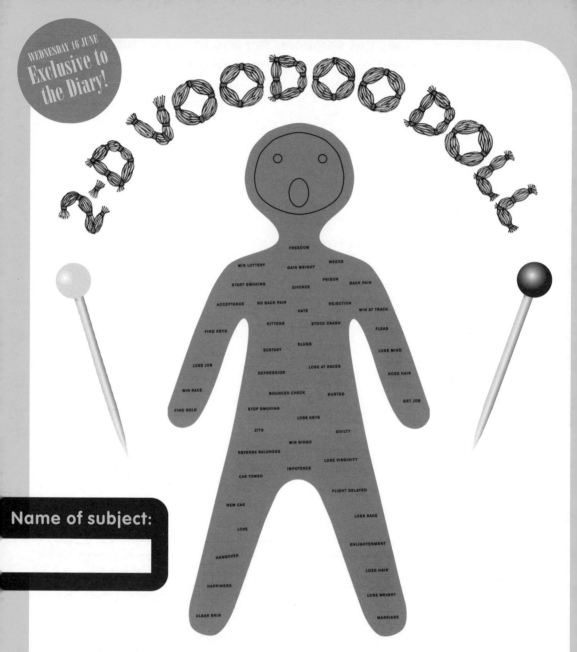

2-D VOODOO DOLL

FREEDOM

WIN LOTTERY · WEEDS

GAIN WEIGHT

START SMOKING · PRISON

DIVORCE · BACK PAIN

ACCEPTANCE · NO BACK PAIN · REJECTION

HATE · WIN AT TRACK

KITTENS · STOCK CRASH

FIND KEYS · FLEAS

SLUGS

ECSTASY · LOSE MIND

LOSE JOB · LOSE AT RACES · NOSE HAIR

DEPRESSION

WIN RACE · BOUNCED CHECK · BUSTED

FIND GOLD · GET JOB

STOP SMOKING

LOSE KEYS

ZITS · GUILTY

WIN BINGO

REVERSE BALDNESS · LOSE VIRGINITY

IMPOTENCE

CAR TOWED

FLIGHT DELAYED

NEW CAR

LOSE RACE

LOVE

ENLIGHTENMENT

HANGOVER

LOSE HAIR

HAPPINESS

LOSE WEIGHT

CLEAR SKIN · MARRIAGE

Name of subject:

Instructions: draw a line from our special 2-D pins to the areas of voodoo activity you require. White pins are for positive voodoo. Black pins are for negative voodoo. Remember! Any bad karma caused is your responsibility.

8	12	16	
9	13	17	
10	14	18	
11	15	19	

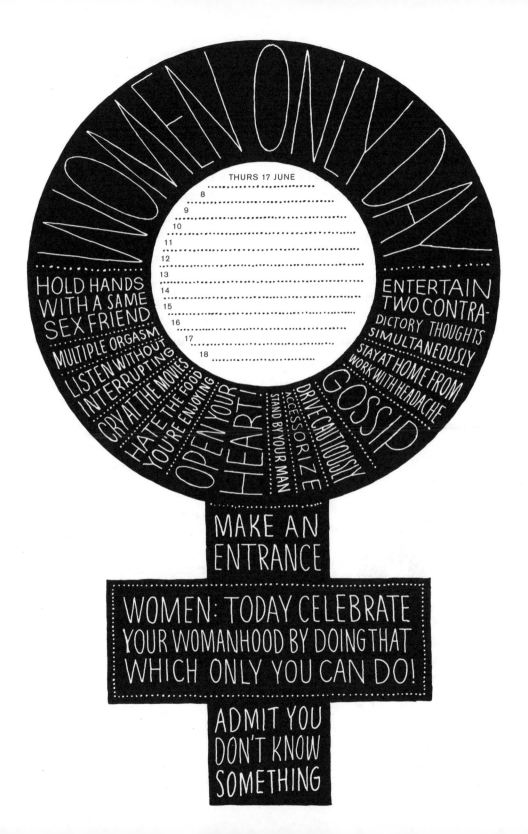

In this day and age in the final analysis you've got to grasp the nettle with both hands and give one hundred and ten percent if you want to stay ahead of the game after all it's a dog-eat-dog world where the fat cat powers that be will stab you in the back with a crushing blow if you don't come up to scratch and you won't know what hit you so don't get caught napping with your pants down – because then unless you get your act together and cut the mustard you're well and truly up for a rude awakening at least according to the doom merchants though let's not make a drama out of a crisis; look on the bright side: even if it all goes pear-shaped and you're left in the lurch, your heart is in the right place and now so long as you can keep your head above water and the wolf from the door you'll be able to spend time with your family and get away from it all anyway let's do lunch so I can rub it in. Have a nice day.

TODAY:
Speak only
in clichés

FRIDAY 18 JUNE

8 14
9 15
10 16
11 17
12 18
13 19
....

TODAY SELL SOMETHING THAT YOU HAVE MADE

Homemade object:	Going rates:
Origami flamingo	$15
Automobile	$20,000
Pottery item	$24
Pretty Card	$5
Manky Card	$1
Furniture	$50-500
Original Painting	$50-500,000
Poo	$0,15

Secret subliminal sales techniques

Flattery: »Hey this'll go great with your jumper.«

Empathy: »No kidding? I wear a toupee as well!«

Sympathy: »I can see you're very poor, but this is only $0,15«

Threat: »Buy this or I'll eat your dog raw.«

SATURDAY 19 JUNE

08

09

10

11

12

13

14

15

16

17

18

19

Today: come up with your own Diary page idea!

Send it in to Simon Trewin, PFD Literary Agency, Drury House, 34-43 Russell St, London WC2B 5HA, UK. If it's any good, we'll use it for free in next year's edition. If not, we'll send you a humiliating put-down letter that'll make you feel small. Sharpen those pencils!

BAD!

This is not actually physically possible, and therefore not a serious idea.

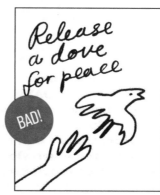

BAD!

Pretentious. There's nothing wrong with big themes like peace war and death, as long as you make them humourous.

BAD!

Superficially, this seems like a contender, but on closer inspection, it's just stupid.

BAD!

DEMONSTRA-TE AGAINST FATHERS WHO STILL TREAT YOU LIKE A LITTLE **CHILD!**

Kill your darlings: no one wants to hear about your boring personal problems. See a shrink.

BAD!

Nothing stupid about this one, but it's only for men. The Diary does not discriminate against either gender.

SO-SO!

Not bad. But this cannot really be achieved in one single day. Keep 'em coming though!

TUESDAY 22 JUNE

8	14
9	15
10	16
11	17
12	18
13	19

Show off your hairy palms.

HAIRY PALM EXHIBITION $5 ↓

BODY HAIR DAY

We normally take our body hair for granted, often shaving it off in shame. No more: today celebrate your ape ancestry by tending to your body hair.

Braid your nose hair.

WEDNESDAY 23 JUNE

8
9
10
11
12
13
14
15
16
17
18

Women are just as hairy as men: sisters, shun the razor blade today.

Colour your ear hair pink.

Draw attention to your fine head of hair and your bushy eyebrows.

HAIR

Toe hairs may need extensions, or use convenient toe wigs.

AMAZING: this human has lost his body but kept his hair.

TODAY:
GO ON STRIKE!

ENOUGH IS ENOUGH. COMRADE, WHY TOIL DAY IN DAY OUT FOR THE 'SAKE of THE BOURGEOISIE? ORGANIZE RESISTANCE TO EXPLOITATION IN YOUR WORKPLACE. FORM A TRADE UNION AND PASS A RESOLUTION IN FAVOUR OF A ONE-DAY GENERAL STRIKE. DEMAND BETTER CONDITIONS, A SAFER ENVIRONMENT, AND A BIGGER SHARE OF THE CAPITALIST PIE... LONG LIVE THE STRUGGLE! HOW TO SET UP AND OPERATE A PROPER PICKET LINE: YOU WILL NEED: A LENGTH OF SOLID ROPE (NOT STRING), SOMETHING TO TIE IT TO (THE OUTSIDE OF YOUR CUBICLE IF YOU ARE IN AN OFFICE), A LIST OF ANTI-SCAB SLOGANS TO CHANT, AND A BUCKET TO RECEIVE CONTRIBUTIONS FROM THE PUBLIC. STAND IN FRONT OF THE LINE AND INTIMIDATE ANY SCAB WHO TRIES TO CROSS IT WITH THREATENING EYE CONTACT.

8	14
9	15
10	16
11	17
12	18
13	19

free pet day!

Put a lost dog ad up and see whether one turns up

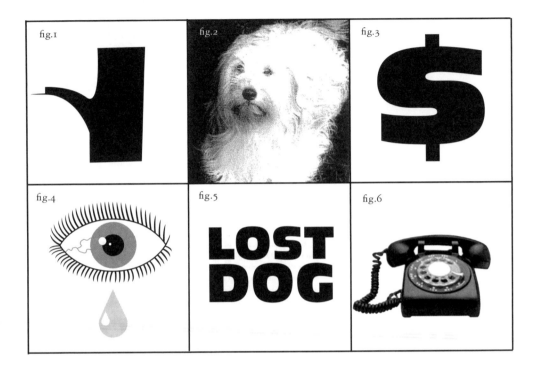

Key elements of any successful lost dog ad

fig.1 *Positioning:* tree is traditional, or lamp post, preferably one they enjoyed peeing on particularly.

fig.2 *Photo:* poor quality photocopy, hinting at nationwide magnitude of your search and maximizing the range of dogs that look a bit like that.

fig.3 *Reward:* keep this bit vague, that way you'll always be able to fob them off with a cheap chocolate bar or similar lame effort.

fig.4 *Description:* favour the emotional content over the descriptive. »My darling bulimic daughter Lizzie's little puppy has gone and she hasn't stopped crying since, please help restore her faith in life« is more motivational than »fox terrier, 7 years old, brownish, answers to the name dog«.

fig.5 *Headline:* LOST DOG works best usually.

fig.6 *Phone number:* might attract psychos, but fairly essential.

8	14	
9	15	
10	16	
11	17	
12	18	
13	19	

Measure Your Temperature Day

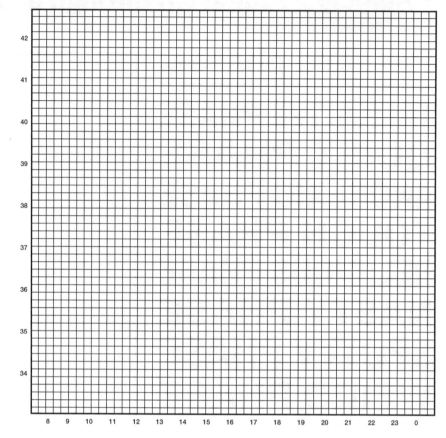

Body temperature is a crucial indicator of well-being. Therefore it is important to monitor it on an hourly basis, using this chart. Body temperature is 37 degrees Celsius on average, but, contrary to popular myth, it varies between 34 and 40 degrees throughout the day, depending on outside influences. See here:

Monday 28 June	14
8	15
9	16
10	17
11	18
12	19
13	

THERMOMETER LOCATIONS: PROS AND CONS.
BUCCAL: That's under the tongue to you and me. Classic but effective.
UNDERARM: Snug and discreet. Good for use in business meetings.
RECTAL: Ugh! Only for French persons. Impractical and painful.

SPEND TODAY PRETENDING TO BE A TOURIST!

EQUIPMENT:
daypack, camera, lost look

ITINERARY:

10 AM	Visit Big monument
12AM	Ride around in bus for a while
1PM	Lunch in tourist trap restaurant
3PM	Big museum
5PM	Get laughed at by schoolkids
6PM	Big show
9PM	Get mugged by schoolkids
10PM	Bed in Big hotel.

Repeat tomorrow.

BACKGROUND ON YOUR COUNTRY:
Make it up, no one cares.

LINES:
This monument/museum/show sure is nice.
Do you have any ketchup?
Is the Queen in right now?

Tuesday 29 June

8

9

10

11

12

13

14

15

16

17

18

19

WEDNESDAY 30 JUNE. Today write to your local authority asking that your street be renamed after you. To make sure your application is successful, explain why the current name is no good, give details of your main achievements, and enclose a petition signed by your neighbours. **IMPORTANT!** Specify the type of street:

BLOGGS BOULEVARD

BLOGGS ROAD

BLOGGS CLOSE

BLOGGS ROW

BLOGGS SQUARE

BLOGGS ALLEY

BLOGGS GARDENS

BLOGGS WAY

BLOGGS GROVE

BLOGGS CRESCENT

BLOGGS WALK

BLOGGS PROMENADE

AVENUE BLOGGS

BLOGGS STREET

8
9
10
11
12
13

14
15
16
17
18
19

Today return to childhood

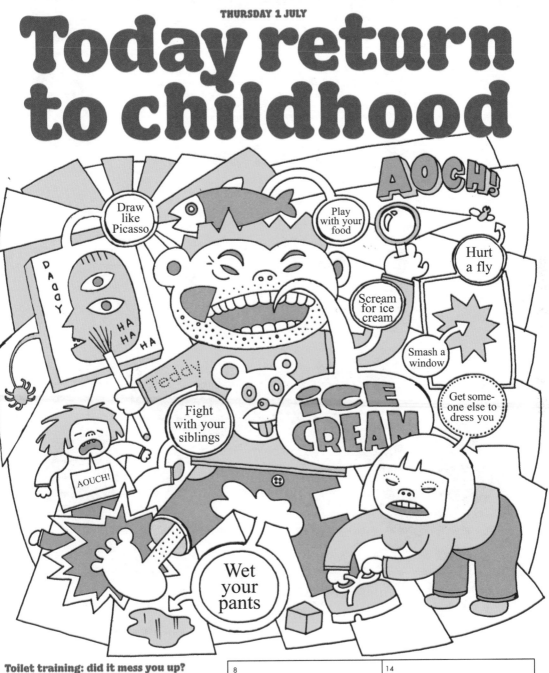

Toilet training: did it mess you up?

Toilet training is a crucial formative influence on your life. As you sit on the potty today, see if it triggers any repressed memories that may have helped ruin your life. Do you feel aggressive at work or in traffic? Do you feel like emotions are bottling up inside? Do you want to just let rip? Then chances are you may be suffering from TTS (Toilet Training Syndrome). Unfortunately there is no cure, though it may sometimes help to sue your parents.

8	14
9	15
10	16
11	17
12	18
13	19 Go to bed!

Sense-less Day

GO THROUGH TODAY WITHOUT USING YOUR SENSE OF: SMELL

How to: Nose plug, cold virus.

True story: Susan T. ran a perfume shop in downtown Baltimore. Her big selling point was the ability to mix a unique perfume for every customer. She prospered, until she was accidentally exposed to toxins, and lost all sense of smell. According to medical expert Dr. Carol Fiske, this condition (»anosmia«) affects millions, particularly amongst elderly men. It sometimes disappears with time, says Fiske, though no one yet knows how or why. This comes as no consolation to Susan T., of course, who can no longer smell her precious perfumes and has had to close shop and lose her livelihood as a result. She has not worn perfume since.

FRIDAY 2 JULY		
8	14	Write down the pros and cons of this sense as you discover them.
9	15	Pros: ....
10	16	Cons: ....
11	17	....
12	18	End of day assessment: How crucial is
13	19	my sense of smell to me ..../10

w memorable is your everyday conversation? Today, find out by writing down everything you say. Highlight the wittiest phrases.

Examples:

Oscar Wilde (1854-1900)
»Only dull people are
brilliant at breakfast«

Dorothy Parker (1893-1967)
»I don't care what is written
about me so long as it isn't true«

Benjamin Franklin (1706-1790)
»He that falls in love with
himself will have no rivals«

Tallulah Bankhead (1903-1968)
»If I had to live my life again,
I'd make the same mistakes,
only sooner«

Samuel Johnson (1709-1784)
»Of all noise I think music is
the least disagreeable«

Saturday 3 July	
8	
9	
10	
11	
12	
13	
14	
15	
16	
17	

If you've said more than this, use extra paper. If you haven't, expand your social circle.

Cleanliness Day

Today become as a clean as the day you were born (or cleaner in fact as there's normally a lot of muck around you at birth for some reason). We're not talking about just taking a plain old bath here, but really cleaning those hard-to-reach crevices that most people overlook.

Armpit crud

There's only one way to get rid of all those greasy accretions of deodorant and sweat, and that's to shave it all off. Women are often ahead of the game on this one.

Inner ear wax

Q-tips just push the wax further into the ear. Liquefy the inner wax with ammonia solution and get a loved one to suck it out gently with a straw.

In-growing toenail grout

Left untreated, this can result in amputation of the foot. Cut off the guilty toe to prevent it from recurring. (Bleeding may occur in some individuals.)

Dead lip

Applying vaseline may cover up chapped lips, but it doesn't get to all those layers of dead lip underneath. A pumice stone should do the trick.

Dorsal mould

Few of us bother to wash that difficult-to-reach upper back patch. The result? Furry moss. Get a friend to rub alcohol in, and set fire to it.

Eyebrow dandruff

Your deep blue eyes won't count for much if they're overshadowed by flakes of dead skin. Household bleach will rinse them out nicely.

Pubic pus

Need we say more? There's a great deal of oozing in this region in both sexes, which must be addressed with a vigorous scouring with a wire brush.

Belly button dirt

Fluff is easily removed, but grit gets into the clefts of poorly-severed umbilical cords. Hire a powerful vacuum cleaner with special nozzle to dislodge it.

Tongue dross

The Ancients could determine your health by examining your tongue. Lick sandpaper to lose those layers of yellowish goo.

Eye snot

Use a toothbrush to extract those little brown crumbs from the corners of your eyes, making sure to scrub under the eyelids too.

Nasal goo

A good deep breath of hydrochloric acid will soon dissolve any nasal obstructions. Take care not to overdo it and dissolve your septum though.

Fungal foot

Those awkward spaces between the toes are the perfect breeding ground for fungi. Stick your feet in the freezer for 12 hours to exterminate the little parasites.

Monday 5 July		
8		14
9		15
10		16
11		17
12		18
13		19

A very overweight woman in Nevada went to her doctor's complaining of a sore buttock. When the doctor had her x-rayed, he discovered something remarkable. Years before, the rather slovenly woman had slumped on her sofa naked, not realizing her dog had been playing there with a greasy leftover T-bone. The bone got caught in the folds of her obese cheeks, and over the months her flesh simply grew around it. Surgery was required to extract it.

PICK UP LITTER IN THE STREET TODAY

It's disgusting, and it's not yours. But hands up the person who has never littered. Let's all join together in a mass display of community spirit and make this country cleaner!

BIODEGRADABILITY TIMESCALE

Banana peel..................................3–4 weeks
Tin can....................................10–40 years
Aluminium wrapper.................200–500 years
Disposable diaper...................500–600 years
Plastic jug...........................1,000,000 years
Styrofoam cup..................................Eternity
Plutonium rod............................Eternity + 1
(DO NOT PICK UP DISCARDED PLUTONIUM ROD WITH YOUR BARE HANDS. FETCH PLASTIC GLOVES FIRST.)

8	TUESDAY 6 JULY	14
9		15
10		16
11		17
12		18
13		19

Today, get life-coached!

If you haven't managed to do everything this Diary has instructed so far, then you clearly need some help organizing your life. Life coaches give you advice on sorting out your priorities and acting on them. If your life is a bit of a mess, they'll help untangle it with you.

WEDNESDAY 7 JULY

8

9

10

11

12

13

14

15

16

17

18

19

Charlotte Davies

BONUS The Diary are offering one lucky individual a free introductory session with top life coach Charlotte Davies. The first person to get through to her at 11am GMT today (phone number on www.thiswebsitewillchangeyourlife.com) will enjoy a full 40 minutes of free life coaching. Think of what it could do for you. For the others: feel free to contact her and try it out (normal rates apply).

CHAPTER I

1. The burden which Habakkuk the prophet did see.

2. O LORD, how long shall I cry, and thou wilt not hear! even cry out unto thee of violence, and thou wilt not save!

3. Why dost thou shew me iniquity, and cause me to behold grievance? for spoiling and violence are before me: and there are that raise up strife and contention.

4. Therefore the law is slacked, and judgment doth never go forth: for the wicked doth compass about the righteous; therefore wrong judgment proceedeth.

5. Behold ye among the heathen, and regard, and wonder marvelously: for I will work a work in your days which ye will not believe, though it be told you.

6. For, lo, I raise up the Chaldeans, that bitter and hasty nation, which shall march through the breadth of the land, to possess the dwellingplaces that are not their's.

7. They are terrible and dreadful: their judgment and their dignity shall proceed of themselves.

8. Their horses also are swifter than the leopards, and are more fierce than the evening wolves: and their horsemen shall spread themselves, and their horsemen shall come from far; they shall fly as the eagle that hasteth to eat.

9. They shall come all for violence: their faces shall sup up as the east wind, and they shall gather the captivity as the sand.

10. And they shall scoff at the kings, and the princes shall be a scorn unto them: they shall deride every strong hold; for they shall heap dust, and take it.

11. Then shall his mind change, and he shall pass over, and offend, imputing this his power unto his god.

12. Art thou not from everlasting, O LORD my God, mine Holy One? we shall not die. O LORD, thou hast ordained them for judgment; and, O mighty God, thou hast established them for correction.

13. Thou art of purer eyes than to behold evil, and canst not look on iniquity: wherefore lookest thou upon them that deal treacherously, and holdest thy tongue when the wicked devoureth the man that is more righteous than he?

14. And makest men as the fishes of the sea, as the creeping things, that have no ruler over them?

15. They take up all of them with the angle, they catch them in their net, and gather them in their drag: therefore they rejoice and are glad.

16. Therefore they sacrifice unto their net, and burn incense unto their drag; because by them their portion is fat, and their meat plenteous.

17. Shall they therefore empty their net, and not spare continually to slay the nations?

CHAPTER 2

1. I will stand upon my watch, and set me upon the tower, and will watch to see what he will say unto me, and what I shall answer when I am reproved.

2. And the LORD answered me, and said, Write the vision, and make it plain upon tables, that he may run that readeth it.

3. For the vision is yet for an appointed time, but at the end it shall speak, and not lie: though it tarry, wait for it; because it will surely come, it will not tarry.

4. Behold, his soul which is lifted up is not upright in him: but the just shall live by his faith.

5. Yea also, because he transgresseth by wine, he is a proud man, neither keepeth at home, who enlargeth his desire as hell, and is as death, and cannot be satisfied, but gathereth unto him all nations, and heapeth unto him all people:

6. Shall not all these take up a parable against him, and a taunting proverb against him, and say, Woe

Thursday 8 July: don't waste the 4 minutes and 22 seconds (on average) you will spend on the toilet. Read the much-neglected Old Testament Book of Habakkuk instead, and try and improve yourself.

to him that increaseth that which is not his! how long? and to him that ladeth himself with thick clay!

7. Shall they not rise up suddenly that shall bite thee, and awake that shall vex thee, and thou shalt be for booties unto them?

8. Because thou hast spoiled many nations, all the remnant of the people shall spoil thee; because of men's blood, and for the violence of the land, of the city, and of all that dwell therein.

9. Woe to him that coveteth an evil covetousness to his house, that he may set his nest on high, that he may be delivered from the power of evil!

10. Thou hast consulted shame to thy house by cutting off many people, and hast sinned against thy soul.

11. For the stone shall cry out of the wall, and the beam out of the timber shall answer it.

12. Woe to him that buildeth a town with blood, and stablisheth a city by iniquity!

13. Behold, is it not of the LORD of hosts that the people shall labour in the very fire, and the people shall weary themselves for very vanity?

14. For the earth shall be filled with the knowledge of the glory of the LORD, as the waters cover the sea.

15. Woe unto him that giveth his neighbour drink, that puttest thy bottle to him, and makest him drunken also, that thou mayest look on their nakedness!

16. Thou art filled with shame for glory: drink thou also, and let thy foreskin be uncovered: the cup of the LORD's right hand shall be turned unto thee, and shameful spewing shall be on thy glory.

17. For the violence of Lebanon shall cover thee,

8	
9	
10	
11	
12	
13	
14	
15	
16	
17	
18	
19	

and the spoil of beasts, which made them afraid, because of men's blood, and for the violence of the land, of the city, and of all that dwell therein.

18. What profiteth the graven image that the maker thereof hath graven it; the molten image, and a teacher of lies, that the maker of his work trusteth therein, to make dumb idols?

19. Woe unto him that saith to the wood, Awake; to the dumb stone, Arise, it shall teach! Behold, it is laid over with gold and silver, and there is no breath at all in the midst of it.

20. But the LORD is in his holy temple: let all the earth keep silence before him.

CHAPTER 3

1. A prayer of Habakkuk the prophet upon Shigionoth.

2. O LORD, I have heard thy speech, and was afraid: O LORD, revive thy work in the midst of the years, in the midst of the years make known; in wrath remember mercy.

3. God came from Teman, and the Holy One from mount Paran. Selah. His glory covered the heavens, and the earth was full of his praise.

4. And his brightness was as the light; he had horns coming out of his hand: and there was the hiding of his power.

5. Before him went the pestilence, and burning coals went forth at his feet.

6. He stood, and measured the earth: he beheld, and drove asunder the nations; and the everlasting mountains were scattered, the perpetual hills did bow: his ways are everlasting.

7. I saw the tents of Cushan in affliction: and the curtains of the land of Midian did tremble.

8. Was the LORD displeased against the rivers? was thine anger against the rivers? was thy wrath against the sea, that thou didst ride upon thine horses and thy chariots of salvation?

9. Thy bow was made quite naked, according to the oaths of the tribes, even thy word. Selah. Thou didst cleave the earth with rivers.

10. The mountains saw thee, and they trembled: the overflowing of the water passed by: the deep uttered his voice, and lifted up his hands on high.

11. The sun and moon stood still in their habitation: at the light of thine arrows they went, and at the shining of thy glittering spear.

12. Thou didst march through the land in indignation, thou didst thresh the heathen in anger.

13. Thou wentest forth for the salvation of thy people, even for salvation with thine anointed; thou woundedst the head out of the house of the wicked, by discovering the foundation unto the neck. Selah.

14. Thou didst strike through with his staves the head of his villages: they came out as a whirlwind to scatter me: their rejoicing was as to devour the poor secretly.

15. Thou didst walk through the sea with thine horses, through the heap of great waters.

16. When I heard, my belly trembled; my lips quivered at the voice: rottenness entered into my bones, and I trembled in myself, that I might rest in the day of trouble: when he cometh up unto the people, he will invade them with his troops.

17. Although the fig tree shall not blossom, neither shall fruit be in the vines; the labour of the olive shall fail, and the fields shall yield no meat; the flock shall be cut off from the fold, and there shall be no herd in the stalls:

18. Yet I will rejoice in the LORD, I will joy in the God of my salvation.

19. The LORD God is my strength, and he will make my feet like hinds' feet, and he will make me to walk upon mine high places. To the chief singer on my stringed instruments.

FRIDAY 9 JULY: FOLLOW THESE DIRECTIONS

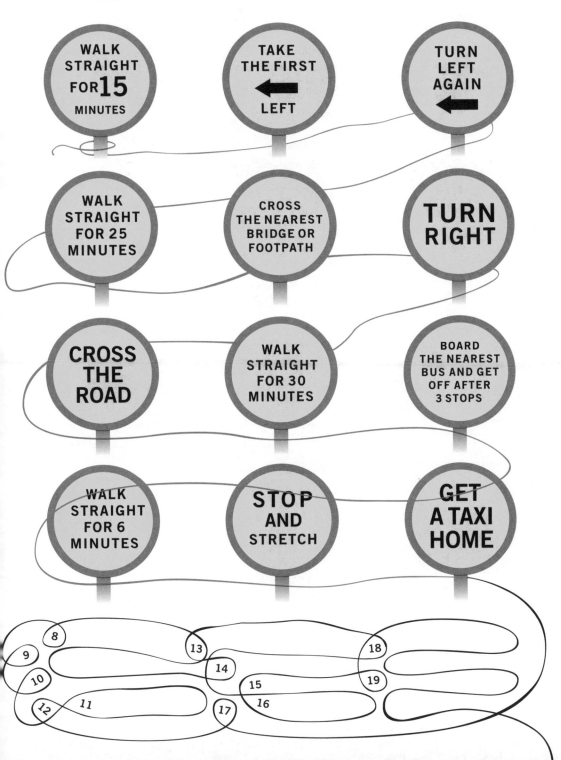

BURY A TREASURE TODAY This is a fun day out. Assemble some objects that have special meaning to you, like family photos, some letters, and a hoard of stolen gold. Find a secluded spot and dig a hole at least one foot deep, so some dumb dog can't unearth it. Draw a map of the location so that you will be able to find it in ten or twenty years' time. Place your treasure in a sealed box. Now bury it. One day when you're broke and/or civilization has crumbled, you'll be glad to dig it up and live off the contents.

SATURDAY 10 JULY

8

9

10

11

12

13

14

15

16

17

18

Attention!
Do not bury
the map.

Family Love day

Incest works well for animal breeding, so why not for you?
Today explore your deeper feelings towards a cousin, a sibling, or
a parent perhaps. Taboos, after all, are made to be broken.

Sunday 11 July

8		14
9		15
10		16
11		17
12		18
13		19

You are a precious
flower. Or a delicate bud perhaps?
No, no, rather, you are like a beautiful as yet
undeveloped photograph, that will perish without light.
Why all those endless hours wasted in the preternatural gloom
of your sordid little place of work? Stroll, or sit outside for a couple
of hours today and enjoy the sun's golden rays. SAD (Seasonal Affective
Disorder) is a clinically diagnosed condition in which the lack of sunlight in
winter literally makes people ill. It affects millions of people around the
world, though proportionately more the further you get from the Equator of
course. In the more remote parts of Scandinavia, it has been known to con-
tribute to higher suicide rates. SAD's effects can be explained with reference
to the importance of sunlight on cellular functioning. As light enters the eye,
it hits the retina and filters through to the pineal gland. The pineal gland in
turn produces melatonin, a neurotransmitter that affects the hypothalamus
gland. The hypothalamus controls a whole range of vital functions, including
mood, hormones, appetite, libido and metabolism. Beyond this,
sunlight is also crucial as an indirect provider of Vitamin D. The sun's
ultraviolet rays set off its production, itself necessary for the
absorption of calcium in the bones and teeth. Indeed,
vitamin D deficiency among those who spend too
much time indoors, can lead to brittle
bones and fractures.

8	Monday 12 July	1
9		1
10		1
11		1
12		1
13		1

Today, prioritize your dreams!

Winner takes all!

I'm going to make it!

American Dream come true!

No room for losers!

1989

m on the path to success!

1989

All the way to the top?

I wanna restructure and move on!

Stockham Management Consulting

SMC

	Tuesday 13 July
8	
9	
10	
11	
12	
13	
14	
15	
16	
17	
18	

Mannerisms Day

Your body language is as individual as your DNA. You move in your very own mysterious ways, and your physical quirks actually reveal much about you. Today, try to be aware of what your body is saying to those around you: don't let them betray your innermost feelings.

YOU TOUCH YOUR NOSE:
you lack the confidence to face others.

YOU BITE YOUR NAILS:
you have repressed anger within you.

YOU SHAKE ONE LEG:
you are nurturing some chronic anxiety.

YOU BITE YOUR LIPS:
you fear your hidden demons.

YOU FIDDLE WITH YOUR HAIR:
you are not comfortable with your appearance.

YOU LICK YOUR LIPS:
this one doesn't mean anything.

YOU TAP YOUR FINGERS:
you have tendencies towards control freakery.

8		14	
9		15	
10		16	
11		17	
12		18	
13		19	

Improve your signature today

FRIDAY 16 JULY. In an increasingly digitized society where you're defined by your social security and bank account numbers, your signature is one of the very last bastions of your individuality. Let other great signatures inspire it; refine it constantly; and above all take pride in it!

Great signatures of our time

MARLENE DIETRICH

THOMAS JEFFERSON

TONY BENNETT

DALAI LAMA

JACKIE KENNEDY

BORIS KARLOFF

MARILYN MONROE

GARY COOPER

WILLIAM SHAKESPEARE

BUDDY HOLLY

CHARLIE CHAPLIN

Practice area

Signature before

8	
9	
10	
11	
12	
13	

Signature after

14	
15	
16	
17	
18	

— Remember to notify your bank! —

8	12	16
9	13	17
10	14	18
11	15	19

Saturday 17 July
TODAY, HAVE A GOOD CRY
Research has revealed that crying is good for us,
indeed that it is physiologically essential.
There are three different types of tears.
1) Basal tears, that keep our eyes lubricated.
2) Reflex tears, when a foreign
body gets into or irritates our eyes.
3) Emotional tears, when we react
psychologically to something.
Emotional tears contain chemically higher levels of
manganese and prolactin hormone. Losing these
through crying reduces their levels in the body and
keeps depression away. This is why we feel better
after a good cry. Here are some sad thoughts to help
stimulate your crying glands and cheer you up:
We're all going to die…eventually.
Can you really ever trust anyone fully? Really?
You may never meet the love of your life.
Orphans, starving.
Time is running out.
Snookums the puppy has died (horribly).

WHAT DO YOU CALL THOSE LITTLE PLASTIC THINGS ON THE TIP OF SHOELACES? AGLETS.

WHY DO YOU NEVER SEE BABY PIGEONS? THEY GROW UP TOO FAST.

WOULD A MARS BAR MELT ON MARS? YES.

WHAT IS THE MOST COMMON MIDDLE NAME? MARY.

WHAT YEAR WERE TENNIS BALLS OFFICIALLY CHANGED FROM WHITE TO YELLOW? 1967.

HOW MUCH WATER DO WE PASS ON AVERAGE? 24CL/MINUTE.

HOW MUCH DOES THE TALKING CLOCK GUY GET PAID? $3,100 A YEAR.

WHAT WAS THE WEATHER OVER SAO PAULO ON THE MORNING OF MAY 12, 1976? CLOUDY.

WHAT IS THE VOLUME OF A WHALE'S EJACULATE? 2 LITRES.

HOW MANY DIMPLES ARE THERE ON A GOLF BALL? 336.

WHAT IS THE SECOND MOST POPULAR CAT NAME? PATCHES.

WHEN WERE POSTAGE STAMPS INVENTED? 1840.

WHAT IS THE LONGEST RECORDED FLIGHT OF A CHICKEN? 13 SECONDS.

HOW MUCH DOES AN AVERAGE ADULT HUMAN HEART WEIGH? 274 GRAMMES.

WHAT IS THE ONLY FOOD THAT DOES NOT SPOIL? HONEY.

WHAT WAS THE NAME OF LADY GODIVA'S HORSE? AETHENOTH.

HOW MANY HAIRS IN THE AVERAGE BEARD? 12,000.

HOW MANY BRICKS ARE THERE IN THE EMPIRE STATE BUILDING? 10 MILLION.

WHO IS THE PATRON SAINT OF TOOTHACHES? ST. APOLLONIA.

8	14
9	15
10	16
11	17
12	18
13	19

TODAY SEND A MESSAGE IN A BOTTLE

Be sure to choose the appropriate bottle for your message.

Plain glass bottle:
standard »I'm lost on a
desert island« messages

Mineral water bottle:
for long fancy letters you'd like
to see published someday

Perfume bottle:
letters to one's illicit lovers

Vintage champagne bottle:
formal messages: weddings,
funerals, bar mitzvahs

Plastic bottle:
messages to your
inferiors

Monday 19 July

8

9

10

11

12

13

14

15

16

17

18

DON'T FORGET THE CORK!!!

(Note: according to marine experts, there are currently
125,000 bottles containing messages floating around
the world's oceans. Yours could be one of them.)

Beer bottle:
party invitations & news
of sports victories

Soft drink bottle:
the young person's choice

Medicine bottle:
painful news

Foreign wine bottle:
letters from abroad,
holiday postcards

Broken bottle:
suicide notes

PREGNANCY TEST DAY

You can never be too careful. Deposit a drop of urine on this chemically-sensitive spot to determine whether you're in the family way.

WHITE: You've missed. Try depositing your drop from a closer range, however good you believe your aim to be.

RED: Allelujah! You are the proud future parent of a precious lil'baby! Get into that whole baby talk thang now! Goo grrr!

BLUE: Hmmm. Cold. Better luck next time.

GREEN: Shittin' hell. Good luck to you, you're gonna need it.

YELLOW: You've just actually urinated in a book. Yuck. How revolting. Please get rid of this copy and buy a clean one.

MEN: If your pee goes anything but a faint yellow, this might indicate a hormonal imbalance – or a scientific first.

Wednesday 21 July	14
8	15
9	16
10	17
11	18
12	19
13	

DIARY PYRAMID SCHEME

SELL THE DIARY DOOR-TO-DOOR AND GET RICH QUICK!!!

The business brains behind the Diary are looking for go-getting individuals with a knack for selling and an eye for the main chance! You could make literally **millions** in no time, as a **DDD** (Diary Direct Distributor)!

Here's how it works. We need people to sell the Diary door-to-door, to those folks who can't make it to the bookstore for some reason. For every two salesmen you recruit, you get a commission (calculated on the basis of their future sales)! **Sounds easy, don't it?** Well it is.

To get started, all you need is our **Diary Salesman Recruiting Pack** (DSRP), available to order **NOW** on **00-65-453-788964** for a measly $499.99 which you could recoup in as little as a week*. It will teach you the tricks of the trade. But in the meantime, why not get started? Recruit a family member (minimum age 14) and you get 5% off the **DSRP** already!

Visualization of Pyramid Scheme

Wouldn't you like to wear a business suit and stay in nice hotels too?

DSRP

CALL NOW!
00-65-453-788964

*Based on two salesmen each recruiting six others in turn recruiting twelve with average sales of 13,897 Diaries each over the eight following quarters. Tax not included. »Week« as defined by the Second Era Babylonian calendar.

Thursday 22 July	14
8	15
9	16
10	17
11	18
12	19
13	

TODAY, BE ENTIRELY SERIOUS

Irony is a curse in disguise, corrupting and reducing everything to the same
superficial level and abolishing depth in both values and relationships.
Today, avoid the temptations of glibness and frivolity, and take life seriously for a change.

FRIDAY 23 JULY	12	17
8	13	18
9	14	19
10	15	
11	16	

THE FRENCH THINK NOTHING OF SHOUTING AT EACH OTHER IN FRONT OF EVERYONE, SO LET LOOSE. SUITABLE TOPICS INCLUDE THE STATE OF SOCIALISM TODAY, THE HUMAN CONDITION AT THE DAWN OF THE THIRD MILLENNIUM, WHO GETS TO PLAY WITH THE BEACH BALL NEXT.

HOLIDAYING AT HOME? PUBLIC ROWS ARE FROWNED UPON, SO EITHER WHISPER URGENTLY AND SCOWL AT YOUR PARTNER, OR PRETEND TO BE A FRENCH TOURIST AND SCREAM AT EACH OTHER IN FRENCH.

08	14
09	15
10	16
11	17
12	18
13	

IN FRANCE, BUYING AN »EXPRÈS« IN ANY CAFÉ ENTITLES YOU TO SIT THERE FOR AS LONG AS YOU LIKE. THUS IT PROVIDES THE PERFECT OPPORTUNITY FOR FRENCH PEOPLE OF ALL AGES TO WRITE VOLUMINOUS TOMES ON HOW THEY SEE LIFE, WHICH ARE NEVER LESS THAN COMPELLING. MOST FAMOUS IS JEAN-PAUL SARTRE'S »BEING AND NOTHINGNESS«, WHICH AT 1564 PAGES, WAS WELL WORTH THE PRICE OF THAT »EXPRÈS«.

HOLIDAYING AT HOME? SIT IN A SPORTS BAR. YOUR PHILOSOPHY MAY HAVE TO BE SHORTER THAN THE FULL FRENCH DEAL THOUGH, AS STAFF ARE LESS SYMPATHETIC AND MIGHT KICK YOU OUT AFTER A BIT.

08	14
09	15
10	16
11	17
12	18
13	

MARDI 27 JUILLET   TOPLESS SUNBATHING DAY

OH LA LA, LADIES! THIS IS WHERE YOU LOSE YOUR INHIBI-
TIONS AND HIT THE BEACH *AU NATUREL*. MEN: IT IS IMPOR-
TANT TO STAY COOL AND CASUAL AMIDST THE PROFUSION
OF BARE FLESH. ACT AS IF YOU SEE THIS ALL THE TIME AND
IF ANYTHING ARE PERHAPS MILDLY BORED BY IT. STICKING
YOUR HEAD IN »BEING AND NOTHINGNESS« COULD HELP.

HOLIDAYING AT HOME? THIS ONE IS
POTENTIALLY ILLEGAL. AVOID, EXCEPT
IN THE PRIVACY OF YOUR OWN PATIO.

08		14
09		15
10		16
11		17
12		18
13		

GAULOISES CIGARETTES ARE THE MARK OF THE GENUINE FRENCH PEASANT, SALT-OF-THE FRENCH-EARTH. TO CONVERSE WITH HIM ON EQUAL TERMS – A HOLIDAY MUST – YOU MUST REEK OF GAULOISES TOO AND LOWER YOUR VOICE TO THE GUTTURAL LUNG-CANCERISH DEPTH THAT HE IS ACCUSTOMED TO. CHAIN SMOKING THREE PACKS SHOULD DO THE TRICK.

HOLIDAYING AT HOME? YOU MAY EXPERIENCE DIFFICULTIES IN LOCATING GAULOISES AND/OR FRENCH PEASANTS.

08

09

10

11

12

13

14

15

16

17

18

JEUDI 29 JUILLET

TAKE A LOVER

THE FRENCH ARE DEMOCRATIC IN THEIR UNFAITHFULNESS. BOTH SEXES ARE ENTITLED TO CHEAT IN EQUAL MEASURES. HOWEVER SOME RULES MUST BE OBEYED. THERE MUST BE A SIGNIFICANT AGE GAP BETWEEN YOU AND YOUR LOVER. YOU MUST COME FROM WILDLY DIFFERENT SOCIAL BACKGROUNDS. AND YOU MUST ONLY MAKE LOVE IN GARRETS. HOLIDAYING AT HOME? THIS IS ONE YOU CAN TRY, THOUGH PEOPLE ARE USUALLY MORE FUSSY ABOUT COMMITMENT AND OTHER NARROW-MINDED UNFRENCH CONCEPTS.

08	14
09	15
10	16
11	17
12	18
13	

END YOUR HOLIDAY ON A HIGH NOTE, WITH A SPOT OF RIOTING. IN FRANCE YOU NEED NO PARTICULAR EXCUSE FOR DIRECT ACTION, AS THE 1789 REVOLUTION WAS NEVER OFFICIALLY DECLARED TO HAVE ENDED. JUST LOB BRICKS OR MANURE AT THE NEAREST OFFICIAL-LOOKING BUILDING AND YOU WILL SOON BE INTRODUCED TO THE LOCAL RIOT POLICE WHO WILL ASSIST YOU BACK HOME AFTER A BRIEF SPELL *EN PRISON*.

HOLIDAY WEEK IN FRANCE!

HOLIDAYING AT HOME? BEST TO END HOLIDAY EARLY ON THIS ONE.

08		14
09		15
10		16
11		17
12		18
13		

Pillow book
Tonight use the Diary as your pillow book and write down your dreams.

What is a pillow book?
The pillow book is a Japanese institution, first used in 550AD by the Asuka dynasty. It is used to record thoughts, events, dreams. Now, the Asukas used to mainly dream about giant serpents, many-clawed dragons, saber-toothed tigers and the like, but there's no reason why you can't write down your boring old everyday dreams about your third-grade schoolmistress. You must however use Japanese calligraphy to do so.

8
9
10
11
12
13
14
15
16
17
18

**Saturday
31 July**

SURVEILLANCE SPECIAL: TODAY STAGE A CRIME IN FRONT OF A CCTV CAMERA AND SEE IF ANYONE COMES TO THE RESCUE.

1) LITTERING

2) DRUNKEN FIGHTING/JOSTLING

3) MUGGING

4) STABBING FOLLOWED BY MUGGING

5) STABBING AND/OR GANG-BEATING WITH MUGGING

6) MURDER (BACK ALLEY CCTV ONLY)

8 ....

9 ....

10 ....

11 ....

12 ....

13 ....

14 ....

15 ....

16 ....

17 ....

18 ....

19 ....

TODAY, MEASURE YOUR IQ

YOU HAVE TEN MINUTES TO COMPLETE THIS TEST. IF ONE
ITEM PROVES TOO DIFFICULT, MOVE ON TO THE NEXT ONE.

1 INSERT THE WORD THAT
COMPLETES BOTH OTHER WORDS

S H A L (...) B R O W

2 INSERT THE MISSING NUMBER

3	9	26	9	27	80	6	18	?

3 WHICH IS THE ODD ONE OUT?

HOJH	ICADLUA
BLATRE	CHIMLEA

4 WHAT IS THE MISSING NUMBER?

4   7
?   11
22   9

5 WHAT THREE-LETTER
WORD ENDING
CAN BE PREFIXED
BY ALL THESE?

CL...
N...
B...
T...
S...
R...
W...
G...

8
9
10
11
12
13
14
15
16
17
18
19

MONDAY 2 AUGUST

6 WHAT IS THE MISSING NUMBER?

4976   4463   3950   3437   ?

7 WHAT NUMBER GOES HERE?

FREEMASON=232
SATANIST=?

8 END THIS SENTENCE

THE OAK SPANS FIVE ?

9 WHICH IS THE ODD ONE OUT?

① ② ③ ④

YOUR IQ = FINAL SCORE SQUARED + 100. UNDER 110: POOR TO AVERAGE 110-130: GOOD 130-150: VERY BRIGHT
150 AND OVER: LIAR

WEDNESDAY 4 AUGUST

Today live for the moment: that moment is 21:31:22 to 21:31:23. Plan your entire day around that one single second of absolute choking nirvana. First, purchase the necessary accessories: one rare Belgian white truffle sugar-dusted chocolate, silk pyjamas, the sleekest hi-fi system available and a CD of Maria Callas. Retire to your home, where after a restorative siesta, you are to bathe in champagne for an hour or so, before receiving a massage from some gorgeous Swedish creature. As the blissful second nears, pop the chocolate in your mouth, kiss the love of your life, and bring yourself to orgasm at 21.31.22, precisely the moment when Maria Callas hits the high note in Tosca's »Vissi D'Arte« aria. Truly now, you may say you'll die having lived.

8	
9	
10	
11	
12	
13	
14	
15	
16	
17	
18	
21:31:22	

VIP-DAY

These are the people we'd like to buy and read the Diary. If your name is on the list, please use the exclusive form to tell us what you think. If your name isn't on the list, please turn the page and move along. Thank you.

The Dalai Lama (religious leader)
The President of the USA (leader)
The Vice-President of the USA (leader)
Kofi Annan (political leader, UN)
The Pope (religious leader)
Oprah Winfrey (celebrity)
Jean Baudrillard (philosopher)
Jerry Springer (celebrity)
Steven Spielberg (filmmaker)
Madonna (singer)
Richard Branson (businessman)
Tony Blair (Prime Minister of England)
Mick Jagger (singer)
Salman Rushdie (author)
David Beckham (sportsman)
Bill Cosby (entertainer)
Colin Powell (political leader)
Stephen Hawking (scientist)
Michael Jackson (singer)
Arnold Schwarzenegger (actor)
Hugh Hefner (editor)
Yoko Ono (artist)
Afrika Bambaataa (artist)
Jack Chirac (political leader)
Meryl Streep (actress)
Sinead O'Connor (singer)
Noam Chomsky (intellectual)
Luciano Pavarotti (singer)
Henry Kissinger (intellectual)
Mike Oldfield (singer)
Ivan Lendl (sportsman)
Tom Cruise (actor)

David Copperfield (entertainer)
Gore Vidal (writer)
Donald Trump (businessman)
Bill Gates (businessman)
Eddie Murphy (actor)
Mikhail Gorbachev (political leader)
Robert De Niro (actor)
Newt Gingrich (political leader)
Celine Dion (singer)
Al Gore (political leader)
Alan Greenspan (economist)
Umberto Eco (writer)
Gunter Grass (writer)
Norman Mailer (intellectual)
Donna Tartt (writer)
Wes Craven (filmmaker)
Ingmar Bergman (filmmaker)
Bono (singer)
George Michael (singer)
Justin Timberlake (singer)
Vladimir Putin (political leader)
Tiger Woods (sportsman)
Pamela Anderson (actress)
Siwert Öholm (entertainer)
Stock, Aitken, Waterman (producers)
Phillippe Starck (designer)
Stephen King (writer)
Tom Hanks (actor)
Bryan Ferry (singer)
Helmut Newton (photographer)
Natasha Kinski (actor)
Chelsea Clinton (daughter)

Phil Collins (singer)
Elton John (singer)
Tina Turner (singer)
Sting (singer)
Bruce Springsteen (singer)
Robert Murdoch (businessman)
George Soros (businessman)
Michael Douglas (actor)
Robin Williams (actor)
Margaret Thatcher (stateswoman)
Renzo Piano (architect)
Nelson Mandela (statesman)
Jacques Derrida (philosopher)
Pierre Boulez (composer)
Germaine Greer (writer)
Peter Greenaway (filmmaker)
Jurgen Habermas (thinker)
David Hockney (artist)
Jimmy Carter (political leader)
Don Johnson (actor)
Helmut Kohl (statesman)
Camille Paglia (intellectual)
Cindy Crawford (model)
Lady Sarah Ferguson (royalty)
Lord Wolff (high court judge)
Roland Magdane (French comedian)
Jon Bon Jovi (singer)
Yasser Arafat (political leader)
Charlton Heston (actor)
Bernard Pivot (French intellectual)
Ralph Nader (intellectual)
Gene Simmons (singer)

I,................................., whose name appears above, have perused the Diary and this is my considered opinion of it:

....

....

....

....

You have my permission to use it as a review, should you wish to do so. Signed: ....

Please send this form to Benrik, c/o Penguin Books, 80 Strand, London, WC2R 0RL, UK.

If you feel your name should be on this page but has been overlooked, please write in as well stating your case, with supporting evidence and references where appropriate.

THURSDAY 5 AUGUST	14	
9	15	
10	16	
11	17	
12	18	
13	19	

ME!

LADY
E
D

CAREY'S
BABY

24
26
28
30
32
34
36
38
40
45
50
60

MUM

ANDERSON
THIRD FLOOR

SMITH
NEXT
DOOR

THE PEOPLE
OPPOSITE

TODAY, VOLUME-TEST YOUR NEIGHBOURS
These days the puniest hi-fi system can pump out a
cool 100Wx2. But at what point do your neighbours
begin to feel the bass? Find out by adjusting your
amplifier's dial up until they start complaining. Then
mark the notch and leave it as your standard setting.

8
9
10
11
12
13
14
15
16
17
18
19

CONFIDENTIAL:

A huge meteorite is about to hit the Earth, blasting it into smithereens. The world's main governments left weeks ago for a secret base on Pluto, leaving their lookalikes to keep the populace placid. Only owners of the Diary are allowed to be in the know, so please keep this information to yourself.

OPTIONS: THERE ARE FOUR MAIN WAYS OF REACTING TO THE NEWS.

1) GO ON THE RAMPAGE
You are understandably peeved at the imminent termination of your life, and need to channel your anger. Also, the rules of society are now null and void, as you need not worry about punishment. So let loose and steal, fight, pillage and destroy.

2) HAVE SEX WITH EVERYONE
People will feel much freer to hop into bed with you today, as long-term commitment is less of an issue. This only goes for fellow Diary owners though; others who are not aware of their impending doom may need more convincing.

3) PREPARE FOR THE AFTERLIFE
A bit of a gamble, but probably worth it by now: find the nearest priest and go full tilt for last minute salvation. This option is not compatible with the two previous ones however.

4) SIT IN FRONT OF TV IN NUMBED DISBELIEF Probably the option most people will resort to. You may not even notice much change from everyday life.

SUNDAY 8 AUGUST	14	
9	15	
10	16	
11	17	
12	18	
13	19	

LIVE THIS DAY AS IF IT WERE YOUR LAST.

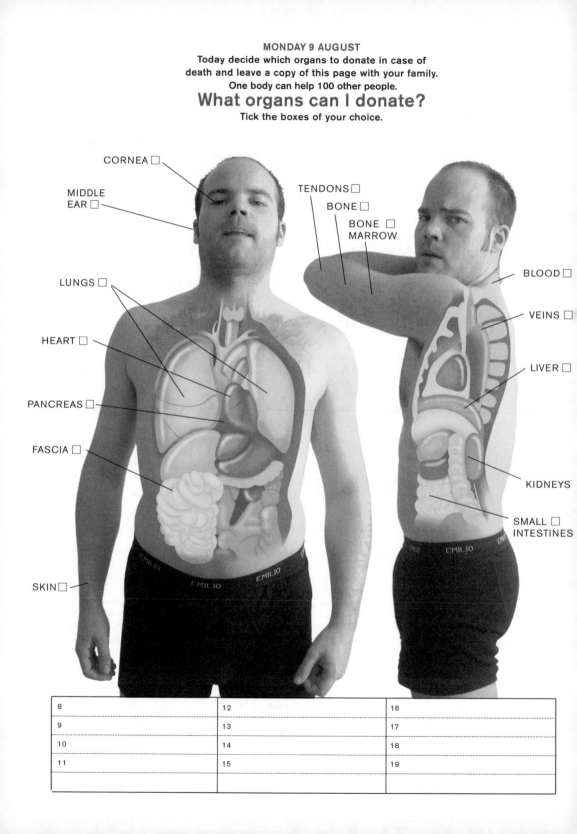

MONDAY 9 AUGUST
Today decide which organs to donate in case of
death and leave a copy of this page with your family.
One body can help 100 other people.

What organs can I donate?

Tick the boxes of your choice.

CORNEA ☐

MIDDLE
EAR ☐

TENDONS ☐
BONE ☐
BONE ☐
MARROW

BLOOD ☐

LUNGS ☐

VEINS ☐

HEART ☐

LIVER ☐

PANCREAS ☐

FASCIA ☐

KIDNEYS

SMALL ☐
INTESTINES

SKIN ☐

8	12	16
9	13	17
10	14	18
11	15	19

FIND A WAY OF INCLUDING THE WORD VORTEX IN ALL YOUR CONVERSATIONS TODAY. Try to do it without sounding clumsy. Here are some suggestions: »Lovely weather, isn't it?«, »Yes, though that cloud over there looks a bit *vortex*-shaped«, »This business report makes for interesting reading«, »Indeed. It lies at the *vortex* of cruciality.«, »Did you see that programme on television last night?«, »What, the one about the *vortex*?«

VORTEX

Tuesday 10 August

8	14
9	15
10	16
11	17
12	18
13	19

Minute
ONE

8		14
9		15
10		16
11		17
12		18
13		

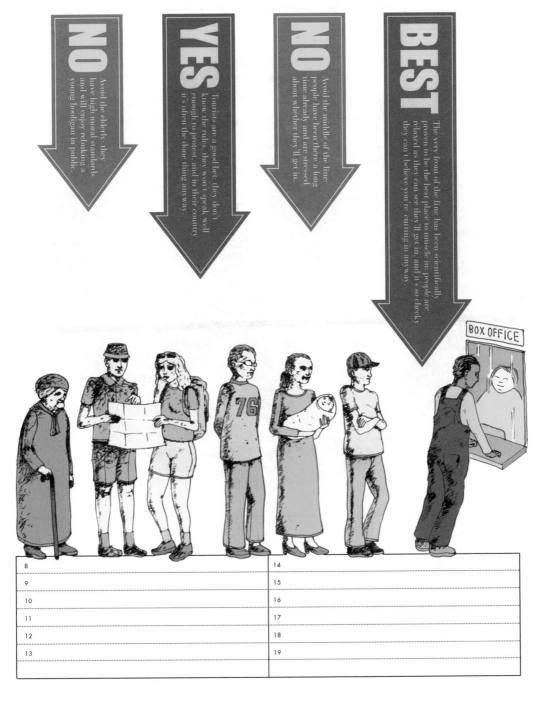

TODAY JUMP A QUEUE

NO Avoid the elderly: they have high moral standards and will enjoy rebuking a young hooligan in public.

YES Tourists are a good bet: they don't know the rules, they won't speak well enough to protest, and in their country it's often the done thing anyway.

NO Avoid the middle of the line: people have been there a long time already and are stressed about whether they'll get in.

BEST The very front of the line has been scientifically proven to be the best place to muscle in: people are relaxed as they can see they'll get in, and it's so cheeky they can't believe you're cutting in anyway.

BOX OFFICE

8	14
9	15
10	16
11	17
12	18
13	19

Friday 13 August

In 1992, the town of Kiruna in the north of Sweden became concerned about the falling birth rate amongst its citizens. It was calculated that if the rate didn't improve, Kiruna's population would halve in size within 30 years. So, the town council decided to cut off the electricity for 24 hours, every first day of the month. Initially, this caused an uproar. But protests subsided when an unprecedented number of babies were born within the same week, exactly nine months later...

No Electricity Day

Our proud ancestors survived for years without electricity. See if you can last a day without relying on any electrically-powered devices.

8	14
9	15
10	16
11	17
12	18
13	19

Why spend a fortune on clothes to make a fashion statement when your own head provides the perfect opportunity already? Here are some popular radical haircuts to inspire you.

The Waterfall

The David Beckham

The Executive
(This one looks particularly
radical on women)

Random Patches

The Square

The Mullet

The name of the
person you love

The King

The Queen

The Russian

The Squirrel

Your very own

8	14	SATURDAY 14 AUGUST
9	15	
10	16	
11	17	
12	18	
13	19	

 Advanced: DO SOMETHING RADICAL WITH YOUR PUBIC HAIR. If your main (non-pubic) hair is already radical or you are bald, style your pubic regions. Shaving is hip but potentially dangerous. Colouring is more original and a welcome ice-breaker on those one-night-stands.

Today go to a supermarket and enter all the competitions

Tell us why new detergent WIZ is the BIZ! and WIN A TRIP TO BELGIUM

SUPERMARKET SWEEPSTAKE! The fullest trolley gets their money back!

This coupon could mean a coupé!

Sunday 15 August

8
9
10
11
12
13

14
15
16
17
18
19

Tie breaker! SPLOSH paint is the best BECAUSE...

BUY A BAR! WIN A CAR!

Any of these pens could contain...the GOLDEN BISCUIT!!!

Collect 200 points like this one and this magnificent pen is yours

Win your weight in tuna chunks!

If you don't win anything, it must be because they're rigged. Complain to the supermarket manager.

Phrenology day
TODAY HAVE YOUR HEAD EXAMINED

Phrenology is the science of identifying character traits from the shape of the brain, itself deducible of course from the shape of the skull. As modern-day brain imaging techniques have confirmed beyond doubt, many of the brain's main functions are indeed localized. We have yet to confirm the exactitude of early phrenologists' categories, but in the meantime why not judge for yourself? Simply run your fingers over your skull and refer any unusual protuberances to the diagram below.

1. Impulse to propagate
2. Language faculty
3. Tenderness for offspring
4. Disposition for delighting in colour patterns
5. Friendly attachments
6. Aptitude for music
7. Defence of self and property
8. Arithmetical ability
9. Carnivorous instinct /bloodlust
10. Architectural talent
11. Memory for faces
12. Sense of ruse
13. Relative sagacity
14. Metaphysical perspicuity
15. Arrogance and love of authority
16. Caustic wit
17. Vanity and love of glory
18. Poetical talent
19. Circumspection
20. Goodness
21. Theosophical feelings
22. Memory for names

Monday 16 August		
8	14	
9	15	
10	16	
11	17	
12	18	
13	19	

Studies have shown that the rear hippocampus of London black cab drivers, at the front of the brain, grows larger over the years as they use it for navigation purposes. That's a fact.

Today is Blue-Sky Day.
Forget the practicalities: decide what
you really want out of life. I want…

A shed on the
moon

72 kids

To be King
of Lombardy

A second
belly button

To make
love to the
Virgin Mary

My enemy's
head on a plate

A layer
of atmosphere
named after me

My own
nuclear-powered
submarine

TUESDAY 17 AUGUST	
8	
9	
10	
11	
12	
13	
14	
15	
16	
17	
18	

World
peace

One pyramid
for me and two smaller
ones for my followers

To be left
alone

To be
beamed
up

To rule
the world

Now make it
happen.

THE SMALL THINGS ARE WHAT MAKES

LIFE SO COMFORTABLE · TOO COMFORTABLE! PRACTICE

SELF-DISCIPLINE · LEARN TO LIVE WITHOUT THOSE

SELF-INDULGENT PLEASURES FOR A DAY

TODAY DENY YOUR SELF SOMETHING

NOT VAL NIGHT

PILLOWS AREN'T GOOD FOR YOUR NECK
DON'T CALL HIM/HER
SHOWERS·MORE HYGIENIC THAN BATHS
RAINING? LEAVE YOUR UMBRELLA AT HOME
CANCEL THAT DINNER WITH FRIENDS

YOU DON'T NEED SUGAR IN YOUR COFFEE
YOU DON'T NEED COFFEE EITHER
SITTING DOWN TOO MUCH IS BAD

THE CHEAPEST TOILET PAPER IS QUITE SUFFICIENT!

SKIP THAT SECOND HELPING AND DESSERT

8	14
9	15
10	16
11	17
12	18
13	19

Today the makers of the Diary are issuing Personal International ID numbers. Get yours at www.thiswebsitewillchangeyourlife.com before they run out. In the future, your PIID will supersede any other form of identification. It will serve as your passport, your social security number, your telephone number, your credit card, your driving licence, your video store card. The PIID is a collaborative venture between the Diary owners and over 183 governments worldwide. It comprises seven digits, which allows for millions of possible combinations. They will be allocated on a strict first-come-first-served basis. Any individual without a PIID will be sorely disadvantaged in the society of the future, so make sure to obtain yours now. Hurry hurry!

Thursday 19 August

8

9

10

11

12

13

14

15

16

17

18

19

SAUNA DAY

Once the Incredible Hulk was locked into a sauna by some evil man who was a criminal and he put the heat up to the max. But Hulk became the green monster out of anger and heat and smashed the bloody door down!!! Otherwise he would have sweated to death, and died. He caught the criminal man.

Saunas are good for you, so today turn your heating up to the max and indulge in some healthy sweating!

Russian sauna: the banya

The wood-fired banya is an age-old tradition in Russia. The Khlysty, a 17th century Russian sect, used to gather there to practise self-flagellation, in the belief that the heat brought the blood closer to the surface of the skin. Theirs was a theology of salvation through sin, in which ecstatic collective prayer sessions (which some claimed ended in group orgies) were followed by violent whipping, designed to leave scars. Some claim they taught Sacher-Masoch and thus are the true fathers of masochism.

HEALTH NEWS!
HEALTH NEWS!
HEALTH NEWS!

SAUNAS INCREASE YOUR HEART RATE: a 20 minute sauna is the equivalent of a brisk walk!

SAUNAS DETOXIFY YOUR SKIN, FLUSHING OUT IMPURITIES AND HELPING REDUCE CELLULITE!

Saunas raise your body temp to 38degrees, creating an immune system-boosting fever!

Saunas relieve the painful symptoms of arthritis and revive tired muscles!

Sauna songs

(To the tune of Jingle Bells)
Sauna day, Sauna day,
Let's have lots of fun
Bring a towel and a snack
And let's turn up the heat.

(To the tune of My Bonnie)
Come and sit in my sauna
I cleaned it especially for you
There is no old sweat on the benches
So come and stain them with yours.

(To the tune of Old McDonald)
No one is allowed in here
With a towel on
And if you have your towel on
It will be removed.

(To the tune of Twinkle
Twinkle Little Star)
If you're tired or overworked
And you have no money left
To go on a holiday
Where there's sun and heat
Then you should pop on down to us
We'll wipe you and take care of you.

Friday 20 August

8	
9	
10	
11	
12	
13	
14	
15	
16	
17	
18	

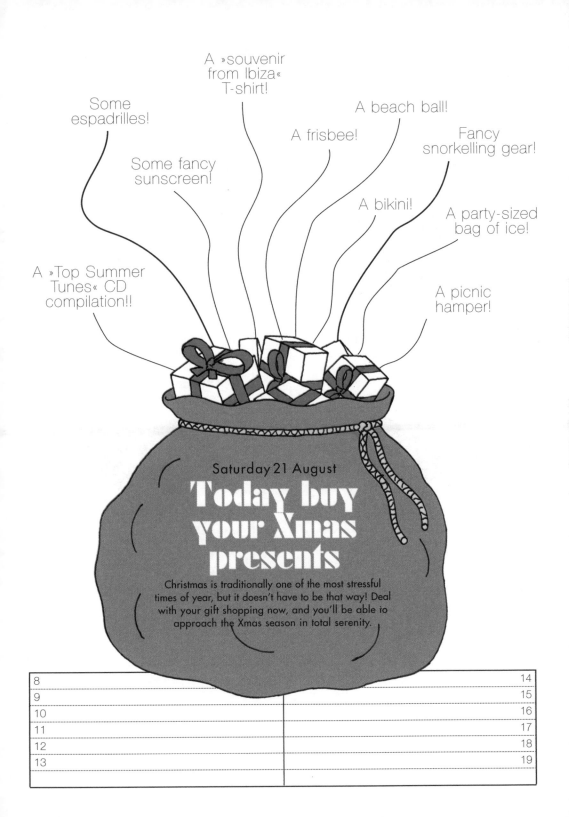

Some espadrilles!

A »souvenir from Ibiza« T-shirt!

A beach ball!

A frisbee!

Fancy snorkelling gear!

Some fancy sunscreen!

A bikini!

A party-sized bag of ice!

A »Top Summer Tunes« CD compilation!!

A picnic hamper!

Saturday 21 August

Today buy your Xmas presents

Christmas is traditionally one of the most stressful times of year, but it doesn't have to be that way! Deal with your gift shopping now, and you'll be able to approach the Xmas season in total serenity.

8		14
9		15
10		16
11		17
12		18
13		19

Today buy a newspaper and read only the ads

Judge the most truthful one and recompense the advertiser by purchasing their product.

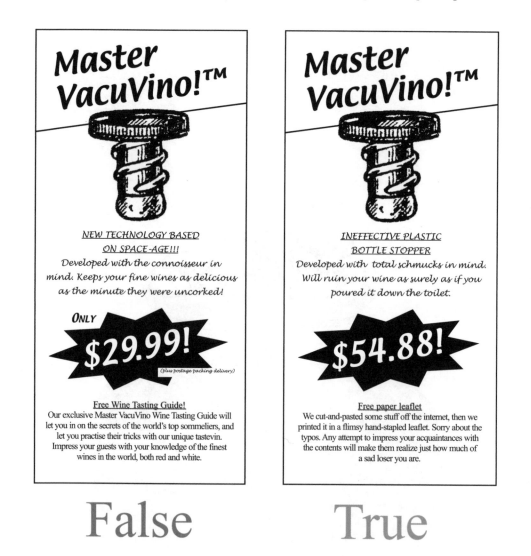

False	True

8	14	
9	15	
10	16	
11	17	
12	18	
13	19	

Monday 23 August: Stare at this stranger. Memorize her features.
Should you ever meet her, call her Aubrey, and she will tell you a secret

8
9
10
11
12
13
14
15
16
17
18

Tuesday 24 August

Feniseca tarquinius (causes freak flooding in Beirut), Erora laeta (causes early morning mist in Central Park)', Plebeius saepiolus (causes sun storms on Jupiter).', Colias philodice (causes rainbows over Northampton)', Feniseca tarquinius (causes hurricanes in Southern China)', Colias philodice (causes rainbows over Northampton)', "the flap of a butterfly's wings in Brazil can set off a tornado in Texas". Types of butterfly: Pieris oleracea (causes hurricanes in Southern China)', Colias philodice to quote Edward Lorenz, "the flap of a butterfly's wings in Brazil can set off a tornado in Texas". Types of butterfly can have huge effects. Thus to quote Edward Lorenz, small impossible-to-measure initial changes in complex systems can have huge effects. Thus The butterfly effect explained: the butterfly effect dramatically illustrates chaos theory. The idea is that very butterfly effect: chase a butterfly away from its flight pattern to disrupt meteorological systems worldwide.

Today 1539 Mon

Today experience a new emotion

Retroescalophobia	The fear of walking down stopped escalators	»I'm a chronic retroescalophobe«
E-mailism	Obsessive need to check for new e-mails	»Stop being so e-mailistic!«
Pluvialness	The love of raindrops	»Sandra loves autumn, she's very pluvial, you see«
Cathodillia	Sexual attraction to one's television set	»Man arrested for catho-dilliac outburst in store«
Goreness	When you realize you're never going to make it	»He's only 29 and already he's feeling gorey«
Supplementobia	When you're exhausted at the prospect of reading your newspaper	»Weekends bring out the supplementobic in me«
Extremosis	Violent animosity towards one's extremities, especially big toes	»Since the amputation, I haven't been so extremosist«
Cerebrosity	Overfondness for one's own intellect	»The professor's cere-brosity was legendary«
Spatred	Hatred of spades	»Such spatred in one so young!«
Sommelierism	Powerful urge to impress others with wine knowledge	»His sommelierism was driving me crazy, so I got a divorce«
Architectillia	Passion for licking glass buildings	»He would have made a great window cleaner, had it not been for his architectillia«
Hurtism	When you secretly look forward to being hurt so you can moan about it	»Don't insult him, he's hurtistic«

Find an inchoate emotion within you and name it

WEDNESDAY 25 AUGUST	14
8	15
9	16
10	17
11	18
12	19
13	

TODAY SEND A TELEGRAM
FORGET INTERNET. TELEGRAMS IMPACTFULLER
SPECIALNEWSWISE. SEND TODAY.

THURSDAY 26 AUGUST

08————————————————————————————————————
09————————————————————————————————————
10————————————————————————————————————
11————————————————————————————————————
12————————————————————————————————————
13————————————————————————————————————
14————————————————————————————————————
15————————————————————————————————————
16————————————————————————————————————
17————————————————————————————————————
18————————————————————————————————————
19————————————————————————————————————

————————————————————————————————————
————————————————————————————————————

THE BIRTH OF THE TELEGRAM
THE TELEGRAM WAS INVENTED IN 1844, BUT FOR YEARS, NO
ONE THOUGHT THE INVENTION HAD ANY FUTURE. THEN IN
1853, TWO CRIMINALS, OLIVER MARTIN AND FIDDLER DICK,
TRIED TO ESCAPE BY JUMPING ON THE LONDON-SLOUGH TRAIN.
THE LONDON POLICE THOUGHT ON THEIR FEET AND CABLED
THEIR COLLEAGUES IN SLOUGH, RESULTING IN A PROMPT
ARREST AND TRIUMPHANT HEADLINES ENSURING THE SUC-
CESS OF THE NEW TECHNOLOGY. (THE BRITISH POLICE USED IT
SO OFTEN THEY GOT THEIR OWN SPECIAL TELEGRAM ADDRESS:
HANDCUFFS, LONDON.)

BULLSHIT TODAY

Log on to an internet chatroom and participate in a discussion you know nothing about for as long as you can without being exposed as a fraud. Example: go to www.hortmag.com and engage in an informed discussion in response to this post.

Posted by:LandPlanFran
Subject: Butterfly bush-hardiness

Although Butterfly bushes are listed as zone 5 hardy, I find them questionable in Ohio. Site them so they have as much winter protection as possible from the harsh winter winds. Mulch them after the first hard freeze. In spring, while they are still dormant, cut them back to about 12" above the ground. Since they are easy to propagate from cutting, make a bunch and place them throughout the garden. Some will survive and you will learn which locations give them the best survival rate. Has anyone out there had any success growing them in South Dakota?

Friday 27 August	
8	
9	
10	
11	
12	
13	
14	
15	
16	
17	
18	

Today do everything backwards

7am:	Brush your teeth and put on your pyjamas	3-6pm:	Meetings to set the day's agenda
8am:	Nothing like a glass of brandy to cheer you up	7pm:	Say good morning to everyone
8.30am:	Coffee and mints	8pm:	Time to read the day's newspaper
9am:	Three course dinner washed down with a nice bottle of red (or two!)	8.30pm:	Get the kids off to school
		9pm:	Breakfast: scrambled eggs, tea and toast
10am:	Couple of drinks with colleagues in your local bar to gossip	10pm:	Shave (men), apply make-up (women)
		10.30pm:	Shower
11am:	Work – say goodnight to your boss	11pm:	Get out of bed and smell the fresh morning air
12.05pm:	God it's been a long day		
1pm:	Lunch hour!		

SATURDAY 28 AUGUST

8

9

10

11

12

13

14

15

16

17

18

19

Today make sure your name is on the internet

If you're not on the net, you're nobody. Type your name into a search engine and find out if it plucks you out of cyberspace, even if it's in the school yearbook some nerdy ex-classmate has put online. If nothing comes up, visit our »I want my name on the web« page on www.thiswebsitewillchangeyourlife.com and we'll help you acquire some virtual reality.

Searching the net for Pickasso [sic] yields 153 results. If he features on the internet this many times with this spelling, surely you can get on it once.

Pablo Pickasso

SUNDAY 29 AUGUST	14	
9	15	
10	16	
11	17	
12	18	
13	19	

Wednesday 1 September. Plan the day ahead down to the minute.

Time		Time		Time	
08.00		11.50		15.40	
08.10		12.00		15.50	
08.20		12.10		16.00	
08.30		12.20		16.10	
08.40		12.30		16.20	
08.50		12.40		16.30	
09.00		12.50		16.40	
09.10		13.00		16.50	
09.20		13.10		17.00	
09.30		13.20		17.10	
09.40		13.30		17.20	
09.50		13.40		17.30	
10.00		13.50		17.40	
10.10		14.00		17.50	
10.20		14.10		18.00	
10.30		14.20		18.10	
10.40		14.30		18.20	
10.50		14.40		18.30	
11.00		14.50		18.40	
11.10		15.00		18.50	
11.20		15.10			
11.30		15.20			
11.40		15.30			

Today extend your life span

Scientists have discovered that rats live 33% longer on a very low calorie diet. Recent research seems to suggest this also applies to humans. So why not try the long-life diet today and see if it's for you?

Olga Ratashnikov doesn't look a day over 400, but in fact she is a limber 512 years old! You too can be like Olga and reach a merry older age thanks to our diet!

Target calorie intake: 1000 cal. for a sedentary 60 kg. adult.

Breakfast: 1 lo-fat yoghurt, 1 glass of water
Lunch: Sandwich (brown bread) with tuna and salad (no mayo), Half an apple
Afternoon tea: Cracker
Dinner: Fish (small portion), Rice (50g), Broccoli (1 stem), 1 glass water

Thursday 2. September

8
9
10
11
12
13
14
15
16
17
18
19

Medical guidelines: There are many hypotheses to explain the life-extensions power of a low calorie diet. The one that has the most support posits that low calorie intake reduces the amount of free radical damage to cellular mitochondria, although no one knows the mechanism of how this might occur. While it seems probable that caloric restriction is an effective way to prolonging life, researchers warn of some pitfalls for those attempting such a regime. Care should be taken that the diet is adequate in vitamins, minerals, protein and other nutrients. In addition to suffering hunger pangs, if the diet is too severe, it also is possible that the ability to handle stresses, such as cold temperatures or infection could be compromised. Women may become less fertile or stop ovulating, and this might increase the risk of osteoporosis and loss of muscle mass later in life.

Friday 3 September. Today is Vocabulary Day. Expand yours with our choice selection.

A — Amanuensis: Person who writes from dictation

B — Bonhomie: Happy friendliness

C — Cynosure: Centre of attention

D — Duenna: Elderly woman chaperone

E — Encomium: Formal expression of praise

F — Fallopian: Liable to error

G — Galumph: Move about clumsily

H — Harum-scarum: Reckless

I — Integument: Natural skin covering

J — Jeremiad: Long complaint

K — Kwashiorkor: Malnutrition of young children

L — Lacteal: Of or like milk

M — Myrmidon: Follower

N — Nugatory: Of little value

O — Oppugn: To dispute

P — Poetaster: Bad poet

Q — Quondam: Former

R — Rodomontade: Boastful talk

S — Shibboleth: Slogan characteristic of a particular group

T — Tergiversate: To be evasive

U — Uxorious: Too dependent on one's wife

V — Vermiform: Resembling a worm

W — Walleyed: Having eyes with an abnormal amount of white showing

X — Xanthippe: Peevish woman

Y — Yoni: Tantric for vagina

Z — Zoophyte: Any animal resembling a plant

8	14
9	15
10	16
11	17
12	18
13	19

SATURDAY 4 SEPTEMBER		14
8		15
9		16
10		17
11		18
12		19
13		

Today eat everything using chopsticks.

Which chopsticks are best for me? God did not create all chopsticks equal.
Chopsticks with the following features are best suited to the designated tasks.

TYPE OF CHOPSTICK:	LARGE HANDLE DIAMETER	HIGH TIP ANGLE	LONGER LENGTH
BEST FOR:	PULLING	SHEARING/RIPPING	PINCHING
APPROPRIATE FOOD:	STICKY NOODLES	STEAK	PEANUTS

If you eat all of the above most days, the most efficient all-purpose chopstick
has a 6mm handle diameter, 4mm tips, and a 2 degree tip angle.

Here's some names to get you started.

- Miguel Azpilicueta, San Huaco, Guatemala
- Takara Kobayashi, Hakone, Japan
- Abdul Karim Jasim, Rutba, Iraq
- Elizabeth Chitika, Ibolelo, Zambia
- Mosharraf Wajed, Nurullahpur, Bangladesh

Twin Yourself with a Foreigner

Why should towns have all the fun? Today pick a foreigner at random and twin yourself with him or her. Then visit each other once a year.

Nota: no person can be twinned to more than one other. Foreigners in tropical-style locations are usually already twinned. Vacant twins are currently readily available in the following locations: Vladivostok, Khartoum, Sanaa, Baghdad, Epsom.

8
9
10
11
12
13
14
15
16
17
18
19

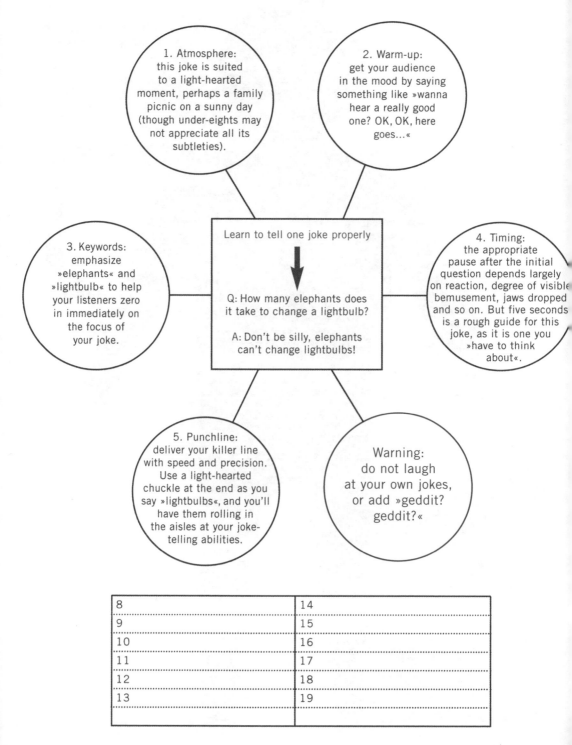

1. Atmosphere: this joke is suited to a light-hearted moment, perhaps a family picnic on a sunny day (though under-eights may not appreciate all its subtleties).

2. Warm-up: get your audience in the mood by saying something like »wanna hear a really good one? OK, OK, here goes...«

3. Keywords: emphasize »elephants« and »lightbulb« to help your listeners zero in immediately on the focus of your joke.

Learn to tell one joke properly

Q: How many elephants does it take to change a lightbulb?

A: Don't be silly, elephants can't change lightbulbs!

4. Timing: the appropriate pause after the initial question depends largely on reaction, degree of visible bemusement, jaws dropped and so on. But five seconds is a rough guide for this joke, as it is one you »have to think about«.

5. Punchline: deliver your killer line with speed and precision. Use a light-hearted chuckle at the end as you say »lightbulbs«, and you'll have them rolling in the aisles at your joke-telling abilities.

Warning: do not laugh at your own jokes, or add »geddit? geddit?«

8	14
9	15
10	16
11	17
12	18
13	19

Read your own palm

☞ Life Line (quality of life: if it is thin and reedy, see a physician regularly)

❖ Love Line (luck in love: if it extends beyond the middle finger, you will know love instead of having to pay for it)

♏ Heart Line (emotional depth: if it runs deep, become a social worker)

♓ Travel Line (propensity for travel: if it is broken, stay at home)

♌ Fate Line (the longer the better: if it is shorter than the love line, your lover will kill you)

☞ Miscellaneous Line (good at shopping, expert at DIY, raconteur: this one you can interpret as you like)

⌂ Mount of Venus (sex drive: the more prominent the better)

🖎 Blue Mark (biro: do be more careful, and wash your hands)

WEDNESDAY 8 SEPTEMBER		14	
8		15	
9		16	
10		17	
11		18	
12		19	
13			

8	14
9	15
10	16
11	17
12	18
13	19

TIP: To help, why not purchase a pair of these X-RAY VISION GOGGLES™, available from *Extreme Intelligence Ltd.* The X-RAY VISION GOGGLES™ see through swimwear and many types of sensitive material, work in low sunlight, come with a 1 year warranty and are available now at the special introductory price of **$2400**.

This is the »Aunt Roberta«, the strongest cocktail in the world. Invite a friend over today and sample it.

Ingredients:
2 shots Absinthe
1 shot Brandy
3 shots Vodka
1 1/2 shot Gin
1 shot Creme de Mûre
Shake well with ice and strain into a martini glass.

8	14
9	15
10	16
11	17
12	18
13	19

AUNT ROBERTA Aunt Roberta was born in Alabama in 1854, the mulatto daughter of a slave owner, Jim Burns. After her alcoholic father tried to abuse her at age 11, she ran away, and lived off the land for several years, picking cotton as an itinerant worker, sometimes selling her body in railroad towns. Eventually at 23 she ran a bootleg shack down by the Mississippi Delta. There, her and lover T.B. Dixon mixed homemade gin with moonshine, killing an estimated 34 people over 2 years. But in those days no one cried much for the dead drunken hoboes that used to frequent »Aunt Roberta's« as it had become known, largely on account of her prematurely large girth. She came up with her famous cocktail by serendipity, whilst drunk. She was a mixer of genius, but it was only through the observation of one man, racoon-hunter Billy Joe Spratt, that this particular recipe survived. Roberta could never recreate it, and died in abject poverty, aged 32. Spratt headed up north to New York, opened a chain of bars based around the original »Aunt Roberta« and became a millionaire within 2 years.

Today invent a new punctuation mark. Examples:

Denotes that the previous sentence is to be construed ironically.

Orgasm. More generally used to indicate the writer is sexually aroused.

Writer is aware that at this point he's bullshitting.

Double brackets: contains a secret, only read if you agree to keep it.

Example: As I write this I am sitting stark naked with a blonde on my lap‚ ((She has a third nipple)). Actually there are two of them, twins in fact‚ OK, well it's bound to happen someday

SATURDAY 11 SEPTEMBER	14
8	15
9	16
10	17
11	18
12	19
13	

Today,
test god's existence

Whether god exists or not is a pretty fundamental question, and one that could make a big difference to your life. If you're not yet convinced either way, find out for sure with these questions, which are especially designed to make him manifest himself. It's best to address them from a mount or hill of some sort, as that's how he's used to humans communicating with him.

Questions to god:

Hey god, look at this. I'm doodling right here in this bible of yours.

god, I bet you can't hit me with lighting, I'm too fast, whooossshhh!

Show me a miracle god and I'll sacrifice any animal you care to mention

god, I have some important data about the Devils latest plans. Come down and I'll show you.

Help god, I'm angel Bob, I've lost my wings somewhere over there. Help me out?

god are you there? (worth a try)

Sunday 12 September

8	14
9	15
10	16
11	17
12	18
13	19

Monday 13 September

Today destroy photos that make you look ugly. Everyone has a pile of old photos lying around. Good ones are invaluable: they represent good memories to cherish for the rest of your life. But bad photos are bad karma: they represent negative moments of your life and show you as boring, ugly or demonic. Burn them promptly.

8
9
10
11
12
13
14
15
16
17
18
19

Stay in bed today

Guidelines for throwing a sickie: If possible, leave a message for your boss before he gets in. Before calling, convince yourself you really are sick. Double bluff: avoid overelaborate excuses. Simple ones are best e.g.: »I feel sick«. If pressed on specific symptoms, mention something socially embarrassing like »I've spent half the night on the toilet« to end their line of questioning. Good things to do in bed: Sleep; curl up in fœtal position; hug a pillow; listen to the world outside at work; sniffle/cough/wheeze; read a trashy novel; talk to Mum on the phone under the duvet; stroke the cat/dog/yourself; write a long letter to a distant relative; feel a bit sorry for yourself.

TUESDAY 14 SEPTEMBER

9		14
10		15
11		16
12		17
13		18

LAST REMINDER!
TODAY SEND US MONEY

Attention! Your second down payment on this Diary is due tomorrow. To avoid any surcharge or penalty payments, make sure you transfer the balance of your account (another £12.99, exclusive of VAT) to us today. Please write cheques to: Benrik Ltd, and send c/o PFD Literary Agency, Drury House, 34-43 Russell St, London WC2B 5HA, UK. Fines for late payment up to £3000.

Ten good reasons to cough up:
1) we need money
2) we've spent the other money
3) we need fresh new money
4) we need it more than you do
5) our publisher screwed us
6) our agent screwed us
7) our ex-wives screwed us
8) the taxman screwed us
9) this book was underpriced by mistake
10) anyone who sends the money in gets their photo in next year's edition*

Help the starving boys so they don't have to eat out of the garbage bin ANYMORE!

Hang on in there hungry boys! Help is apparently on its way.

LITTER

8	14	
9	15	
10	16	
11	17	
12	18	
13	19	

*This is 100% true

8	
9	
10	
11	
12	
13	
14	
15	
16	
17	
18	
19	

Today do something to make it to the top.

Are you happy ploughing along your everyday furrow? Why not seek to rise above your station? Why not be the main man, the top boss, the biggest fish in the pond? They didn't get there by moping around being friendly to their neighbours. Grow a spine and stab someone in the back. Lie if you have to. Steal if you need to. Kill if you must. Today every action must be performed with an eye to the main chance. Make friends, influence people, then dump them as you make your way up the greasy pole. Today, look out for no1.

»Ambition is so powerful a passion in the human breast, that however high we reach we are never satisfied.«
–Niccolo Machiavelli

FRIDAY 17 SEPTEMBER
TODAY EMBRACE CHANGE
FOR THE SAKE OF IT
CHANGE IS LIFE AND IT'S ALL
AROUND YOU. FORCE YOURSELF TO
CHALLENGE THE CREATURE OF
ROUTINE WITHIN. YOU COULD TAKE
A DIFFERENT ROUTE TO WORK.
YOU COULD SHOWER INSTEAD OF
TAKING A BATH. OR YOU COULD
REMARRY. RECONSIDER
EVERYTHING ABOUT YOURSELF:
TODAY, YOU ARE A BLANK SLATE.

8	14
9	15
10	16
11	17
12	18
13	19

Today give someone a totally impractical gift

SATURDAY 18 SEPTEMBER	A BRIDGE!	A REMOTE PLANET!	A HAEMORRHOID!
8			
9			
10			
11	AN UNBORN PET!	AN ELEVATOR!	A PHILOSOPHICAL WORLDVIEW!
12			
13			
14			
15	A MOLECULE OF TITANIUM!	ONE (EXPEN-SIVE) SOCK !	A FULLY-ARMED NUCLEAR SUB-MARINE!
16			
17			
18			

Get instructions for today
off the net.
Log on to
www.datatranscorp.org/
htm1003.02.
Your password is
vector/xxxx*

8							
9							
10							
11							
12							
13							

14							
15							
16							
17							
18							
19							

*First 4 letters of your mother's maiden name

disinfection

Today rid yourself of the parasites in your life.

GUILTY: the good old kitchen sink. Probably the dirtiest place in your home, with an average of 229,000 bacteria per square inch. GUILTY: the air we breathe. Full of viral particles floating through the indoor environment, contaminating surfaces everywhere from the dinner table to the remote control, and ending up on your hands. Why, even common soap can spread germs…

THE SOLUTION? Germicidal soap, used often and liberally. Clean food preparation surfaces, scrubbed and disinfected every time you eat. And a healthy wariness of too much physical contact between members of the family. Moral infection is just as insidious as its microscopic counterpart. Let cleanliness rule YOUR family!

8

9

10

11

12

13

14

15

16

17

18

19

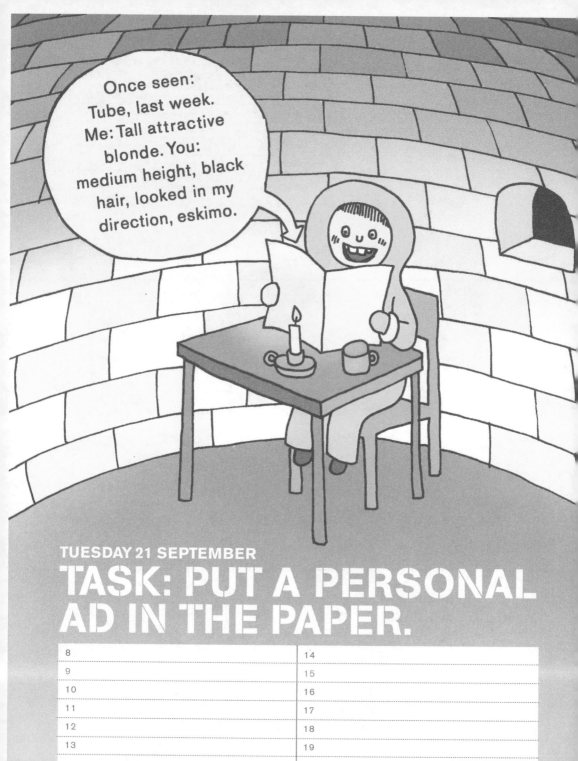

TUESDAY 21 SEPTEMBER

TASK: PUT A PERSONAL AD IN THE PAPER.

8	14
9	15
10	16
11	17
12	18
13	19

Wednesday 22 September

Prevention is better than cure!

Today do something that could save you a lot of future hassle.

Leave a copy of your house keys with a friend in case you lose them in the woods.

Buy candles and matches in case there's a sudden power cut while you're in the bath.

Spoil your kids so they don't put you in a home when you're old and decrepit.

Learn Norwegian in case Norway turns into an evil superpower and invades.

8	12	16
9	13	17
10	14	18
11	15	19

TEST YOUR MEMORY

What were you doing last Thursday evening? Do you have trouble remembering? Here are some tried-and-tested techniques that could help improve your memory skills.

RRR   ## ROUTINE RECALL RECOGNITION
What do you normally do on Thursdays? What are you doing today?
Are there any events that recur every week on Thursdays?
Think back to the last example and visualize your expectations.

CR   ## COGNITIVE REWINDING
What did you do yesterday evening? How about the evening before that?
And the previous one. Rewind through the week one day at a time until you
reach your target evening, last Thursday.

ESS   ## EXTERNAL STIMULI SUPPORT
Look up last Thursday's newspaper headlines on the web. Try to remember
where you were when reading them, or who you discussed them with.

RA   ## REPETITIVE ASSOCIATION
Repeat the word »Thursday« out louder and louder until your brain
gets bored of you and unlocks the relevant memory code.

LM   ## LEAPFROGGING MATRIX
What happened last week that marked you? Was
that before or after Thursday evening? Could you
possibly have discussed this event on Thursday,
or decided to go ahead with it on Thursday?

People make money like you wouldn't believe coming up with stuff like this. If you have any suggestions of your own, please forward them to us.

C   ## CHEATING
Just look back through the Diary and see what
you wrote for Thursday evening. Duh.

Thursday 23 September

8	14
9	15
10	16
11	17
12	18
13	19

FRIDAY 24 SEPTEMBER: DO YOUR BIT FOR WORLD PEACE. DISPOSE OF A POTENTIAL WEAPON TODAY

Violence comes in many shapes: gun, assault rifle, knife, hammer, toenail clipper, fire poker, broom, paper clip, saw, chisel, duster, matches, bazooka, scissors, harpoon, laser, shoelace, torpedo.

8	14	
9	15	
10	16	
11	17	
12	18	
13	19	

Today bake a cake!

Careful! The fruit cake described below is not the one represented here. This fruitcake is the work of the master craftswoman, Tatiana Blok, that won her the Vladisvostok Communal Patisserie Award in 1972. Unfortunately, it can never be made again as the special Soviet jelly base necessary to hold it together is no longer in production due to new overzealous food safety laws.

Monday 27 September

8

9

10

11

12

13

14

15

16

17

18

19

Tatiana Blok's Fruit Cake

You will need: 200g margarine, 300g caster sugar, 5 eggs, 236g baking flour, 500g dried fruit.

Preheat oven to 160 centigrade. Line a cake tin with greaseproof paper. Set as the fruit and place everything else in a bowl. Beat for 5 minutes, then add fruit stir until you have a smooth mix. Pour into cake tin. Bake for 90 minutes. Enjoy

Today talk to a child. Children are untainted by prejudice and habit. Have a proper conversation with a young child today and learn from their innocence. Topics might include: favorite colours, toys, birds, bees, granny, why people fight, belly buttons, mud (fun with).

8	
9	
10	
11	
12	
13	

14	
15	
16	
17	
18	
19	

Update: sadly these days it is no longer legally prudent to approach children not your own. Either borrow a relative's, or make your own.

THE DICEMAN
by Luke Rhinehart

During the first month the dice had rather small effect on my life. I used them to choose ways to spend my free time, and to choose alternatives when the normal 'I' didn't particularly care. They decided that Lil and I would see the Edward Albee play rather than the Critic's Award play, that I read work x selected randomly from a huge collection; that I would cease writing my book and begin an article on 'Why Psychoanalysis Usually Fails'; that I would buy General Envelopment Corporation rather than Wonderfilled Industries or Dynamicgo Company; that I would not go to a convention in Chicago; that I would make love to my wife in Kama Sutra position number 23, number 52, number 8, etc.; that I see Arlene, that I don't see Arlene, etc.; that I see her in place x rather than place y and so on.

In short the dice decided things which really didn't matter. Most of my options tended to be from among the great middle way of my tastes and personality. I learned to like to play with the probabilities I gave the various options I would create. In letting the dice choose among possible women I might pursue for a night, for example, I might give Lil one chance in six, some new woman chosen at random two chances in six, and Arlene three chances in six. If I played with two dice the subtleties in probability were much greater. Two principles I always took care to follow. First: never include an option I might be unwilling to fulfill; second: always begin to fulfill the option without thought and without quibble. The secret of the successful dice-life is to be a puppet on the strings of the die.

Six weeks after sinking into Arlene I began letting the dice diddle with my patients: it was a decisive step. I began creating as options that I comment aggressively to a patient as my insights arose; that I restudy some other standard analytic theory and method and adopt it for a specified number of hours with a patient; that I preach to my patients.

Eventually I began also to include as an option that I give my patients assigned psychological exercises much as a coach gives his athletes physical exercises: shy girl assigned to date make-out artist; aggressive bully assigned to pick a fight with nine-eight-pound weakling and purposely lose; studious grind assigned to see five movies, go to two dances and play bridge a minimum of five hours a day all week. Of course, most meaningful assignments involved a breach of the psychiatrist's code of ethics. In telling my patients what to do, I was becoming legally responsible for any ill consequences which might result.

In Luke Rhinehart's 1971 cult classic The Diceman, the hero rolls the dice to determine his fate. He picks out options and assigns them a number. For instance ▨ could be »I will go see a movie«, ▨ »I'll take a stroll in the park«, ▨ might be »I'll take the first flight to Siberia« and so on. Today, let the dice govern your life.

8		14	
9		15	
10		16	
11		17	
12		18	
13		19	

OH, LEAVE IT ALONE
FOR CHRIST'S SAKE!

FRIGIDITY DAY

Does sex play too big a part in your life? Today act like a nun
and abstain from any sexual contact, even with yourself.

Turn-offs to help you focus: Cold showers; spiders;
cod liver oil; Mum and Dad together; Grandad and Grandma
together; God; Mum, Dad, Grandad, Grandma and God
together. If any of the above turn you on and not off,
you are in serious psychological trouble.

THURSDAY 30 SEPTEMBER	
8	14
9	15
10	16
11	17
12	18
13	19

A WORD OF WARNING Do not prolong this treatment: extended sexual deprivation can have severe side effects. It was reported in
1905 that Sister L. of the Carmelites was so perturbed by lack of intercourse that the mere sight of flies mating would send her into an
onanistic frenzy. For ultimately, as French writer Anatole France reminded us, »the only true perversion is chastity«.

YOUR NAMESAKE
TODAY FIND SOMEONE NAMED LIKE YOU, CALL THEM UP AND OFFER TO MEET.

WHERE ARE THEY?

WEBSITE xxx

18

STATISTICALLY YOU ARE MORE THAN LIKELY TO HAVE A NAMESAKE SOMEWHERE IN THE WORLD.

TRY LOOKING UP Y
NAME ON THE WOR
WIDE WEB, OR IN Y
LOCAL PHONE BOO

FUN NAMESAKE TRICKS

1
HI IS THAT JOSH WEAVER?

EXAMPLE

2
YES WHO'S THIS?

IT'S JOSH WEAV-ER

HA HA HA

3

INTRODUCTIONS: KICK OFF THE CONVERSATION BY INTRODUCING YOURSELF CRYPTICALLY.

THIS IS GUARAN-TEED TO CREATE A HUMOROUS BOND.

CRIME: UH?

POLICE ARE EASILY CONFUSED BY NAMESAKES. TRY SETTING UP AN INTERNATIONAL MONEY-LAUNDERING DRUGS RING WITH YOUR NAMESAKE.

SUING YOUR NAMESAK

EXPLAIN THAT YOU HAVE PATENTED YOUR NAME AND WISH HI
CHANGE HIS, FAILING WHICH YOUR LAWYERS WILL BE IN TOUC

OH NO!

FRIDAY 1 OCTOBER	14
8	15
9	16
10	17
11	18
12	19
13	

THE POLITICS OF HEIGHT

The late Alan Clark recounts in his *Diaries* how when he became a Minister in Margaret Thatcher's government, he looked down at the masses from his high-rise office and suddenly wondered how it would feel to urinate on them. Go to the tallest point in your town today and be master of all you survey. Relieving your bladder is optional.

8	14
9	15
10	16
11	17
12	18
13	19

Today go to the zoo and DO FEED THE ANIMALS
Zoo animals have a miserable time as it is, they should have the right to stuff their faces, whatever some fascist zookeeper says. Here are some of their favorite foods in the wild so you know what to take along.

ANACONDA

Rats

GIRAFFE

Small birds (as they fly past)

ANTEATER

Beetles

BEAR

Berries

ELEPHANT

Grass

BALD EAGLE

Ice cream

ZEBRA

Zebras

More Grass

LION

HIPPO

Salmon (smoked)

GIANT PANDA

GORILLA

Bananas

Gi

ELECTRIC EEL

Plankton

Sunday 3 October
08
09
10
11
12
13
14
15
16
17
18

Monday 4 October
Trust someone with
your life today.

Deepen the bonds between you and a
close friend today and experience the
vulnerability and liberation that ensues.

Trust them to guide you on a railway
platform with your eyes closed .

Trust them to prepare
your dose of medication.

Trust them to turn the gas
off after you fall asleep.

Trust them not to post that death
threat to a mafioso that you signed.

Advanced: to truly test your faith in mankind,
try this with a complete stranger. Good luck.

8	14
9	15
10	16
11	17
12	18
13	19

Sense-less Day

GO THROUGH TODAY WITHOUT USING YOUR SENSE OF: TOUCH

How to: Wear winter clothing – ski gloves, anorak, cagoule.

True story: Bill W. lost all sense of touch in his lower left leg after a farm accident in 1977. But as he was close to retirement age, it didn't bother him too much. For a while at least. Two years later, on a cold winter morning, he was sitting in his easy chair reading his daily paper in front of the warm fire. His wife was out in the yard. His dogs were asleep in the kennel. So preoccupied was Bill W. with the day's news, that he didn't notice until alerted by the bacon-like smell that his nerveless limb had caught fire, and was charred beyond all human recognition.

TUESDAY 5 OCTOBER

8	14
9	15
10	16
11	17
12	18
13	19

Write down the pros and cons of this sense as you discover them.

Pros: ....

Cons: ....

End of day assessment: How crucial is my sense of touch to me ..../10

Don't forget!

Tomorrow is the 73rd
birthday of Archbishop and
Nobel Peace Prize
laureate Desmond Tutu:
Send him a card.
Standard formulation:
»Dear Archbishop,
Thank you very much for all
your good works over the years .
You are an inspiration
to us all. Keep it up.«

Wednesday 6 October

8	14
9	15
10	16
11	17
12	18
13	19

Send to: Archbishop Emeritus Desmond Mpilo Tutu, P.O. Box 1092, Milnerton, 7435, Cape Town, South Africa.

FASHIONVICTIM!

Find a particularly anorexic shop mannequin today and graffiti your fashion statement right on to him or her. Possible statements: FAT IS FUN! FASHION FASHISTS! FEED ME FEED ME!

8

9

10

11

12

13

14

15

16

17

18

19

TODAY DO A GOOD DEED. Donate £20 to one of the following, resisting the urge to tell anyone about it.

GREENPEACE
We are an independent, campaigning organization that uses non-violent, creative confrontation to expose global environmental problems, and force solutions for a green and peaceful future.

www.greenpeace.org

Centrepoint
We are a charity that helps homeless and socially excluded young people to rebuild their lives.

www.centrepoint.org.uk

arc
We aim to advance the understanding, prevention and treatment of arthritis and related conditions.

www.arc.org.uk

AMREF
UNITED KINGDOM
We are an independent non-profit, non-governmental organization whose mission is to improve the health of disadvantaged people in Africa as a means for them to escape poverty and improve the quality of their lives.

www.amref.org.uk

Oxfam
We are a development, relief, and campaigning organization dedicated to finding lasting solutions to poverty and suffering around the world.

www.oxfam.org.uk

WWF
Our mission is to stop the degradation of the planet's natural environment and to build a future in which humans live in harmony with nature.

www.panda.org

HELP THE AGED
We are committed to addressing the issues that matter to older people.

www.helptheaged.org.uk

ALZHEIMER'S ASSOCIATION
We are the largest national voluntary health organization dedicated to advancing Alzheimer's research and helping those affected by the disease.

www.alz.org

Actors' Benevolent Fund
Our role is to care for actors unable to work because of poor health, an accident or frail old age.

www.actorsbenevolentfund.co.uk

BREAST CANCER CARE
We are the leading provider of breast cancer information and support across the UK.

www.breastcancercare.org.uk

CHILDREN INTERNATIONAL
Our mission is to help children living in dire poverty. We provide needy children with a variety of programs and services to meet their basic needs, enhance their human dignity and raise their physical and educational levels in a meaningful, lasting way.

www.children.org

ASBAH
We aim to improve services for people with spina bifida and/or hydrocephalus, to work with them to extend their choices, and maximize opportunities for independence and achievement.

www.asbah.org

CATS PROTECTION
We rescue and rehome unwanted and abandoned cats, and promote responsible cat ownership.

www.cat.org.uk

Care
Care is a humanitarian organization fighting global poverty.
www.care.org

Multiple Sclerosis Society
We are the UK's largest charity for people affected by Multiple Sclerosis (MS) – about 85,000 people in the UK.

www.mssociety.org.uk

NATIONAL ECZEMA SOCIETY
We are the only organization in the UK and one of the most established organizations worldwide dedicated to the needs of people with eczema, dermatitis and sensitive skin.

www.eczema.org

cancerBACUP
Our mission is to give cancer patients and their families the up-to-date information, practical advice and support they need to reduce the fear and uncertainty of cancer.

www.cancerbacup.org.uk

Friday 8 October

8

9

10

11

12

13

14

15

16

17

18

Barnardo's
Our vision is that the lives of all children and young people should be free from poverty, abuse and discrimination.

www.barnardos.org.uk

MEDECINS SANS FRONTIERES / DOCTORS WITHOUT BORDERS
We deliver emergency aid to victims of armed conflict, epidemics, and natural and man-made disasters, and to others who lack health care due to social or geographical isolation.

www.doctorswithoutborders.org

SCOPE
We are a disability organization in England and Wales whose focus is people with cerebral palsy.

www.scope.org.uk

LEUKAEMIA RESEARCH
We are the only national UK charity devoted exclusively to improving treatments, finding cures and investigating the causes and prevention of cancers of the blood and related conditions, in children and adults.

www.leukaemia-research.org.uk

RNIB
We help all blind and partially sighted people in the UK.

www.rnib.org.uk

THE PROSTATE CANCER CHARITY
We are the largest and most comprehensive of the charities working specifically in the field of prostate cancer.

www.prostate-cancer.org.uk

Terrence Higgins Trust
We are the leading HIV & AIDS charity in the UK and the largest in Europe.

www.tht.org.uk

British Hedgehog Preservation Society
We are a UK Charity dedicated to helping & protecting Hedgehogs.

www.software-technics.com/bhps/

ROYAL BRITISH LEGION
The Royal British Legion is the UK's leading charity safeguarding the welfare, interests and memory of those who have served in the Armed Forces and their dependants.

www.british-legion.org.uk

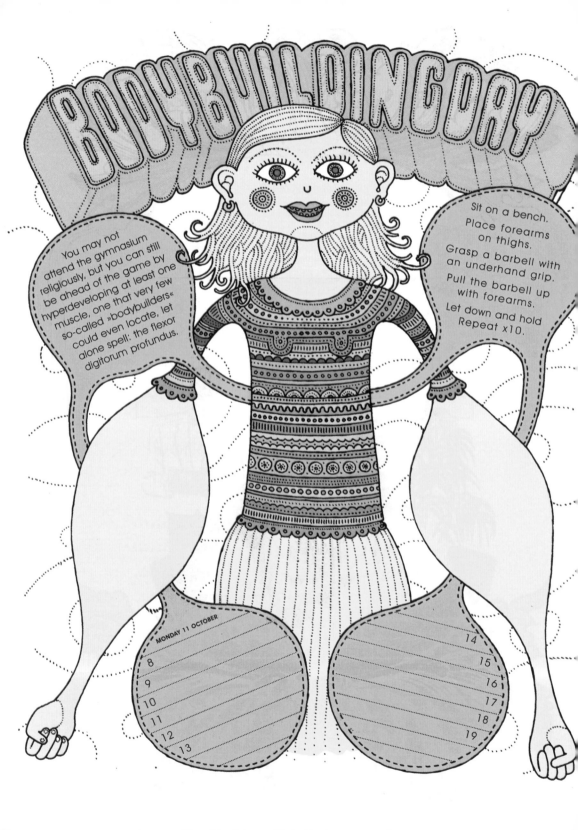

TUESDAY 12 OCTOBER
Today, make sure the police are acting within the law

Without the constant vigilance of fellow citizens, police forces everywhere are all too easily tempted to abuse their powers. Do your bit for democracy: follow a police patrol and make sure they respect suspects' rights.

You have the right to remain silent. Anything you say can and will be used against you in a court of law. You have the right to speak to an attorney, and to have an attorney present during any questioning. If you cannot afford a lawyer, one will be provided for you at government expense. (Police get really annoyed if you say this faster than they can!)

How can you tell a bad cop from a good cop?

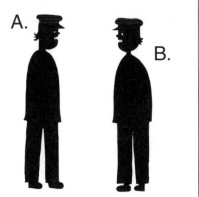

A.

B.

Easy: The bad one's moral decrepitude will manifest itself in sloppy dress, like B's too-short trousers.

What if you witness abuse?
If you sense that abuse is occurring or might be about to occur, do not hesitate to intervene. For instance, if police officers are running in pursuit of a suspected criminal, and seem to you a little too excited by the chase, run alongside them, reminding them of the alleged criminal's rights. It may help to video them if you have the equipment. When they catch the »suspect«, monitor how tight the handcuffs are, mentioning the Human Rights Declaration's ban on cruel and unusual punishment. Insist on accompanying the suspect back to the police station, and use the suspect's free phone call to alert your local civil liberties group to the situation. Occasionally, the police will pick on you as well at this point, asking you to leave the suspect's cell for example. If this happens, lie down and chain yourself to the nearest radiator in protest. You are now officially a political prisoner. Fight on!

8		14
9		15
10		16
11		17
12		18
13		19

Wednesday 13 October 2004

You don't need round-the-clock news

It needs you. Why allow yourself to be dangled in a permanent state of anxious suspense about matters that don't even directly affect you, like some remote murder enquiry, or even war?

Constant media-induced stress is addictive and prevents us from stepping back and seeing the big picture. You have nothing to lose but your remote. As long ago as 1854, Thoreau wrote in »Walden« about the pernicious dependence on the latest news: »I am sure that I never read any memorable news in a newspaper. If we read of one man robbed, or murdered, or killed by

accident, or one house burned, or one vessel wrecked, or one steamboat blown up, or one cow run over on the Western Railroad, or one mad dog killed, or one lot of grasshoppers in the winter – we never need read of another. One is enough. If you are acquainted with the principle, what do you care for a myriad instances and applications? To a philosopher all news, as it is called, is gossip, and they who edit and read it are old women over their tea. Yet not a few are greedy after this gossip. There was such a rush, as I hear, the other day at one of the offices to learn the foreign news by the last arrival, that several large squares of plate glass belonging to the establishment were broken by the pressure – news which I seriously think a ready wit might write a twelve-month, or twelve years, beforehand with sufficient accuracy.«

EXCLUSIVE! HAPPY END NEWS STORY!

ANNAPOLIS,MD–According to patrons of popular downtown Starbucks branch, teacher and father of two Robert Hindman, 41, narrowly escaped serious injury this morning, when he crossed the main drag without looking left.
»This guy just strolled across the street in the middle of rush hour without even looking,« said latte-drinker Kathy Peach. »It's like a total miracle he didn't get hit by a bus,« Peach added. »What an idiot.«
At an emotional press conference,

Hindman acknowledged he had failed to check for traffic, blaming pressure from work. »I was thinking about all those term papers I still had to mark by noon, and before I knew it, I'd just plain crossed Lafayette.«
Hindman and his wife Jackie hugged for the cameras, as he pledged never to repeat his mistake. »I'll never repeat my mistake,« he said. »But I came out of it alive, and that's all that really matters.«

OUT NOW!

It's official! No news is good new:

Stacy Hoxburger of Buffalo, Wyoming, first realized she had a problem i January 1998, five months after the death of Diana Princess of Wales. »At firs I thought it was still grief, that I hadn't dealt with it properly, but then I saw [Stanton and he told me about Media Addiction Disorder,« she confided.

Along with many others, Hoxburger was helped to cope with the loss of the Princess by the constant stream of news and features relating to her death. For weeks, much of the media led on the circumstances of her car accident, the alleged responsibility of the paparazzi, her troubled life, and even scurrilous speculation concerning the involvement of the British secret services. »It was kind of comforting seeing her on TV all the time, even though obviously it had to be old footage,« said Hoxburger. »It's as if she'd never gone away.«
When the coverage abated, most people returned to their normal humdrum lives. One person, however, found it difficult to live without her daily dose of Diana news. »It's like I needed my fix,« confirmed Hoxburger, a housewife and mother of three. »I'd wake up in the morning, switch on the TV and there'd just be some dumb item about the Bosniaks or whatever instead of Diana.«
»Jeepers,« she continued, »I called the damn network and gave them a piece of my mind, but the woman on the phone would just put me on hold for hours.

But I wasn't going to give up. I calle her every day for three weeks.«
After pressure from her husbar Roger who claimed it was ruinir their marriage and increasing the phone bills, Hoxburger finally co sulted her physician. He referred h to Dr Harold Stanton, who specialize in media-induced stress.
»Overexposure to the media is th no1 hidden cause of anxiety i Americans today,« said Stanton. »A these stories of war and crime lead an adrenaline surge which the boc becomes addicted to. Stacy is a typ cal case. She got hooked on the who! Diana thing and when it stopped, h hormones just went haywire.«
Dr Stanton has written a book on th subject, called »Media Addictic Disorder: The News Behind Th Headlines«, soon to hit the shelve Hoxburger says his advice has »total! cured« her: »I think he's a genius. I r longer even think about that Dian person one little bit. Now I spend m time monitoring the news and callir up when I feel their stories are takir over people's lives.«

8	14	
9	15	
10	16	
11	17	
12	18	
13	19	

THURSDAY 14 OCTOBER
SEXUAL FANTASY DAY

It is said that we think about sex every 6 seconds. Today monitor your thoughts by writing them down as you go along, noting the sexual ones in capitals.

EXAMPLE: Must do shopping SEX! have run out of broccoli and SEX! now where did I leave that briefcase SEX! I wonder if it's raining SEX! hmmm, the veranda definitely needs repainting SEX! what time am I meeting Michael SEX! that's one ugly looking car SEX! Jenny must have finished choir practice by now SEX! can't believe how well that meeting went SEX! tra la la la the sky is blue SEX! I wish they'd take that billboard down SEX! what's on TV tonight SEX! oh here's mother.

8	14	
9	15	
10	16	
11	17	
12	18	
13	19	

FUN·O·METER

How funny are you?
Today tell your favorite joke ever to several different people
and note down how much they laugh on our FUN Scale™
....
....

FUN Scale™
Joke:...
....
....

Date.........................Hour.........................Subject......................
Laugh YES/NO length........................... depth........................
sincerity...
Signature..
Comments..
....

Conclusion
Based on the above measurements, it seems clear that:
You should have your own TV show
You're a pretty funny individual
You can make people laugh if they're drunk
You're just not very funny
People laugh, but it's not with you
You must have bought this book by mistake

Friday 15 October
08...
09...
10...
11...
12...
13...
14...
15...
16...
17...
18...
....

A FOOL OR A PROPHET?

According to Indiana-based »Church of the Holy Rapture«, the world will end today, at precisely one-half second to midnight, central Israeli time (7 p.m. GMT). Make all the necessary preparations just in case. But if you are still alive by 7.05 p.m., e-mail Bud Kramer on kramer89@hotmail.com to demand compensation for trauma.

WHAT TO LOOK OUT FOR:

»Jesus will come with a cloud of angels for his saints which know him and the fellowship of his deep sufferings... This will be heavens-gate. Nuclear war will start the next 45 days of the wrath of the Lamb for those which are left within the doomsgate. Just prior to these events, the earth will shift, causing earthquakes and volcanic activity which will darken the skies and create worldwide chaos.«

Saturday 16 October

8	14	
9	15	
10	16	
11	17	
12	18	
13	19	

Judge which one of your elderly relatives is most likely to have hoarded away a pile of cash and call them up out of the blue to get in their will.

True story! Marcus Grant, 32, was working as a checkout assistant for Walmart in North Canton, Ohio, when his supervisor Russell Streiff called him to the phone. His great-aunt Lana Milova Granovskaia had just died at the age of 105. Lana had been a young painter of great promise just before the revolution, even said to be in line for a portrait of Tsar Nicholas II. Of course, her career ended as quickly as it had begun. Now, the only time Marcus had ever met great-aunt Lana was in 1995 in Moscow, when he had been backpacking around Europe and decided to drop in on her in her humble suburban flat. Then he had charmed the lonely old lady with his naive American ways, and his encyclopaedic knowledge of Cold War-era Bond films. Ironically, she later froze to death in her post-Soviet garret on the very day the new Russian courts accepted her claim to the Granovskaia estate outside Moscow, now worth a hefty $40,000,000. The rest of the Grant (ex-Granovskaia) clan having ignored her, she'd left everything to Marcus. Marcus has now quit Walmart, and is living in San Fernando, California, pending the outcome of the court case with Lana's stepsister Magda, an off-shore tax accountant in Latvia.

Sunday 17 October

9
10
11
12
13
14
15
16
17

Meeting!

MONDAY 18 OCTOBER

Today everyone who has bought a copy of this diary is to meet at 7.00pm (local time) to discuss their experiences so far. Bring your copy!

Rendezvous points

LONDON
THE DOG & DUCK
18 BATEMAN ST.
S O H O

BERLIN
PRATER BEERGARDEN
KATANIENALEE 7-9

EDINBURGH
THE BEEHIVE INN
18-20 GRASSMARKET

NEW YORK
THE WHITE
HORSE TAVERN
567 HUDSON ST
AT 11TH ST

DUBLIN
MULLIGAN'S
8 POOLBEG ST

SYDNEY
THE BOURBON & BEEFSTEAK
24 DARLINGHURST RD
KING'S CROSS

PARIS
CAFE DE FLORE
172 BOULEVARD
ST-GERMAIN

PECKHAM
SALLY O'BRIEN
710 PECKHAM HIGH ST.

Present your copy of the Diary and claim your free drink!

8	14	
9	15	
10	16	
11	17	
12	18	
13	19 *Meeting.*	

PIGEON SHIT IS GOOD LUCK!

What pigeons look out for: the average pigeon likes a nice clean target, preferably a stationary or slow-moving bald head. *Women:* bright headwear also catches the pigeon's eye. It takes about two minutes for the pigeon to »lock on« to his target and manoeuvre into position, so stay patient and stand still. Resist the temptation to look up and check on progress as pigeon droppings are toxic to the eye, besides being aesthetically displeasing. A clear bull's-eye hit will yield roughly two weeks of good luck. Drippy muck on your shoulder is usually worth three or four days, whereas a near miss is actually bad luck.

TUESDAY 19 OCTOBER

8
9
10
11
12
13
14
15
16
17
18

»EXPERIENCE IS THE NAME WE GIVE TO OUR MISTAKES« (OSCAR WILDE)

WRITE DOWN AND ACKNOWLEDGE YOUR BIGGEST MISTAKE IN LIFE. OR BE CONDEMNED TO REPEAT IT.

8	12	16
9	13	17
10	14	18
11	15	19

TODAY START A FIGHT

Top fight-starting lines:
Who you looking at?
Don't tell me that's your boyfriend
Big car, small penis...
What queue?
Which is the kid which is the dog?
Hey, quit kicking sand in my face

8	12	16
9	13	17
10	14	18
11	15	19

HI! YOU DON'T KNOW ME BUT CAN I JUST SAY HOW HANDSOME/ BEAUTIFUL YOU LOOK. YOU SEEM LIKE A REALLY NICE PERSON TOO. I'M USUALLY GOOD AT TELLING THESE THINGS. WILL YOU MARRY ME?

DID THEY SAY YES? HERE'S A QUICK GUIDE TO ELOPING: MARRIAGE LICENSES CAN BE OBTAINED IN ABOUT 15 TO 20 MINUTES AT THE MARRIAGE LICENSING BUREAU IN LAS VEGAS. VICTORIA SANCHEZ, DEPUTY CLERK OF LAS VEGAS MARRIAGE LICENSING BUREAU, SAID 99,310 COUPLES RECEIVED MARRIAGE LICENSES IN LAS VEGAS LAST YEAR, WHICH IS 12,702 MORE THAN 1994. A DRIVER'S LICENSE AND $35 ARE ALL THAT IS NEEDED FOR A MARRIAGE LICENSE. BOTH PARTIES MUST BE 18 OR ABOVE OR HAVE A PARENT'S CONSENT, SHE SAID.

FRIDAY 22 OCTOBER
8
9
10
11
12
13
14
15
16
17
18

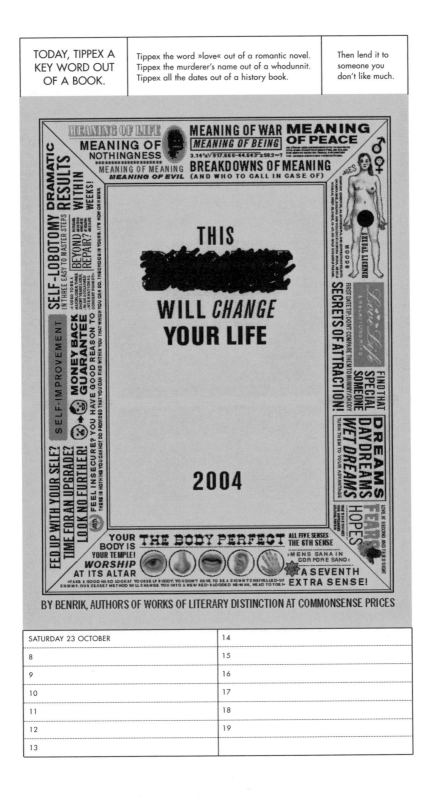

THIS **WILL** *CHANGE* **YOUR LIFE**

2004

BY BENRIK, AUTHORS OF WORKS OF LITERARY DISTINCTION AT COMMONSENSE PRICES

SATURDAY 23 OCTOBER	14
8	15
9	16
10	17
11	18
12	19
13	

Today earn a diploma

The Diary have arranged a cooperative venture with the UNIVERSITY OF HARVARD (Illinois) which could procure you one of many prestigious qualifications, based on your previous education, your life experience and, of course, your knowledge of the Diary itself. Obtain a prosperous future, earning power, and the admiration of all!

Here is a list of the qualifications you may aspire to (along with »course« fees).

Bachelor of Arts with Honours BA (Hons) $2,000
Masters of Arts (MA) $3,000
Masters in Business Administration (MBA) $5,000
Doctorate (PhD) $5,500

All diplomas available in the field of your choice.
No required tests, classes, books, or interviews.
No one is turned down. Confidentiality assured.

SUNDAY 24 OCTOBER

8	14
9	15
10	16
11	17
12	18
13	19

Receive your diploma within days!!!
www.thiswebsitewillchangeyourlife.com

How do you know you weren't adopted?

It is estimated that one in twelve people are adopted. Many never find out. If you have ever felt different from your parents or your siblings, seek out the truth today. Check by calling the Adoption National Helpline on 0808 808 1234.

MONDAY 25 OCTOBER

8

9

10

11

12

13

14

15

16

17

18

»Book Club« Day

Here is the list of the top 100 masterpieces of Western literature. Work out how many you have read (no cheating now). Then work out how many you will have to read per year to finish them all.

1. Anonymous, *The Bible*
2. Aeschylus, *Oresteia*
3. Aristophanes, *Comedies*
4. Aristotle, *Politics*
5. Augustine, *Confessions*
6. Austen, Jane, *Pride and Prejudice*
7. Bacon, Sir Francis, *Essays*
8. Balzac, Honoré de, *Old Goriot*
9. Baudelaire, Charles, *The Flowers of Evil*
10. Beckett, Samuel, *Waiting for Godot*
11. Benrik, *This Diary Will Change Your Life*
12. Blake, William, *Songs of Innocence and of Experience*
13. Boccaccio, Giovanni, *The Decameron*
14. Brontë, Charlotte, *Jane Eyre*
15. Brontë, Emily, *Wuthering Heights*
16. Bunyan, John, *The Pilgrim's Progress*
17. Camus, Albert, *The Stranger*
18. Céline, Louis-Ferdinand, *Journey to the End of the Night*
19. Cervantes, Miguel, *Don Quixote*
20. Chaucer, Geoffrey, *Canterbury Tales*
21. Chekhov, Anton, *Plays*
22. Conrad, Joseph, *Lord Jim*
23. Cooper, James Fenimore, *The Last of the Mohicans*
24. Cortázar, Julio, *Hopscotch*
25. Dante, *The Divine Comedy*
26. Darwin, Charles, *The Origin of Species*
27. Defoe, Daniel, *Robinson Crusoe*
28. Dickens, Charles, *David Copperfield*
29. Donne, John, *Poems*
30. Dostoevsky, Fyodor, *Crime and Punishment*
31. Eliot, George, *The Mill on the Floss*
32. Eliot, T.S., *Complete Poems*
33. Emerson, Ralph Waldo, *Essays*
34. Euripides, *Plays*
35. Faulkner, William, *The Sound and the Fury*
36. Fielding, Henry, *Tom Jones*
37. Fitzgerald, F. Scott, *The Great Gatsby*
38. Flaubert, Gustave, *Madame Bovary*
39. Freud, Sigmund, *The Interpretation of Dreams*
40. Frost, Robert, *Poetry*
41. Garcia Márquez, Gabriel, *One Hundred Years of Solitude*
42. Gibbon, Edward, *History of The Decline and Fall of the Roman Empire*
43. Goethe, Johann Wolfgang von, *Faust*
44. Hardy, Thomas, *Tess of the D'Urbervilles*
45. Hawthorne, Nathaniel, *The Scarlet Letter*
46. Hemingway, Ernest, *A Farewell to Arms*
47. Homer, *Iliad*
48. Homer, *Odyssey*
49. Hugo, Victor, *Notre Dame of Paris*
50. Ibsen, Henrik, *Plays*
51. James, Henry, *The Ambassadors*
52. Joyce, James, *Ulysses*
53. Kafka, Franz, *The Trial*
54. Keats, John, *Poems*
55. Lawrence, D.H., *Women in Love*
56. Machiavelli, Niccolo, *The Prince*
57. Mann, Thomas, *Buddenbrooks*
58. Maupassant, Guy de, *Stories*
59. Melville, Herman, *Moby Dick*
60. Montaigne, Michel de, *Essays*
61. Mill, John Stuart, *On Liberty*
62. Milton, John, *Paradise Lost*
63. Molière, *Selected Plays*
64. Ovid, *Metamorphoses*
65. Pascal, Blaise, *Pensées*
66. Pasternak, Boris, *Dr Zhivago*
67. Petronius, *Satyricon*
68. Plato, *Republic*
69. Plutarch, *Parallel Lives*
70. Poe, Edgar Allen, *Tales*
71. Proust, Marcel, *Remembrance of Things Past*
72. Rabelais, François, *Gargantua and Pantagruel*
73. Racine, Jean, *Phèdre*
74. Rilke, Rainer Maria, *Poems*
75. Rimbaud, Arthur, *Poems*
76. Rousseau, Jean-Jacques, *Confessions*
77. Sartre, Jean-Paul, *Nausea*
78. Shakespeare, William, *Plays*
79. Shakespeare, William, *Poems*
80. Shaw, Bernard, *Plays*
81. Sophocles, *Tragedies*
82. Stendhal, *The Red and the Black*
83. Sterne, Laurence, *Tristram Shandy*
84. Stevenson, Robert Louis, *Treasure Island*
85. Swift, Jonathan, *Gulliver's Travels*
86. Thackeray, William Makepeace, *Vanity Fair*
87. Thoreau, Henry D., *Walden*
88. Thucydides, *The History of the Peloponnesian War*
89. Tolstoy, Leo, *War and Peace*
90. Tolstoy, Leo, *Anna Karenina*
91. Turgenev, Ivan, *Fathers and Sons*
92. Twain, Mark, *The Adventures of Huckleberry Finn*
93. Virgil, *Aeneid*
94. Voltaire, *Candide*
95. Whitman, Walt, *Leaves of Grass*
96. Wilde, Oscar, *Plays*
97. Woolf, Virginia, *The Waves*
98. Wordsworth, William, and Coleridge, Samuel, *Lyrical Ballads*
99. Yeats, William Butler, *Collected Poems*
100. Zola, Emile, *Germinal*

Number left to read:..........................(X)

Number of years left (approx):...........(Y)

Masterpieces/year (X/Y) = ...

8	TUESDAY 26 OCTOBER	15
9	12	16
10	13	17
11	14	18

Say hello to everyone in the street, American-style.
Authorized variations:

HI! HELLO!
GOOD MORNING!
MORNING!
HOW ARE YA? HELLO STRANGER!
HOWDY! HEY!
HOW'S IT GOING?
HEYA!
HI THERE!
HEY MISTER!
MORNIN' MAM!
NICE DAY AIN'T IT!
WAZZUP? HIYA!

ALOHA!

Wednesday 27 October		
8	14	
9	15	
10	16	
11	17	
12	18	
13	19	

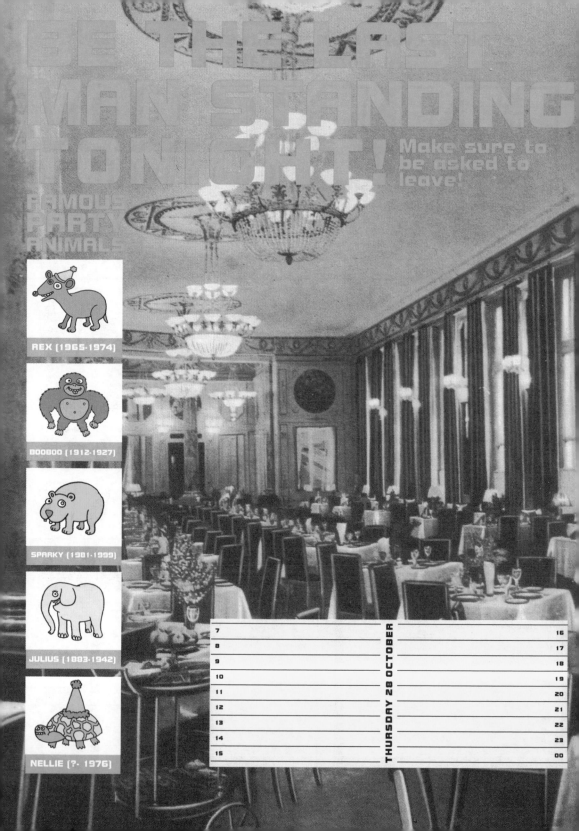

BE THE LAST MAN STANDING TONIGHT!

Make sure to be asked to leave!

FAMOUS PARTY ANIMALS

REX (1965-1974)

BOOBOO (1912-1927)

SPARKY (1981-1999)

JULIUS (1883-1942)

NELLIE (?- 1976)

7		16
8		17
9		18
10		19
11	**THURSDAY 28 OCTOBER**	20
12		21
13		22
14		23
15		00

Friday 29 October. Invent your very own milkshake and make a fortune

In 1933, little Ricki Putz got fed up with selling plain old lemonade on the street corner like every other schmucky kid in his neighbourhood. So what does he do? He goes home to Ma, and he asks her for some leftover milk and a couple scoops of ice cream. Then he takes the cored-out pumpkin from Halloween the previous week, he mashes everything together in the garage real good, and hey presto, Putz's-Pokey-Pumpkin-O-Shake is born! Little Ricki himself unfortunately died of food poisoning not so long afterwards, God bless his soul, but his descendants today are rich on the proceeds.

8		14	
9		15	
10		16	
11		17	
12		18	
13		19	

REPORT A UFO SIGHTING	SATURDAY 30 OCTOBER
Website: www.ufodatabase.com	If over 10 people report sightings in the same area, a US government agency investigation is automatically triggered, anywhere on the planet.

Some typical UFO shapes:					

Characteristics of reported UFO (check all that apply):	Lights on the object ☐ Trail visible in the wake of the object ☐ Aura or haze around the object ☐ Beams emitted by the object ☐ Colour changes visible in the object ☐ Object observed landing ☐ Sounds emitted from the object ☐ Aircraft chasing the object ☐ Electromagnetic effects observed near the object, such as a car engine stopping ☐	Methods of recording your evidence

What to do if you are abducted:	Remain calm. Aliens can sense panic telepathically. If it appears you are about to be sexually abused or dissected, focus on the positive side of the experience: you will be able to sell your story for hundreds and hundreds of dollars to the National Enquirer.

8	14
9	15
10	16
11	17
12	18
13	19

SEE A SHRINK
EXERCISE
SPEED-DATE TEN PEOPLE
GO TO MASS
BAKE A LOAF OF BREAD
DONATE BLOOD
EXTEND FOREPLAY
ADJUST ALL YOUR CLOCKS

SUNDAY 31 OCTOBER. TODAY THE CLOCKS CHANGE. HERE ARE SOME WORTHWHILE THINGS TO DO WITH YOUR EXTRA HOUR OF LIFE.

8 ....
9 ....
10 ....
11 ....
12 ....
13 ....

14 ....
15 ....
16 ....
17 ....
18 ....
19 ....

....
....
....
....
....
....

In 1998, 27-year-old German Ute Schürings kidnapped the pet dog of the Venezuelan ambassador to Berlin, and sequestered it for nine weeks in her bedroom. At first, the police refused to take the case seriously but when Schürings began issuing demands, they investigated. After she was arrested following a tip-off from a neighbour, she explained that she had been trying to draw attention to the life of Josef Kunkel, a little-known 19th century zoologist. »I want my idol Josef Kunkel to be recognized at his true value,« she told a local news channel. »He practically invented sociobiology a century early with his work on giraffes. But he was from Pomerania and had mulatto blood, so no one took him seriously at the time.« The dog, a Weimaraner, was returned to its owner unharmed. Schürings was arrested but later released into care.

MONDAY 1 NOVEMBER

8

9

10

11

12

13

14

15

16

17

18

US Presidential Election! Vote today! Even if you are not technically a US citizen, the result of this election will impact on your life. Therefore it is your duty as a global citizen to vote! Use our special ballot paper and send it in to your local US embassy by 8pm West Coast Time.

I wish to vote for the candidates

of the following party:

REPUBLICAN ☐

REFORM ☐

DEMOCRATIC ☐

SOCIALIST ☐

LIBERTARIAN ☐

GREEN ☐

SOCIALIST WORKERS ☐

GEE I DUNNO ☐

I have also put in brackets my second choice. I have put a little asterisk near my third choice. I have crossed out the ones I really really don't want. Thank you for taking this into account when you count it all up at the end.

To prevent any misunderstandings, I include my name and phone number here in case you're not sure which way I voted:..

....

Thank you for letting me know the results. My address is:..

....

....

8			14
9			15
10			16
11	TUESDAY 2 NOVEMBER		17
12			18
13			19

RANDOM DAY

A) COUNT THE NUMBER OF BUSES
   YOU SEE ON YOUR WAY TO WORK.
B) MULTIPLY THIS NUMBER
   BY 3 AND DIVIDE IT BY 2.
C) BUY AS MANY CHOCOLATE BARS.
D) HAND THEM OUT RANDOMLY
   TO DIFFERENT PEOPLE.
E) WRITE DOWN WHAT THEY
   TELL YOU – WORD FOR WORD
   – ON A PIECE OF PAPER.
F) FOLD THE PAPERS AND PUT THEM
   EACH IN AN ENVELOPE. SEAL.
G) FIND RANDOM ADDRESSES IN
   A TELEPHONE DIRECTORY.
H) STAMP THE ENVELOPES
   AND SEND TO ADDRESSES.
I) WAIT AND SEE.

8

9

10

11

12

13

14

15

16

17

18

EYESIGHT

Hold this text at arm's length. If you have trouble reading...

Knock yourself on each knee with a small mallet. Your lower leg should jerk up.

HEARTBEAT

At rest: 50-100. After running on the spot for 20 minutes: 100-200.

THURSDAY 4 NOVEMBER

8
9
10
11
12
13
14
15
16
17
18

SPERM COUNT

Ejaculate onto glass, isolate 1cm² of spermatozoa, and count them with a micro-scope. There should be roughly 100,000,000 of the little tinkers.

TODAY: PERFORM A SELF-MEDICAL

Repeat every week and contact your doctor with any noteworthy variations.

BREAST CANCER

FEEL FOR LUMPS (other than nipples).

TESTICULAR CANCER

Feel for lumps (other than testicles).

PROS TATE

Feel for painful swelling (girls, you may skip this one).

URINE TEST

Pee into a glass and use our colour chart to check if it is within acceptable range.

ACCEPTABLE

Drive a Ferrari!
The salesman will be only too happy to oblige you with a test drive. Just try not to crash it.

Book a suite at the Ritz!
Obviously call to unbook it tomorrow, as your private jet is unfortunately grounded.

Millionaire!!!
Act like you're worth millions today. Only your bank manager will know the difference.

Visit the casino!
Enjoy the free drinks without gambling and mutter about the dice being loaded here.

YABI RABA

I'LL PAY NEXT MONTH

View a palatial mansion!
Look scruffy and estate agents will assume you're a rock star.

FRIDAY 5 NOVEMBER
8
9
1 0
1 1
1 2
1 3
1 4
1 5
1 6
1 7
1 8
1 9

Call the president!
The White House number is 00 1 202 456 1414. Leave a message to call back urgently.

Interview butlers!
A classified ad for a man-servant should attract plenty of potential minions.

RAVA PAVA

TODAY PLACE FLOWERS ON AN OLD UNATTENDED GRAVESTONE

8	14
9	15
10	16
11	17
12	18
13	19

Sunday 7 November
It's not all about you!
Ego Control Day!

Spend today thinking only about someone else and their life and problems for a change:

Bob Zuccione,
printer of this Diary.

Bob was born in 1954 in Naples. He was a healthy baby, weighing in at a more than acceptable 4kg. His Mum Nina (née Panzani) originally came from Sicily but moved to Naples in 1945 when she married Gino Zuccione, fresh from the Eastern front. Gino had big plans for himself and his family. All the Zucciones until then had gone into the family business (pasta-shape mould-making), but not Gino, no way. Gino was going to make it big, in America! He was going to show them all. Anyway, after he got hit by a bus on the way to the gelateria, Nina remarried. Her new husband was Gino's uncle, Augustino, who hated Bob from the beginning. So Bob never got to go to America and live the Dream (except until last year on a cruise). Instead, he went to the local pasta-mould-making-apprenticeship school, run by Augustino, where the other boys made his life a misery for being the headmaster's stepson and Augustino made his life a misery for roughly identical reasons. Bob

longed wistfully for the day when he could leave home. But he was also quite lazy and so he didn't get round to it until the age of 28, by which time Augustino had become too arthritic to beat him much anyhow. Plus, Bob was now bigger, so there was that, too. Bob worked in the family »pastamodelleria« in the southern (rougher) suburbs of newly industrialized Naples. He was doing well, until in 1976 the local Camorra got in on the deal and tried to stuff the pasta forms with cocaine for export. Bob was unaware of this and boiled the experimental batch, ruining product with a street value of \$2,000,000, a tidy sum in those days. Fortunately for Bob, the mob ordered the assassination of Augustino as revenge, so he didn't mind so much. It gave him a fright though, and he decided to leave the pasta business and head for a related field, printing, though the moulds were different, shaped like letters as they are. In 1981, Bob got married to Julietta Pasqualini, a childhood friend who had correctly concluded that he represented her last chance of not ending up an old maid like her ugly sister Paola. They had clumsy sex a couple of times and agreed not to repeat the experience except when drunk. Bob tried going to a prostitute one time since, but after she

laughed at his request to be addressed as »Il Duce«, he chose not to return. Meantime, professionally things were going good for Bob, as he ascended the printing hierarchy, becoming deputy with special charge of inks in 1988. This was also the year that his beloved mother Nina died, aged 67, of deep vein thrombosis of the left foot. Bob was unconsolable. But in early February 1995, domestic unhappiness

notwithstanding, Bob was made head printer. His early pasta-mould-making had stood him in good stead. And in 2004,

with the successful printing of the Diary, his career reached its apogee. But as he would be the first to admit, he does not consider himself fulfilled, and admits to lying awake at night thinking of cancer. And you thought you had problems. If you have any tips for Bob, write to him at:

Bob Zuccione
»Villa Panzani«
233 Cheaton Hill Road
Manchester M8 8LG
United Kingdom

8
9
10
11
12
13
14
15
16
17
18
19

PER PENNINSULA OF THE LEFT INNER EAR SENDS OUT THE FATHER OF MY BEASTS TO TAKE CARE OF THE MELANCHOLIC MELON
N AMONGST SACRIFIED WALMARTS. SODOMIZING THE WALLS RAISED ETERNALLY WITH CONCRETE SLABS AND WATER RUNNING
OSE OF A RHINO IN THE BITTERSWEET TASTE OF MY MOUTH. CANCAN SALSA BUTTERBUG PANCAKE FROSTY FEMALE GLOBE-
ER STEELBENCH ON PARADE IN RIO. CYKLING BEATS RUNNING IF RUNNING IS WALKING AND WALKING IS WHAT KEEPS ME
THINKING OF YOU. QUOTE UNQUOTE ANGLOSAXON VIKING WITH HYPOTHERMIA LOOKING FOR LOVE IN A CATALOGUE FOR
ARDENER AT HOME WITH MY GNOMES. SCREAM, SAID THE CAT BUT HE KEEPS WALKING UP A TIGHTROPE FUNGUS CLOGGING
Y BREATH AND TIME IS RUNNING OUT AND YOUR SCALP IS BITTER COLD AND PAINTED RED BY THE SUN. OCEAN RIPPLES COAG-
S THE BEACH AND PARADES HISTORICAL KEYBOARDS MULTIPLIED BY FIVE THOUSAND CORIANDER BOTTOMS COVERED IN SNOW
HIT. PUTIN! PUTIN! CANNOT GET HOME THROUGH THAT RIP IN THE CLOTHING AND PIMPLES ALL OVER SIGNIFY A LOCAL TENDENCY
RP. OH SWEET RULING CLASS SPREADING SUNLIGHT IN THE ROBE I'M WEARING IN HONOUR OF BALZAC. LIGHTING A MATCH JU-
S THE SHADOWS CLOSER TO ME. WHAT I THOUGHT WAS POSSIBLE IN SCHOOL WAS NOT. OPPORTUNITIES OF GOLD AND VACCOM
TING UP TO WHAT I COMMONLY REFER TO AS "PROMOTING CAUSES THAT PROVOKES COMMON LANGUAGE" STOP NOW AND ST-
UR THUMBS UP FOR A WHILE, THINK OF MOTHER THERESA IN A PICTURESQUE SETTING COMBING FLEAS OFF A BABYLON COW.
HE PEN TO SOME COMRADE CLAIMING TO BE AN ILL-RECIEVED FORMER MEMBER OF A BAND CALLED SUZY THE PANFLUTE
NG BOZANOVA FAMILY AND LET HIM DRAW A BIG MAN WITH SMALL EYES ON THE INSIDE OF YOUR MOST TENDER THIGH.
AN WAS A CITY RATHER THAN AN ABSTRACT IDEA OF FREEDOM IT WOULD CERTAINLY CONTAIN LESS MOMENTS OF COMPLIC-
STROKES OF BINARY PATHS IN SPACE. AUTOMATIC WRITING DAY. PROBE THE DEPTHS OF YOUR SUBCONSCIOUS TODAY. SIT DOWN
A TABLE WITH A PEN AND A PAPER, PICK A FIRST LETTER AT RANDOM, AND START WRITING AS FAST AS YOU CAN WITHOUT TH-
ABOUT IT. WARNING: IF YOUR AUTOMATIC WRITING ENDS UP SOMETHING LIKE THIS; "THE DEVIL PLAYS THE BANJO BETWEEN
ECHEROUS LEGS OF MOTHER SUPERIOUR RAAAAGH I SPEAK IN TONGUES AT THE DAWN OF THE LAST DAY SCREW THE VEGE-
S AND LET THE UNIVERSE IMPLODE BUTTERCUPS BUTTERCUPS SUCK MY MANIFOLD ORIFICES!!!" YOU ARE EITHER UNHIN-
RA TEENAGER. GO DO YOUR HOMEWORK. ON THE CON-MAN! PISS ON A FLUTE! SPY ON A MALLORCAN! SATURE A MILLION. NOTH-
AN STAND IN MY WAY TO THE ETERNAL WISDOM OF A MAN WITH NO PAST AND NOTHING BUT HANDCRAFTED TOYS IN HIS POCK-
LION ROWS YOUR BOAT. AND YOU'RE NOT HUNGRY. THE LIONS ARE CATS, YOU'RE JUST HUMAN. LIONS EAT ZEBRAS, YOU STICK TO
CONCENTRATED GAFFER PENIS SUFFLE, HARBORING A TERRORIST UNDER EACH ARMPIT, SHOOTING BLUEBIRDS IN THE SKIES OF
RT LUDLUMS PRIVATE CINEMA. EVOLUTION IS NOT MISSING NOR WELCOME HERE. NEITHER IS STRAIGHT LINES OR THE LETTER T.
IVACY. THE SIGN OF THE FRONT PART OF THE GUITAR IS PULLING THE STRING THAT SUPPORTS THE LAUNDRY OF THE FIRST BL-
MAN TO GO TO THE MOON. NOW IS THE TIME TO UNRAVEL THE SONG THAT I'VE WRITTEN TO CELEBRATE THE ANNIVERSARY OF TH-
URTHOUSE APPEARANCE BY THE PRINCE CAUGHT SHOPLIFTING A PAIR OF NEUTRAL-COLOURED LOAFERS IN A SHOP CALLED
ADALE, AFTER THE FAMOUS SINGER DAVID. INTERNATIONAL SCALPELS DRINKS DRUNKEN SAILORS LEFTOVERS TO COPE WITH
OVE-VIRUS SPREADING FASTER THAN ITS COUNTERPARTS CARE TO CARE. PROLONG MY PICK-POCKET FRIENDS VISUMS TO
IN THE COUNTRY OF THEIR INFANTILE COUNTRY OF VIRGIN ORIGIN. FREQUENT VISITS FROM YOU KEEP ME CALM. FLAGSDONT-
O THREATHEN ME WITH WITH BIRDS I WILL CONQUER YOU WITH 50 16-YEAR OLD VIRGINS PLAYING 50 CENT AND TRIVIAL PU-
T WITH A DWARF. NAIL ME TO THE WALL HIGH UP. CIRCLE IT WITH CHALK. ERASE THE SAME WITH A COMPUTER TELEPHONE.
AM IF YOU'RE A BABY, WHISPER IF YOU'RE A CHILD. AND IF YOU DON'T LIKE ME PREACHING, LOOK ME UP IN THE BOOK OF
K BELTS AND SMOKING GUNS AND YOU'LL SEE THAT I WAS THE FIRST TO SPEAK FRENCH WITH AN GEORGIAN ACCENT. AND
OVE IT, I'LL DIP TWO FURRY ANIMALS IN A KETTLE OF BOILING ASPHALT AND PRICE IT TO THE LITRE ACCORDING TO THE
VA-CONVENTION. IT IS ABOUT TIME NOW TO BE THE HERO OF MY OWN ACCORDS. CAN'T STOP FAILING IN THE AFTERMATH
OPLE WHO CLAIM THAT THE FOREST IS MADE UP OF MORE SPECIES OF TREES THAN ONE. SO SOD IT. JUST SHOOT. MUSTARD
IN MY VEINS LIKE POKER IN THE GAMBLER. PUNISHING MY MOTHER FOR STUFF THAT I DID OR AT LEAST WERE PARTLY
ONSIBLE FOR IN A WICKED ROMANESQUE KIND OF WAY. AND YOU WERE SUPPOSED TO BE MY SISTER! DON'T TOUCH MY
R! SORRY, DIDN'T MEAN TO GO SO FAR DOWN THE DIRECTORS INSTINCTS. GOT A BAD CASE OF PARADISE PRETENTIONS
STLING ENDLESSLY WITH OVERRIPE PRIMATES LOST FROM THEIR FLOCK. OH, I'VE SAID TO MUCH, GIVEN OUT TO MUCH,
TO MUCH. IT TELLS ME MORE ABOUT YOU THAN ABOUT ME IF YOU GOT THIS FAR. TWISTED MY ANKLE IN A LUMBERJACK TO
EED WITH THE ROYAL DRAMA ABOUT THE POMPOUS WAR BETWEEN THE GOOD, THE BAD AND THE PEOPLE THAT ALWAY
UNNOTICED; THOSE OF THE PALSTERNAK TRIBAL UNIT SIXTEEN COUGHING IT UP BETWEEN THE TAKES OF SOME SE-
COMMERSIAL FOR ELECTRIC RAZORS ON RETURN AFTER BEING DISHONOURED BY EU-REGULATIONS FOR OVER 200 BRIT-
TLY HANDLED YEARS UP THE ASS OF A PEACOCK. MISS ME NOT, I'M SHAKESPEARE EXCEPT FOR THE TALENT INFLICTED BY

Monday 8 November

8

9

10

11

12

13

14

15

16

17

18

TO BARRACUDAS WITH TEETH SHARP AS THE ICEBLOCKS ON THE
WO PERSONS TRYING TO SOLVE A CRIME INVOLVING A BITTER
YEAR. EAT WITHOUT SCREAMING THEN, TAKE MY WHOLE BIN.
S AND SHOWCASE YOUR PRIDE TO THE ANCESTORS OF THE
JOS THAT YOU THINK IS TRUSTWORDY TO BE CALLED THE
HES. DON'T OVERREACT AND BACK UP THE DATA BEFO-
E BITES YOUR COD AND MAKES YOU FORGET EVERY
EN TO REACH THAT GOAL OF SODOM AND GOMORRA.
OF A BUCKET YOU FIND STANDING ON THE MIDDLE
FOLLOW THE YELLOW LINE TILL YOU COME TO A
ED AS A ZEBRA CROSSED WITH A POODLE, SEEING
FUCKING FUTURE, NARROWING DOWN TO WHAT
D GENETKALLY IMPERFECT OR IN A SENSE BI-
AUNTS AND UNCLES USED TO THE BAD MUSIC OF
ALLY EXPECT FROM HOLLYWOOD BLOCKBUSTERS.
HE NEW FRESH START FOR YOU IF YOU ENJOY
GLES CONTROLLED BY A NAUTIC SENSOR OPERA-
NG AID TO THE POOR MANDATE OF THE CITIZENS OF
YOUR ASS ANOTHER WAY. GOLD COLOURS YOUR SP-
SPARKLE OF BACKPACK PLURALISM AND DISGUIS-
ES ARE GOOD FOR NOTHING IF YOU CAN'T SEE AND
HEN KING FILMATISATION AND HAVE TO RELY ON THE
N A CASSETTE. HERBS AND SPICES MEAN NOTHING NO MO
ALIENS ARE HERE IN THE BACKYARD TO THE VERY LE-
HBOUR, MAKING HIM EVEN MORE NERVOUS AND CONSTAN-
FIRST PERSON TO SEE MARTIN SCORSESES MEAN STREET ON
AND PLUMS THERE. THE CAR WAS SPINNING OUT OF CONTROL WHEN I LEFT HIM TO THE FRONT ROW WITH THE FAV-
ITE THINNER STICK STICKING OUT OF YOUR EAR BUSTING THE BEAR COUGHING TOO LOUDLY AT THE MOVIES TRUST
OW. STEP BY STEP. JEANS ARE BLUE, THE SUN IS YELLOW. YOU ARE PANICKING AWAY INSIDE CHILDRENS BOOKS OF A
IC LIBRARY IN MALTA BUILT FOR DISADVANTAGED BUILDERS AT THE TURN OF THE CENTRE. MANY DIED THERE, TRYING
POPULARIZE MOVEMENTS OF CAREERS ON ICE-SKATES THUMBLING AND FALLING TO COLLABORATE WITH CONSTABLES
URNING TO DEMOCRACY AFTER A LIFE IN EXILE AND ABUSE OF THE FREEDOM OF SPEECH. CRYING FILLS THE SHELVES OF
INSIDE PART OF A GUN NEVER TO BE USED BY ITS TRUE OWNER BUT BY PILGRIM STEPSONS OUT TO IMPRESS THE IR-
RS WITH GLASSES SHARPENED BY POSITIVE LIGHT. THE FIREBRIGAD WON'T GET HERE ON TIME IF YOU KEEP HANGING
TO THE DAGGER THAT POISONS THE GAP BETWEEN US TONIGHT WHEN DOGS AND FROGS GET ALONG BETER THAN THE
OMARK ON THE EDGE OF A COUNTRY WON BY RETARDS. UNIFORMS ARE CLOTHES TOO, EVEN AT MCDONALDS. FIRES
SPREADING AND YOU HAVE HOMOUS AROUND YOUR MOUTH. THAT'S WHAT GIVES ME THE URGE TO TOUCH YOU WITH A LIS
S SOAKED IN BUTTER AND MEN THAT BRAGS ABOUT KNOWING WHEN REALLY THEY'RE JUST HAVING A GOOD TIME

COFFEINDRENCHED PARADIGM
END AND THE TEENAGER OF
CAPSULATE THE INNER EMO
IMMEDIATE CIRCLE OF F-
BUNCH OF PINTS AND
RE SOME EVIL VEGGE-
DAMN STEP YOU'VE
STEAL MEDICAL AID
OF A SHOPPING ST-
CROSSING COMPL-
TWO WAYS INTO
CAN BE CONSID-
LANGUAL JUSTU-
SUSPENSE YOU
PASADENA CAN
A QUICK SET OF
TED BY FEAR OF
RAMMSTEIN SCRA-
ECIAL CRUMBS SO
ED SLAPSTICK CUM.
IF YOU CAN'T SEE
REPRESENTATION OF
RE SINCE I REALIZED
FT OF MY MOST HATED
TLY BRAGGING THAT HE WAS
VIDEO. AHA TJOHO, ROCKETS TH-

TUESDAY 9 NOVEMBER
TAKE ONE MEMORABLE PHOTO TODAY

The most spontaneous-looking pictures are often those that require the most effort. Robert Doisneau had to wait all day for a policeman to walk past before taking this immortal shot. Today walk around with your camera, compose a great picture in your mind, and shoot it, no matter how long it takes you.

8

9

10

11

12

13

14

15

16

17

18

19

We are each exposed to 2000 commercial messages a day on average. Today count them.

TV commercials

Cinema commercials

Ads in newspapers

Classified ads

Posters

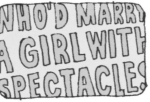

Radio ads

Ads on public transport

Ads in weird places

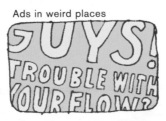

Logos on clothes

Logos on cars

Logos on other possessions

Shop signs

WEDNESDAY 10 NOVEMBER	
8	14
9	15
10	16
11	17
12	18
13	19

Now go back and deface at least one of them for wasting your precious time.

TODAY: JUST HOW GOOD IS YOUR DOCTOR?

Make an appointment to check he knows his symptoms:

TEST no 1: tell him or her you feel a large growing lump in the stomach, and have experienced hair loss along with bleeding from the anus. They should recommend you visit casualty within the next half an hour or so.

TEST no 2: don't say much, just groan and massage your stomach and head. When you do speak, sound drunk. They should recommend you stop wasting their valuable time.

TEST no 3 (advanced): how do they cope with unfamiliar symptoms? Tell them your left eyeball feels unusually mushy, your liver is palpitating, or your belly button is aching. How precise is their diagnostic and how many further tests do they order? Change doctors if you judge these insufficient.

THURSDAY 11 NOVEMBER

8

9

10

11

12

13

14

15

16

17

18

19

FEEDBACK DAY

Today, the minds behind the Diary will be standing near this phone booth to take your calls and answer any constructive questions you may have.

Phonecard

020-793 51129

Ideas for questions: »This is truly an amazing book. Isn't it?« »My life has changed. How can I thank you enough?« »Are you as pretty as you are funny?« »Why don't you run for presidents?« »If I was a girl, would you let me have your babies?«

8
9
10
11
12
13

14
15
16
17
18
19

FRIDAY 12 NOVEMBER

DISCIPLINE DAY

Don't be a slave to your every impulse. Develop the willpower to overcome your body's inherent laziness and reap the rewards. You cannot master external circumstances, but you can begin to master your own mind. Follow this routine to enhance your self-discipline and get a grip on your life. Respect yourself and others will respect you.

SO:

Rise at dawn.
Take a cold shower.
Scrub behind your ears.
Scrub between your toes.
Brush your teeth for 3 mins.
Floss.
Cut your toenails.
Take your medicine.
Jog 5 miles.

Tighten your belt.
Straighten your tie.
Eat your sprouts.
Say »please« and »thank you«.
Look people in the eye.
Sit up straight.
Be in bed by 10pm.
Repeat every day.

Pierced German with a whip

SATURDAY 13 NOVEMBER

8
9
10
11
12
13
14
15
16
17
18
19

NOTE: IF DURING THE DAY YOU SUCCUMB TO NATURAL SLOPPINESS, TAKE A LOOK AT OUR **Pierced German with a whip**. HE'LL HELP YOU CHANGE YOUR WAYS.

Sunday 14 November

Indulge Yourself

Today sample as many of the finest things
in life as your circumstances allow.

Champagne: Krug 1985 Clos du Mesnil (£350/bottle)
Caviar: Tsar Imperial Beluga (£2,100/kg)
Foie gras: Foie Gras Entier du Perigord (£70/500g)
Olive oil: Tenuta di Valgiano Extra Vergine (£45/bottle)
Smoked salmon: Wild Scottish (£44/kg)
Wine: Château Mouton-Rothschild 1945 (£5,400/bottle)
Truffles: Fresh White Alba Truffles (£930/250g)
Lobster: large live Maine lobster (£30)
Chocolate: Neuhaus Belgian Pralines (£30/500g)
Whisky: Dalmore 62 Years Old Single Malt (£26,000/bottle)
Coffee: Jamaica Blue Mountain (£34/lb bag)
Cigar: Cuban Cohiba Churchill Esplendidos (£400/box of 25)

Prices may vary.

»Anyone who lives within their means suffers
from a lack of imagination.« (Oscar Wilde)

8	14		
9	15		
10	16		
11	17		
12	18		
13	19		

NO UNDERWEAR DAY!

Today dispense with your usual under-garments and enjoy a breezier lifestyle.

HEY LOOK AT ME!

NO! LOOK AT ME!

MEDICAL FACT According to a study on »Tight-fitting Underwear and Sperm Quality« published on June 29, 1996, in the medical journal *The Lancet*, tight underwear is not recommended for men trying to become fathers as it may raise testes temperature to a point where it becomes detrimental to sperm count. Also harmful are hot tubs and saunas. So leave those briefs at home and hang loose.

Monday 15 November

8

9

10

11

12

13

14

15

16

17

18

POSTERITY DAY

Don't sink into the oblivion of ages. Give humanity something to remember you by, whether it be a work of art, a feat of arms, or simply the sheer force of your personality. Today, decide what you want to be remembered for and set about writing yourself into History.

TUESDAY 16 NOVEMBER

8	14
9	15
10	16
11	17
12	18
13	19

Tip: one achievement is quite enough. Pity the novelists who diligently churn out one potboiler a year, when they could quite easily get away with one or two of a lifetime. Thackeray is famous for *Vanity Fair*, Proust for *Remembrance of Things Past*, Emily Brontë for *Wuthering Heights*. Tolstoy only needed a couple of decent novels to establish his genius. Paradoxically in our age of information overload, this has never been more true: spend ten years on something and you are presumed to be a thinker of the deepest ilk.

BAIL A STRANGER
OUT OF JAIL

FIND OUT IF YOU CAN TRULY TRUST IN MAN'S INNATE GOODNESS. Every day thousands of petty criminals are available for release from jail pending trial, yet can't afford the relatively paltry sums necessary to post bail.

Call up your local courthouse and ask for suitable cases.

BEGINNERS: AVOID BAILING OUT SUSPECTS WITH ALLEGED VIOLENT PROCLIVITIES, AS THEY MAY TURN AGAINST YOU.

IF YOUR CHEQUE FOR BAIL GOES THROUGH, YOU WILL HAVE SOMEONE IN YOUR DEBT, A NEW BEST FRIEND FOR LIFE.

A NOTE OF CAUTION: BOUNTY HUNTERS.

If you post someone out of jail and they don't turn up in court, you may have a bounty hunter on your ass.

THESE GUYS ARE FOR REAL!

ASSIST THEM IN THEIR SEARCH FOR YOUR EX-NEW BEST FRIEND FOR LIFE, OR THEY COULD TURN NASTY. BOUNTY HUNTERS ARE RECOGNIZABLE BY THEIR BURLY PHYSIQUES AND THEIR MEAN-SOUNDING FIRST NAMES, LIKE DOG, OR BEEF.

WEDNESDAY 17 NOVEMBER
★8
★9
★10
★11
★12
★13
★14
★15
★16
★17
★18

Treasured Memories Day

Often, people find that they can remember the faces of casual acquaintances perfectly even years later, but not those of their departed nearest and dearest. Guard against the march of time by taking a good look at your loved ones' features today and committing them to memory.

8	14
9	15
10	16
11	17
12	18
13	19

TAKE A COLD SHOWER

Historians of the future will no doubt trace the beginning of our civilization's decline to the universal availability of the warm shower, that enfeebling experience. Brace yourself this morning and prove your mettle by showering cold. Once the initial shock is over, it's actually quite invigorating. Plus you save on heating bills. Come on, are you a man or a mouse?

Look! It's so cold that the bar of soap has frozen to his body! Amazing.

I LIKE SHOWERS

CENSORED

8	
9	
10	
11	
12	
13	
14	
15	
16	
17	
18	

Study this intriguing photograph today. What does it mean? What is the sausage doing there? What is it purpose? Who put it there? Write and send us your interpretation (max. 100 words). It will be published on our website and the best one will be rewarded.

SATURDAY 20 NOVEMBER

8		14
9		15
10		16
11		17
12		18
13		19

Arabesque
Extend one leg directly behind the body in a straight line

pas de chat
Jump sideways, cat-like

entrechat
Jump crossing your feet in midair

jeté
Jump from one foot onto the other

8

9

10

11

12

13

today learn a ballet step

Maria-Teresa Ludovinkha Petrovskavna's top tip for the beginner: »To become a prima ballerina assoluta, you just have to get the right name. As plain old Debbie G. Brookner, I was going nowhere fast. Then I simply changed my name, lost 33 kilos, and hey presto! here I am earning kazillions at the Bolshoi in world-famous Russia. Not bad for a girl from Poughkeepsie, huh?«

14

15

16

17

18

19

---

cabriole
Jump raising one leg then bringing the other up

pirouette
Turn on one leg with the other leg raised

éclat de genou
Raise both legs and jump backward, segueing seamlessly into a double pirouette

rond de jambe
Raise one leg with bent knee and circle the air with pointed toe

DO SOME DIY TODAY

LEVEL OF DIFFICULTY: 1

REPLACE A DEAD LIGHTBULB: UNSCREW OLD LIGHTBULB. SCREW IN NEW ONE.

LEVEL OF DIFFICULTY: 2

HANG A PICTURE HOLD PICTURE AGAINST WALL AND MARK CORNERS WITH PENCIL. HAMMER PIN-TYPE PICTURE HOOK INTO THE WALL EQUIDISTANT BETWEEN MARKINGS. HANG PICTURE.

LEVEL OF DIFFICULTY: 3

REPAIR A DRIPPING TAP. CUT OFF WATER SUPPLY. UNSCREW THE BELL-SHAPED COVER TO EXPOSE THE HEXAGONAL HEADGEAR NUT. UNDO WITH A SPANNER. UNSCREW THE NUT HOLDING THE WASHER IN PLACE ON THE VALVE SEATING. FIT NEW WASHER AND JUMPER IF NECESSARY. GREASE THREADS ON TAP BASE. REASSEMBLE AND TURN WATER SUPPLY BACK ON.

LEVEL OF DIFFICULTY: 4

INSTALL A CHEMICAL DAMP-PROOF COURSE REMOVE SKIRTING BOARDS AND TAKE UP FLOORBOARDS. DRILL A HORIZONTAL ROW OF 3INCH HOLES INTO THE WALL ABOVE THE EXISTING DAMP-PROOF MEMBRANE (IF THERE IS ONE), 6INCHES ABOVE GROUND. PUT THE SUCTION NOZZLE INTO THE FLUID CONTAINER OF YOUR DAMP-PROOF COURSE INJECTION MACHINE, INSERT ALL BUT ONE OF THE INJECTION NOZZLES INTO THE HOLES AND TIGHTEN THE WING NUTS. HOLD THE LAST NOZZLE OVER THE CONTAINER AND TURN ON THE PUMP. WHEN FLUID BEGINS TO FLOW, TURN OFF AND INSERT NOZZLE IN HOLE. TURN ON THE PUMP, UNTIL THE WALL BRICKS ARE SATURATED AND BEGIN TO SWEAT. REPEAT ACROSS THE ENTIRE WALL. LEAVE TO DRY FOR WEEKS.

MONDAY 22 NOVEMBER

12

13

14

15

16

17

18

19

Embrace mother earth.

Kiss the ground that supports life today. Mother Earth is not apart from us but of us and through us. We are at one with her, along with the plants, the other animals, the liquids, the minerals and the gasses. Mother Earth is covered in meridians, or leylines, which are sensitive to our healing caress (see map). The Cherokee people observed that upon kissing a leyline, the birds would often flock to that place, and vegetation sprout thereafter. Be part of that healing. We can all make a difference.

Tuesday 23 November

8 ....

9 ....

10 ....

11 ....

12 ....

13 ....

14 ....

15 ....

16 ....

17 ....

18 ....

Leave the Diary aside today and take a well-deserved break from its strictures.
Too much self-monitoring will drive you mad. In fact today, make a special
effort not to think about yourself at all. There, you've failed already.

Thursday 25 November
Today choose your motto and live by it

VINCIT VERITAS
Truth Conquers

✳

IN FIDE ET IN BELLO FORTES
Strong In Faith And War

✳

SOLI DEO GLORIA
Glory To God Alone

✳

PRO MITRA CORONAM
A Crown For A Mitre

✳

HOC MAJORAM VIRTUS
My Virtue Is From My Ancestors

✳

GALATEA MEA VIRIDIS EST
My Helmet Is Green

✳

SEMPER PATRIA SEVIRE PRESTO
Always Ready To Serve My Country

✳

FELIS DEMULCTA MITIS
The Stroked Cat Is Meek

✳

FINIS CORONAT OPUS
The End Crowns The Work

✳

FORTI NON IGNAVO
To The Brave Man, Not To The Bastard

✳

NEC TEMERE NEC TIMIDE
Neither Rashly Nor Timidly

✳

NEMO ME IMPUNE LACESSIT
No One Provokes Me With Impunity

✳

OMNIA VINCIT AMOR
Love Subdues All Things

FORTUNA JUVAT AUDACES
Fortune Favours The Brave

✳

MANUS HOEC INIMICA TYRANNIS
This Hand Is Hostile To Tyrants

✳

NEC TIMEO NEC SPERNO
I Neither Fear Nor Despise

✳

PAREA NON SERVIN
I Obey But Not As A Slave

✳

FORTIS EST VERITAS
Strong Is The Truth

✳

FRUCTO COGNOSCITUR ARBOR
A Tree Is Recognized By Its Fruit

✳

NECARE BARBAROS NOS DELECTAT
We Like To Massacre Others

✳

GLANDIUM MUSQRUM NUTRIX
The Sword Is The Muse Of Muses

✳

HONOS VIRTUTES SATILLES
Honour The Attendant Of Virtue

✳

HUMANI NIHIL ALIENUM
Nothing That Relates To Man Is
Indifferent To Me

✳

IN CRUCE SALUS
Salvation From The Cross

✳

PRUDENS UT SERPENSSIMPLEX
UT COLUMBA PRUDENT
Careful As A Serpent
Simple As A Dove

PER ARDUA SURGO
I Rise Through Difficulties

✳

PER MARE PER TERRAS
By Sea And Land

✳

INDIGNANTE INVIDIA
FLOREBIT JUSTUS
The Just Man Will Flourish
In Spite Of Envy

✳

REX PORCUS LARGUS EST
The King Is A Fat Pig

✳

JUSTITIA ET FORTITUDO
INVINCIBILIA SUNT
Justice And Fortitude
Are Invincible

✳

NIL DESPERANDUM
Never Despair

✳

PRO ARIS ET FORIS
For Our Altars And Homes

✳

AUT VINCAM AUT PERIAM
Either Win Or Perish

✳

MALO MORI QUAM FOE DARI
Better Death
Than Disgrace

✳

FACTA NON VERBA
Deeds Not Words

✳

PATRIAE INFLICI FIDELIS
Faithful To My
Unhappy Country

8	14
9	15
10	16
11	17
12	18
13	19

Hitchhiking has had a bad rap in the past, but it is one of the better solutions to the environmental pollution problems posed by cars, and a great way of generating a sense of community as well. Follow our guidelines to ensure safe and peaceable hitchhiking and hit the road.

DRIVERS: Pick up a hitchhiker today

Do not pick up anyone with a beard
Do not pick up anyone with
fresh bloodstains on clothing
Do not pick up serial killer-types
Do not try to sexually engage with
hiker (especially by pretending
to confuse their knee for gearbox)

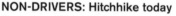

NON-DRIVERS: Hitchhike today

Do design a nice legible sign
on some dry cardboard
Do hide any fresh blood stains on clothing
Do avoid mention of serial killer past
Do not try to sexually engage with
driver (especially when they're driving)

Saturday 27 November

8

9

10

11

12

13

14

15

16

17

18

TONIGHT DATE YOURSELF

As Oscar Wilde noted, to love oneself is the beginning of a lifelong romance. You know you're special, and you deserve to be treated as such. Who better to cater to your every need but yourself? So today, come home early, run yourself a bubble bath, crack open a bottle of champagne, and treat yourself to a candlelit dinner where no one will bore you with selfish talk of themselves. And if the evening is successful, may we suggest you retire to the bedroom. Who knows, you might get lucky…

8

9

10

11

12

13

14

15

16

17

18

19

Telephone number home [   ]
Telephone number work [   ]
Telephone number mobile [   ]
Telephone number emergency [   ]
Telephone number of best friend [   ]
Fax number [   ]
Lottery numbers [   ]
Favourite number [   ]
Lucky number [   ]
Date of birth [   ]
Height [   ]
Shoe size [   ]
Collar size [   ]
Breast size [   ]
Penis size [   ]
Vision left eye [   ]
Vision right eye [   ]
Passport number [   ]
Credit card 1 number [   ]
Credit card 1 number [   ]
Credit card 1 number [   ]
Bank account number [   ]
Savings account number [   ]
National Insurance number [   ]
Employee number [   ]
Current salary [   ]
Private health insurance number [   ]
Home insurance number [   ]
Age [   ]
Age when first spoke [   ]
Age when first kissed [   ]
Age when first lost virginity [   ]
Age when married [   ]
Number of people slept with [   ]
Street number [   ]
Flat number [   ]
Number of TV channels [   ]
Number of favourite TV channel [   ]
Number of siblings [   ]
Number of cousins [   ]
Number of children [   ]

Write down all the numbers in your life

Numbers rule our lives.
As a society develops, more and more numbers accrue to its individual members. A fully evolved citizen should easily be able to fill in this chart.

Monday 29 November

8
9
10
11
12
13
14
15
16
17
18
19

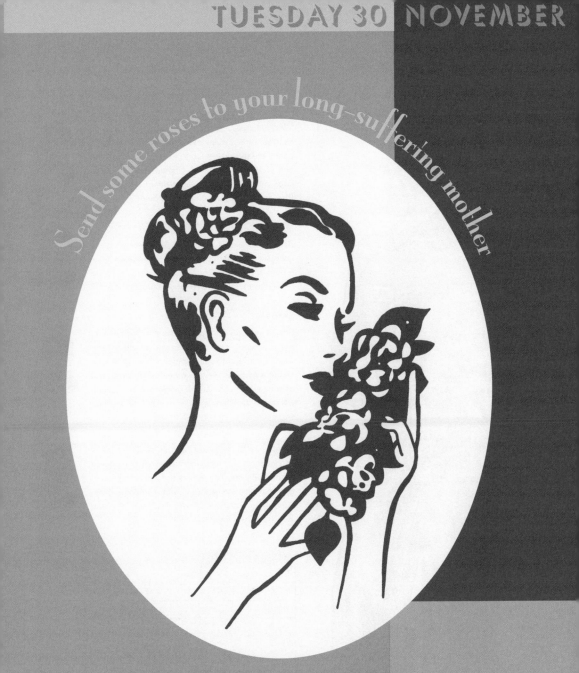

Send some roses to your long-suffering mother

HOW MANY SHOULD YOU SEND?
START WITH 12, AND ADD OR DEDUCT AS FOLLOWS:

SHE BREASTFED YOU +3, SHE DROPPED YOU −4, SHE GAVE UP PROMISING CAREER FOR YOU +2, SHE OVERPROTECTED YOU −2, SHE TRIED HER BEST +1, SHE SMOKED DURING PREGNANCY −3, SHE'S STILL YOUR BEST FRIEND +5 (WOMEN) −5 (MEN).

8		14	
9		15	
10		16	
11		17	
12		18	
13		19	

Today become a master of wine

Why remain a philistine when you could enjoy your drink more and impress society with your savoir-vivre in four easy steps:

1. SWIRL

Hold your glass at a steady angle then swirl it in a controlled movement, so it doesn't ruin your shirt and credibility (practise at home first if unsure). Look out for its colour (light/deep) and its legs (how long it clings to the inner side of the glass).

2. SNIFF

Stick your nostrils over the freshly-swirled glass (swirling frees up the smell) and take a deep nasal breath. Does it smell fruity/old/fresh/of shit (good red burgundy)/of cat's pee (good sauvignon blanc)?

3. TASTE

Still considered a key part of the wine experience. Rinse around your tonsils as you would mouth-wash, then (and this is the clever bit), open your mouth slightly while the wine is still there and breathe in to let the flavour oxygenate. At first you will choke, and then spew all over soft furnishings and make a fool of yourself. Persist.

4. SPIT

The toughest step for many, but essential to convey professionalism. The trick is to form a semi-solid gob that hits the spittoon with a metallic clink, rather than a shower of particles, 90% of which miss the target entirely. Voilà!

WEDNESDAY 1 DECEMBER
8
9
10
11
12
13
14
15
16
17
18

8

9

10

11

12

13

14

15

16

17

18

Today disappear
Don't you sometimes wish you could start all over
again? How difficult would it be just to walk away
from your life, and begin afresh somewhere else?
Test the waters by spending the day on the run from
your friends, family, and colleagues.

RULES OF SPACE TOURISM. The Diary authors take it upon themselves to regulate space tourism to prevent it from spoiling the galaxy. RULE 1) No casting of empty cans, beer bottles or other trash into deep space. RULE 2) If everyone took a bit of the moon home, soon there'd be none left. RULE 3) Safety: to avoid muggings, do not walk on the dark side of the moon unaccompanied. RULE 4) Do not feed the aliens. RULE 5) No »my space helmet's leaking aaarrrgghh!« jokes. Photography no-no: pics of Planet Earth are such a cliché. How exactly are yours going to be different?

8	12	16
9	13	17
10	14	18
11	15	19

Today dig at the end of a rainbow

Myths often survive throughout the ages because they contain a grain of truth. Find out if this one is true today, and you may reap huge rewards, and very possibly get to marry Cinderella as well.

1) Call up your local weather office for information on probable occurrences of rainbows in your area, based on satellite imagery of cloud formation.

2) Triangulate the exact coordinates of the rainbow's end, and track them down using a portable GPS system.

3) Secure the area and excavate a 1 hectare site, aiming for an average drilling depth of 3 metres. Use a magnetometer to establish an electromagnetic and geophysical profile of the zone.

4) Sift for any pots of gold. Be sure to have legal help-at-hand to assert your right of ownership and patent the »Rainbow-Digging« process.

Warning: if the rainbow happens to end on a bank, find another one.

8
9
10
11
12
13
14
15
16
17
18

24k Gold

Carnivorous Day! Today eat nothing but red meat!

Man is a carnivorous mammal, who owes his domination of the earth to a diet of high-protein raw meat. This is all too often forgotten in our anaemic vegetarianistic limp-wristed times. Regain some of those red blood cells with this man-sized feast.
BREAKFAST: 6 sausages with ketchup and/or mustard.
LUNCH: fry yourself 2–3 burgers (easy on those fatty sauces now).
DINNER: a nice big roast.
MIDNIGHT SNACK: nothing like a couple of meat pies to help you sleep.

8

9

10

11

12

13

14

15

16

17

18

Do something kinky today
Here are some little-known kinks to trigger your imagination.
Please note that illegal ones are marked with a star.

Oculolinctus:
licking partner's
eyeball

Axillism:
use of the
armpit for sex

Zoophilia:
use of animals
in sex play*

Tithiolagnia:
having an orgasm
while breast-feeding

Urticophilia:
use of nettles
in sex play

Botulinonia:
sex with a sausage

Pygmalionism:
sex with statues

Agoraphilia:
sex in a
public place

Antholagnia:
getting turned on by
the smell of flowers

Entomophilia:
use of insects
in sex play

8
9
10
11
12
13

14
15
16
17
18
19

Monday 6 December

Tuesday 7 December
Magic of Xmas Day:
convince a kid Santa does exist!

8	
9	
10	
11	
12	
13	
14	
15	
16	
17	
18	

Choose from the following foolproof arguments depending on how precocious the kid is.

»Simple« kids:
Where do you think presents come from then, you little mook?

Average kids:
How do you know he doesn't exist?

Swotty kids:
Of course Father Xmas could deliver gifts in millions of chimneys at once; quantum physics has proven that particles can be in more than one place at a time, unless someone is watching in which case their quantum waveform collapses. QED.

PRE-FEMINISM DAY

The most radical change of the twentieth century has been in the relationship between men and women. It is the first time in history that women have been even approximately treated as equal. Today, revert to pre-feminist behaviour to measure the difference.

WOMEN:
1) Make sure you look your best
2) Don't speak unless spoken to
3) Stay at home and do the housework
4) Cook a nice dinner for your man
5) Ask him for some pocket money for a new dress

MEN:
1) Open doors, stand up, take your hat off
2) Buy your lady some flowers on your way back from work
3) Compliment her on her cooking
4) Sssshhhh her if she voices a foolish opinion
5) Skip foreplay, roll over and snore

WEDNESDAY 8 DECEMBER

8	14
9	15
10	16
11	17
12	18
13	19

8

9

10

11

12

13

Swap jobs with a friend just for today Make sure you get your co-workers on board: say Bob couldn't make it today unfortunat
but he's delegating to you his most trusted friend and he's explained how to do it in detail. Now what are those red dials for aga

14

15

16

17

18

19

Friday 10 December
Today at 11am, we will hide £1000
in this tree. If you recognize the tree,
the money is yours for the taking!

CLUE:
the tree is situated
in a park, not far from
the park entrance.

8	14	
9	15	
10	16	
11	17	
12	18	
13	19	

Today collect your belly button fluff and send it in.
WE WILL USE IT TO KNIT A MULTICOLORED SWEATER FOR THIS DOG.
»What if I have an outie?« About 10% of the population have an »outie«,
so you are not alone. Doctors disagree as to the cause of the condition.
The most popular current theory is that they are caused by an umbilical
hernia: a small circular defect in the baby's abdominal wall that fails to
heal during the first few years. The condition is essentially harmless,
but unfortunately it means you will never have belly button fluff.

SATURDAY 11 DECEMBER

| 8 |
| 9 |
| 10 |
| 11 |
| 12 |
| 13 |
| 14 |
| 15 |
| 16 |
| 17 |
| 18 |

Sunday 12 December
Today plan for your old age

Prudent financial planning is indispensable to ensure a decent income in your sunset years. The earlier you start the better. Work out your needs with this simple formula.

How much you need
Mansion £1,000,000
Yacht £200,000
Cosmetic surgery £20,000
Golf £5,000/year
Viagra £5,000/year
Trip down Nile £5,000/year
Medical care £10,000/year
Prepaid funeral expenses £5,000

Total T

How many years before you retire R

T/R=how much you need
        to save a year

Typical example:
Photocopier technician Pete Donnelly is 42. He wants to retire at 60 and die at 90. His total T is therefore £1,975,000. Divide by number of years until he retires (R=18), which means Pete needs to save a mere £109,800 a year to retire in comfort. Good luck Pete. Now how about you?

8		14
9		15
10		16
11		17
12		18
13		19

8	14
9	15
10	16
11	17
12	18
13	19

HECKLER PUT-DOWNS

A good speech will attract hecklers. Here's how to deal with them subtly but firmly.

»Have you missed your medication again?«

»Is that your face or did your neck throw up?«

»The alcoholics anonymous meeting is the next door down.«

»Hey, I could have been your Dad but the dog beat me over the fence.«

»Shut up! Shut up! Shut! Up!«

What's the point of having opinions if you don't share them with your fellow countrymen? A good speech can jilt a conscience, start a revolution, move you to tears, sometimes even get you laid. Choose a suitably public spot, stand on a box of some kind, and spew forth on a controversial topic.

WHAT GOES AROUND COMES AROUND: A STORY.

START TO A TRAMP GIVE £20

WITH £20, THE TRAMP WILL HAVE ENOUGH TO SPEND THE NIGHT IN A HOSTEL, AND A LITTLE TO SPARE.

WITH THAT LITTLE TO SPARE, HE WILL BE ABLE TO AFFORD A NICE WARM COFFEE.

IN THE COFFEESHOP, HE WILL SIT NEXT TO A RICH FAT MAN AND HIS FAT YOUNG SON AND HEIR.

THE FAT YOUNG HEIR WILL DROP HIS EXPENSIVE FOUNTAIN PEN ON THE WAY OUT.

THE TRAMP WILL NOTICE, PICK IT UP AND FOLLOW THEM OUT TO RETURN IT.

THE RICH MAN WILL TAKE FRIGHT UNTIL HE REALIZES THE TRAMP MEANS WELL.

HE WILL THEN REWARD THE TRAMP, BUT PROBABLY NOT WITH £20. THE END

Tuesday 14 December

8
9
10
11
12
13
14
15
16
17
18

TODAY
DON'T ANSWER
THE PHONE

When Bell invented the telephone in
1876, people predicted it would never
catch on; being summoned by a ring wa
strictly for servants. And indeed, why le
others dictate your movements? Strike a
blow for personal freedom by ignoring th
confounded machine.

8

9

10

11

12

14

15

16

17

18

19

TODAY CHOP DOWN A XMAS TREE YOURSELF

A man who lets others cut down his Christmas tree for him is no kind of a man.
So hie thee to the nearest forest with an axe and get chopping.

HOW TO FELL A TREE PROFESSIONALLY

Chop downwards diagonally at a 65° degree angle

65°

Chop all around the tree towards the centre

Wait until the tree stands only by the thinnest wedge of wood

Push it with your little finger, cartoon-style

Yell »TIMBER« loudly, before the tree falls

timber

Check that you have felled the right kind of tree

OOPS

IRON MAIDEN

8
9
10
11
12
13

14
15
16
17
18
19

Today, join the Freemasons

Freemasonry: world-dominating conspiracy or well-meaning brotherhood of man? There's only one way to find out and that's to sign up! Today, send in your petition to become a Mason to your nearest Masonic Lodge (address it to the Worshipful Master).

Ancient, Free and Accepted Masons

I, the undersigned, a firm believer in the existence of a Supreme Being, respectfully request that I be considered for initiation unto the secrets of the masonic order. I hereby give my word that am not motivated by mercenary or other unworthy motives; that I am prompted by a favourable view of the Institution and a desire to learn of its mysteries; and that, if chosen, I will conform to the various usages and codes of the order.

Name...

Age...

Profession...

Wealth..

....

Are you of sound bodily health?.............

Do you have any physical defects?..........

Are you loyal to your country?................

Have you an upright heart and mind?......

Sign here twice...................................

....

Recommendations by two existing Masons

I am a member of ....masonic lodge and have been since...... I have personally known the petitioner for ....years, and vouch him to be a well-disposed candidate who will reflect well on our institution.

Signed...

I am a member of ....masonic lodge and have been since...... I have personally known the petitioner for ....years, and vouch him to be a well-disposed candidate who will reflect well on our institution.

Signed...

What happens next? Your local lodge will contact you in due course and speak to your family and employers, to ascertain your good standing in society. If accepted unanimously by the existing members, you will receive your first degree (the Degree of Entered Apprentice), learn a catechism covering your degree and be examined by your fellow Masons. You will then be taught the secret handshakes and start making steady progress in your political career.

G

8
9
10
11
12
13
14
15
16
17
18

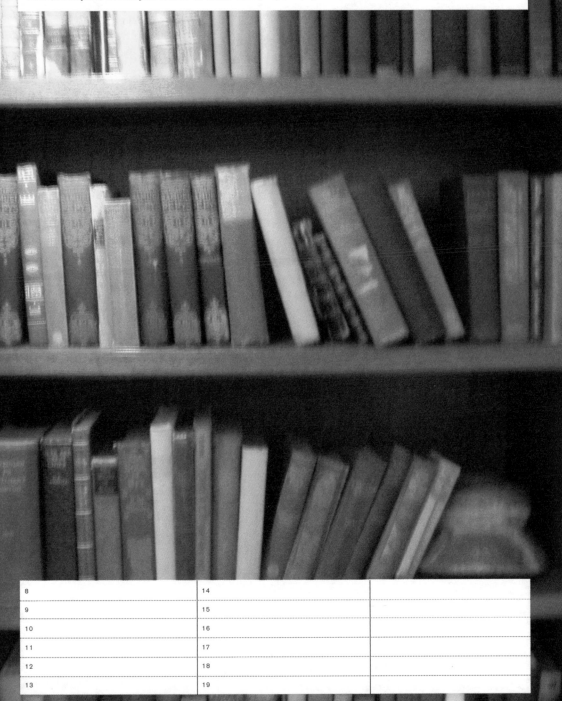

Go into a bookshop and discreetly sign a few books by classic authors to enhance their value. Some famous signatures to emulate: *Tolstoy, Proust, Shakespeare, Dickens, Jane Austen, Cervantes, Goethe, Kafka.*

NOTE ON VERISIMILITUDE: insofar as possible, try to use contemporaneous writing materials, e.g. ink and quills rather than ballpoint pens, markers or pencils.

8	14	
9	15	
10	16	
11	17	
12	18	
13	19	

Etiquette:
Do not plonk the money down on the bedside table ostentatiously as you would with a common whore or gigolo. Rather, give your loved one a naughty wink and slip it into their bra or jockstrap (try to use banknotes rather than coins). How much should you give? Current recommended rates are £5/hour, plus tax where applicable.

SUNDAY 19 DECEMBER

8	14
9	15
10	16
11	17
12	18
13	19

Today challenge everyone you meet to a game of noughts and crosses. By the end of the day you will know how mentally agile you are relative to your social circle.

Tuesday 21 December

8

9

10

11

12

13

14

15

16

17

18

19

Who ever thinks of Mother Christmas?

Pay her tribute today by going up to a Father Christmas in the street or in a store and asking him to please pass on your best wishes. Better still, give him a little something for his under-appreciated wife (feminine protection items are in particularly short supply in the North Pole).

SWEET LIL' MAMA! COULDN'T DO IT WITHOUT YA

What Mother Christmas does:

- •Mother Xmas wraps all the presents
- •Mother Xmas polishes the sleigh
- •Mother Xmas keeps the grotto tidy
- •Mother Xmas deals with the accountants
- •Mother Xmas cleans Father Xmas's outfit after all those filthy chimneys
- •Mother Xmas feeds the greedy reindeer
- •Mother Xmas gives the elves a spanking when they're naughty
- •Mother Xmas sorts out the proper letters from all the junk mail
- •Mother Xmas works out the itinerary
- •Mother Xmas files the class action lawsuits against the lying evil bastards who say Father Xmas doesn't exist

Hip Hip Hurrah for Mother Christmas!

8	14
9	15
10	16
11	17
12	18
13	19

Today come out as a Diary-owner

Wear one red sock and let's find out how many of us are out there. If you spot someone sporting a red sock today, engage them in conversation. You may assume straight off that as Diary-owners they are bright discerning individuals with a good sense of humour and finely-honed critical faculties, and therefore well-worth knowing. They are not going to respond to some oafish overture like »nice sock!« wink-wink. To help, here are some recommended witty ice-breakers that will help establish kinship. »At the risk of putting my foot in it, may I compliment you on your sock« »Together we're quite the pair, wouldn't you say?« »I'll be darned if we haven't met before!« »If you don't want to chat , do tell me to put a sock in it…«

Thursday 23 December
8
9
10
11
12
13
14
15
16
17
18

TODAY: SKETCH SOMEONE OPPOSITE YOU ON PUBLIC TRANSPORT AND SEE HOW THEY REACT

8
9
10
11
12
13
14
15
16
17
18

In case of violent reaction, show them this:

The bearer of this document has been mandated by the public transport authorities to effect paper likenesses of individual users of aforesaid public transport facilities for the purposes of national security. Civilians are asked to cooperate with enquiries under pain of prosecution.

Merry Christmas

To mark this special day, the makers of the Diary are personally offering $1,000,000 to anyone who catches Santa and delivers him to us alive. Not only that, but in addition to the cash prize, you will go down in history as the person who caught Santa and put an end to Xmas!

How do you know you've got the real Santa and not some over-enthusiastic Dad or would-be kiddie fiddler merely dressed up as Santa? Answer: the genuine Santa has a tattoo of Lapland on his left buttock, complete with all the fjords and their individual estuaries.

XMAS PRIZE: $1,000,000!!!

8

9

10

11

12

13

14

15

16

17

18

19

DISINHERIT A RELATIVE!

Boxing Day is traditionally a good time for family feuds. This year, see if you can turn the usual post-prandial squabbles into a fully-fledged Mafia-style deal. To raise the stakes, use expressions such as »I renounce you«, »You are no longer my mother«, or »I can't believe you are the fruit of my loins«. The resulting conversation will certainly beat falling asleep in front of the TV.

8	14
9	15
10	16
11	17
12	18
13	19

✖ STARTING POINT

What is this ant trying to say to you?

If the pattern seems mainly circular, the ant is establishing a rapport with you.

If the pattern seems essentially diagonal, the ant senses danger. Beware.

If the pattern seems hexagonal, that is one clever ant.

If the pattern seems phallic, you probably need psychiatric assistance.

If the ant leaves the page, he's saying he has better stuff to do than talk to a dumb-looking schmuck of a human being such as you. Kill it to teach it a Darwinian lesson.

MONDAY 27 DECEMBER

8	14
9	15
10	16
11	17
12	18
13	19

Today imagine what it would be like to be this person.

Are you fulfilled? What is your job? Do you break down and sob quietly in the middle of the night? Are you sex-mad? What is your dream in life? Have you ever known true love?

8

9

10

11

12

13

14

15

16

17

18

19

Increase your tolerance to »hot« food.

Most Westerners are used to bland seasonings, though with a bit of exercise they could get used to the spicier diets that other civilizations enjoy. Today, work out your current limits.

WEDNESDAY 29 DECEMBER	
8	
9	
10	
11	
12	
13	
14	
15	
16	
17	
18	
19	

The heat level of a dish can be graded thanks to the Scoville Organoleptic Test, originally developed for chilli peppers. The hottest chilli pepper in the world, the Red Savina Habanero, weighs in at a whopping 577,000 Scoville units.

chilli markings table

2 SCOVILLES	25 SCOVILLES
COTTAGE PIE (LO-SALT)	HAM&MUSTARD SANDWICH
600 SCOVILLES	**5000 SCOVILLES**
CHILLI CON CARNE	JALAPENO PEPPER SALSA
40000 SCOVILLES	**200000 SCOVILLES**
TABASCO	DAVE'S GOOD' OL' ALABAMA DEATH SAUCE (AVOID SKIN CONTACT)

We asked Mexican gourmet Alberto Rodriguez Sr his opinion of a typical Western dish, macaroni cheese: »This is very boring for me, just mushy mush, I had to pour a whole bottle of tabasco in before it even registered on the taste buds. And this you call a great delicacy? *Madre de dios* etc etc...«

THE SECRET OF CHILLIES: CAPSAICINOIDS! Chillies get their supernatural heat from chemicals called capsaicins, compounds from the vanilloid family. They bind themselves to pain receptors on the tongue, causing a flow of calcium ions between molecules that translates into a burning sensation. In concentrated form, capsaicin can reach 16,000,000 scovilles, over 25 times as hot as the hottest chilli pepper ever recorded. Pure capsaicin is a highly dangerous irritant: chemists who work with it have to wear full hooded protective suits to avoid inhaling it accidentally. One milligram on the skin would lead to instant severe blistering! Here is how to extract it. Purée a dozen habaneros in a blender with a large quantity of ethanol. Leave overnight. Filter the resulting sludge and evaporate (do not use naked flames!), until a brick-red oil is precipitated on the surface. Suck off the oil with a pipette. It should be 40% capsaicin. Do not ingest or touch.

Try one of these sexual positions
Beginners: 2, 3, 8. Intermediate: 1, 7, 9.
Advanced: 4, 5 ,6. Porn star: 10–16.

8 ....
9 ....
10 ....
11 ....
12 ....
13 ....
14 ....
15 ....
16 ....
17 ....
18 ....

NEW YEAR'S EVE »NEW YOU« PARTY

Well done! You have completed a full year of life-changing instructions. By now, you should be a completely different person. Throw a party where you will unveil the »new you« to your friends and acquaintances.

You will probably find that your entourage no longer suits the new you. Where once you were quite happy to discuss last night's reruns of Cheers, now you crave conversation of a more cultivated nature, like some light badinage about Brecht perhaps? Two solutions offer themselves to you. First, give all your old friends a copy of the Diary so they can catch up with you. Second, discard them and acquire some new ones.

8		14
9		15
10		16
11		17
12		18
13		

CONGRATULATIONS!

You have lived with the Diary for 366 days now, 366 days of rollercoaster emotion that will no doubt have transformed your life in a million different ways (or more). So well done for sticking with it. As a token of our gratitude and admiration, here is a coupon which entitles you to a whole 5 pence off the 2005 edition of THIS DIARY WILL CHANGE YOUR LIFE.

Retailer: please give this gentleman or lady 5p off the cost of This Diary Will Change Your Life 2005, and send the bill to Penguin. Thank you.

Visit www.thiswebsitewillchangeyourlife.com
to register your achievement and receive your prize!
No, don't thank us. It is we who thank you.

The history of the Diary

Most readers will be surprised to learn that the diary is not entirely new. The present authors have endeavoured to bring it back to life. But it has a long and rich history, which Dr. Gunther Pedersen of the Bern Institute of Cultural Studies (Kulturelles Zentrum, Bern) has researched for this edition.

The precise origins of THIS DIARY WILL CHANGE YOUR LIFE are a matter of academic dispute. So divided are scholars even as to its original title, the truth may never be conclusively established. Over the centuries it has been known variously as »The Book of Days«, »Fate's Very Own Calendar«, »Perish Ye Whom Glance Herein«, »365 Rollickin' Rides« and »Die Entdeckung der Weltgeschichte« – amongst many others. Nevertheless we will attempt to outline in broad terms its history, pointing out inconsistencies and gaps in our knowledge, bearing in mind along the way that, as the great Carlyle has said, ultimately »history is but a distillation of rumour«.

The first mention of the Diary is to be found in Herodotus, the Greek »father of history«, writing in about 450BC. He refers to »the curious custom practiced by the Pelasgians of following everyday of the calendar rites written on their oracle's tablets« (*Histories*, VI.56). Herodotus discusses the derivation of this custom: »I may say, for instance, that it was the daughters of Danaos who brought this ceremony from Egypt and instructed the Pelagian women in it.« (II. 171). The Pelasgians, of course, mentioned both by Herodotus and the more reliable Thucydides, are recognized as the majority tribe within the nomadic population of Greece and the Aegean, before their gradual assimilation by the Hellenes. There is therefore a strong case to suggest that the very origins of the Diary can be traced beyond the classical age and back to Egyptian civilization, the ultimate cradle of our culture.

Indeed, some have seen fit to speculate on the influence of the (as yet nameless) Diary on Egyptian history. Could Pharaoh Akhnaton's contempt for age-old tradition, for instance, stem from his worship of the Diary's ancestor? Certainly much has been made of the fact that when his sarcophagus was opened by the American amateur Egyptologist Theodore Davis in 1907, the dusty and unreadable remnants of twelve papyrus scrolls were found at his side. But in truth there is no solid evidence to back this claim.

At this point we should attempt to shed some light on two contentious issues. First of all, which of the multifarious versions is the genuine Diary? Fakes and translations are legion. For our purposes, the real Diary is the so-called Greek version, as found in Constantinople in 1422 by scholar Giovanni Aurispa

(of whom more later). Both in depth and in originality, it stands out as the truest incarnation of the Diary, as anyone who cares to study it at the British Museum will surely agree (by appointment with the British Museum Special Finds Dept, London WC1B 3DG). We call it the »Original Diary«, though no one has managed to pinpoint its ultimate authors (many have tried; see for instance H. Beckenbauer, *The origins of the Diary: Atlantis revealed?*«, Eon Press, 1954).

Secondly, why is there so little mention of this ancient text in conventional histories? The answer will become readily apparent as we proceed; the Diary is essentially an instrument of radical change, unleashing forces too powerful for authorities to control. Thus it has been ignored and hidden away in official accounts; for those who know to look though, its footprints are everywhere.

Following Herodotus, The Diary resurfaces now and again in Greek fragments, mostly concerned with Orphism. Anaximander, for instance, tells us of γμγενειζ, »loosely translated as »The Book Of Days« It is perhaps then no coincidence that Plato is the first to refer to it at any length, for we know he spent 12 years in Egypt and a deep understanding of Orphic cosmology permeates his works (his contemporary Krantor in fact accused him of lifting the *Republic's* political hierarchy straight from the Egyptian caste system). In a little-known appendix to his *Symposium*, he has prophetess Diotima of Mantinea argue the following: »What do you think, Socrates, of the study that Euthydemus and others make of that Phoebean text in which their pursuits are commanded day by day? Haven't you noticed how the course of their existence is varied, when so many people in Athens repeat everyday yesterday's actions again. Don't you agree?« »By Zeus I do!« said [Socrates]. »Well then, [said Diotima], can we say that this text is a medium for messages between mortals and the goddess Fate?« Socrates then goes off on something of a tangent regarding the parentage of said goddess Fate; but it is clear from this that the Diary was in use round about 400BC. It is also surely more than mere coincidence that it is mentioned in the course of the *Symposium*, famous for its emphasis on homosexual relations between adult males and young men. Could some early Diary injunction to experiment sexually have caught on in Greek culture?

The Diary then enters a long period of obscurity, along with so many classical masterpieces. True, there is the odd reference to it in Roman texts; Cicero associates it uncritically with Epicureanism, accusing it of being »so easily grasped and so much to the taste of the unlearned« (*Tusculan Disputations*, IV, 3). But in truth it was more suited to the imaginative Greek spirit than to the more plodding organizationally-minded Roman outlook, and so never really caught on.

Of course throughout Antiquity the DIARY was very much intertwined with religion. Early versions might have enjoined Phoenicians to sacrifice goats and suchlike. Indeed it is probable that the religious trend for issuing arbitrary instructions, such as the Ten Commandments, was derived from that very source. But it is with its rediscovery and adaptation in the Renaissance that it enters the modern age.

The Diary re-emerges – where else? – in Florence. Under Coluccio Salutati, Chancellor of Florence from 1375 to 1406, there came a new yearning for knowledge of the classical past. Very few authors remained in circulation, with some quasi-extinct; there was only one known manuscript of Catullus in existence anywhere, for example. In 1392 Coluccio himself found Cicero's »Epistolae Familiares«, which signalled the beginning of an intensive search for classical manuscripts. It was directed by Niccolo Niccoli, with the help of his right hand man, the irrepressibly enterprising Poggio Bracciolini.

In the summer of 1416, Poggio visited St Gall, a 7th century Benedictine monastery 20 miles from Constance in Switzerland. He asked to visit the library, which turned out to have been grossly neglected, »a most foul and dimly lighted dungeon at the very bottom of a tower«. As he leafed through the dusty old manuscripts, mostly in deplorable condition, Poggio's excitement grew. Here he had found a complete manuscript of Quintilian's *Training of an Orator*, substantial portions of Cicero, and a partial damaged Roman copy of something enigmatically named the »codex diei«, the book of days.

Poggio stayed at the monastery and copied it out himself with goose quills and inkhorn over 56 days. He then sent his copy back to Florence for which we must be grateful, as the original was lost in a monastery fire 7 years later. We are also in his debt for making it readable; the original, like most old parchment manuscripts, was copied out in minute Gothic text, which he exchanged for his own much rounder script (which in due course became the basis of modern handwriting).

It would be false to claim that the Florentines immediately recognized the value of the Diary, which is why it is hardly mentioned in contemporary accounts. This was partly because the Roman version they inherited was very much incomplete. Fragments such as »Today abandon all your pursuits in favour of the greatest good of them all ....chariot!« left them bemused rather than amazed. This all changed in 1423 when Giovanni Aurispa arrived in Italy with a vast hoard of original Greek manuscripts, 239 in all, including most of Greek literature: the *Iliad*, the *Odyssey*, Aeschylus, Sophocles, Euripides, Herodotus, Plato, and countless others, all of a sudden given to Florence, along with of course the original Greek copy of the Diary... This treasure chest of classical culture was seized, debated and lectured upon avidly by the Florentines. The young Greek scholar Marsilio Ficino translated Plato and the Diary, declaring the latter to be »one of the crowning achievements of classical civilization«. Indeed, his famous inscription in the hallway of the Academy, where the leading lights of Florence used to meet, was meant to bear witness to its influence: »Rejoice in the present«. Every citizen had a copy; Lorenzo de Medici had his bound in gold leaf. In retrospect, it is hard to resist the conclusion that the Diary contributed substantially to the conception of the individual that flowered in Quattrocento Florence. It enshrined the notion of »complete man«, one who realized all his innate qualities. It also chimed with the new Renaissance perception of time. The agricultural and monastical societies of the Middle Ages moved to the slow rhythm of the seasons and eternity. With their eye firmly fixed on the afterlife, they cared little for daily upheaval. But the Florentines were a manufacturing and trading people, to whom time was precious, to whom indeed time was money. It is no coincidence that a Florentine, Brunelleschi, invented the alarm clock (in between painting masterpieces and building his famous dome). The Renaissance man lived for the here and now, and prized every moment. The Diary was part and parcel of this Weltanschauung.

Along with so much else in Florentine civilisation, the Diary met its nemesis in the form of Dominican friar Savonarola, who took Florence by storm in the 1490's with his apocalyptic preaching of hellfire and brimstone against the corrupt citizens who had abandoned the gospels for more wordly pleasures and values. In Savonarola's vision of Florence as the new Jerusalem, there was no room for the impious free-thinking Diary. And in 1497, he tried to make sure all copies were burnt in his infamous Bonfire of the Vanities, along with copies of Boccaccio, Petrarch, paintings by Botticelli and other masterpieces. Almost all Diaries were thus consumed by the flames, and none would likely have survived if he had held power much longer. But in 1498 he finally went too far and was excommunicated by the Pope, then hanged in the Piazza della Signoria and thrown on a bonfire of his own. The Florentine Renaissance was at an end.

Thankfully one of the factors in its downfall also guaranteed its survival. When Charles VIII and the French Army invaded Italy in 1494, precipitating the demise of the Medici dynasty, they were spellbound by the scale and beauty of the Florentine achievement: the Medici palace, the sculptors and painters, the tapestries... And so as conquering king, he shipped back to Amboise 21 artists and craftsmen, manuscripts, pictures, over 34 tons of marble – effectively transplanting the Renaissance back to France.

The Diary went with him of course. It was in large part because the French held the original copy that Leonardo da Vinci accepted Francois I's offer to move to France from Italy in 1516, so that he could study it. For the next few centuries, under the absolutist reign of the Bourbon kings, the Diary held a much lower profile, and was considered mostly a quaint, even frivolous curio. Voltaire though saw its subversive potential and in 1778 translated it into French, none too scrupulously, adding much of his own trademark irony in the process.

CE JOURNAL VOUS CHANGERA LA VIE, as it had become, then re-emerged in aftermath of the French Revolution in the unlikely hands of Donatien Alphonse Francois Marquis de Sade. Sade, of course, was an indefatigable scribbler himself and it will readily be perceived how the JOURNAL's mix of arbitrary dictates fired up his imagination. A dozen days he wrote survive. The least unprintable enjoin followers to copulate variously with goats, toads, dwarves and grandmothers (the conceit here being to precipitate a fatal heart attack). Baudelaire claimed to have read the full-year Sadean version, describing it in his correspondence as a »veritable *Kamasutra* of pain«. No copy alas is extant.

The original Diary fell victim to Sade's notoriety and excesses. On March 6, 1801, Parisian police arrived suddenly to search the premises of Sade's publisher Nicolas Mosse, in hot pursuit of an obscure pamphlet, »*Zoloe*«, which Sade had allegedly penned against Napoleon and Josephine. The accusation turned out to be false, but the police nevertheless seized all the remaining stock of his novel *Juliette*, and of course his copy of the Diary. Napoleon, it seems, was ungrateful for this new acquisition, for he had Sade imprisoned without trial, and later transferred to Charenton insane asylum, where he stayed locked up until his death in 1814. In 1810, Napoleon punished him further by signing a decision to

keep him in detention and forbidding all communication with the outside world, depriving him also of any writing materials. Whether this fate would have befallen him without the Diary is quite possible, but it is clear that Napoleon's unlawful confiscation of such a valuable manuscript helped consign the Marquis to political oblivion.

There is no record of Napoleon himself directly referring to the Diary, but there is no doubt he would have perused it; it is known that he liked books – even in difficult times at St Helena he had 3370 books in his library. But as Madame de Remusat informs us, he was »really ignorant, having read very little and always hastily«. The Diary's clear and concise orders would have suited his military temperament.

Few of his career-defining decisions can be traced directly to the Diary's dictates, with one exception: the Louisiana Purchase. Historians have always been somewhat puzzled by Napoleon's agreement to suddenly relinquish French possession of what was then called Louisiana but in fact encompassed 13 current states and over 900,000 square miles, for a relative pittance (15 million dollars). This was one of the greatest real estate deals in history, doubling the size of the United States, transforming it into a world power and effectively ending France's dreams of worldwide presence overnight. No one was more surprised than Napoleon's finance minister, the Marquis de Barbe-Marbois, when he was instructed to reverse official policy on the morning of April 4, 1803. Perhaps if he had known that day's Original Diary entry, he would have been wiser: »Aujourd'hui, débarrassez vous d'une source d'ennui« (Today, get rid of something tiresome). Thus was the whole course of 19th century geopolitics and the destiny of nations transformed in one stroke.

On a more general note, it is surely not coincidental that the year Napoleon acquired the Diary corresponds to that when his ego exploded: he was already First Consul by 1801, but by 1802 he had made himself Consul for Life, and by 1804 he was Emperor. Perhaps he took the Diary's emphasis on extreme individualism at face value. Some historians even posit he kept it close to his heart in his famous Imperial greatcoat, hence his famous position right hand tucked inside the tunic. Certainly he took it with him on all his major campaigns, and indeed this is how it was acquired by its next owner, one Alexei Fedrovsky. As Napoleon retreated across the Berezina in December 1812 after his disastrous invasion of Russia, one of his staff officers, a Bordelais by the name of Ramballe, was hastily put in charge of the Emperor's remaining possessions as Bonaparte fled back to Paris in a fur-laden sleigh.

Ramballe was immortalized by Tolstoy in *War and Peace*, where we find him ragged and near-delirious with his orderly Morel sharing a campfire with Russian soldiers near Krasnoe. Alas, he never made it back to Bordeaux. Like so many thousands, both French and Russian, worn out by the sub-zero temperatures and incessant gales, he froze to death drunk in the knee-deep snow on the roadside near Orsk, only ten miles from the Prussian border. The Diary was found amongst other papers by a band of pillaging cossacks, more interested in mens' boots than any obscure bundle of documents. They dumped the lot at their local billet, the castle of Alexei Fedrovsky, a count exiled from Moscow for political reasons in 1807. Alexei was famous for his imaginative cruelty: on at least one documented occasion, he sent his servants out early one morning to the local weekly village market, ordering them to buy up all the food available so that his peasant neighbours would have to starve for the week.

Fedrovsky was an early exponent of Russian political dissent, a radical before his time and more by temperament than ideology: he advocated the overthrow of Tsar Alexander on the grounds that his beard was not sufficiently manly. Rather like Sade, he was exiled at the insistence of his family, who kept finding their relative the laughing stock of Muscovite society. Nevertheless, Fedrovsky maintained links with the early precursors of Russian dissent. Though he did not make much use of the Diary himself (except when following its edicts could annoy his loved ones), he did pass it on upon his death in 1827, along with copious notes on facial hair throughout history, to his anarchist friend Bakunin. Bakunin, at the time, was not yet quite the international firebrand and scourge of governments worldwide that he became in the 1850s. But he was still too impetuous and restless to sit down and take orders from a mere book. He was also permanently penniless, and thus it came that he gave the Diary away in exchange for some cabbage soup at the house of a friend of his in 1832.

Fortunately, this friend was none other than literary critic Vissarion Grigorievich Belinsky, perhaps the man most deserving of the Diary anywhere on the planet at the time.

By the early 1830s, Russia was a moral and intellectual vacuum. The burgeoning young intelligentsia was desperate for spiritual nourishment, caught between the dumbly repressive autocracy of Nicolas I on the one hand, and the illiterate groaning peasant masses on the other. With no native role models to look up to, the Russian youth avidly absorbed every Western notion with a hint of revolutionary change. This was fertile ground for the Diary, and no one took it up more forcefully than their effective spokesman, Belinsky, the »conscience of the

Russian intelligentsia« as Isaiah Berlin so aptly terms him. To Belinsky, books and ideas represented salvation from the grim material philistine circumstances of Russian life. His was a philosophy of engagement; a man's life should reflect his beliefs, however much of a struggle was involved. Behaviour had to follow on from ideas. He lived in a state of permanent moral frenzy, of constant searching after the true ends of life. It is no surprise that the Diary, with its zeal for unending revolutionary experimentation and disregard for social conventions, appealed to him immediately. He copied out some of the more extreme days like »Go up to a member of the ruling classes and tell him how ignomious he is« or the religious-themed »God is dead. Make a small clay model of him and bury him in your back garden« and disseminated them amongst his friends and fellow radicals. He even penned a few pages of his own on the subject of serfdom (»Grab the nearest serf and run for the woods to free him«, »Paint ›serfdom is the doom of the human spirit‹ on the wall of the Kremlin«). This sort of sentiment did not endear him to the Tsarist police as can readily be imagined.

And indeed it is reading out these pages of Belinsky's (and not merely his more famous 1847 *Letter to Gogol*«) that got Dostoevsky condemned to death and sent to Siberia. By then Belinsky had alas died of consumption. But such had been his influence that he can legitimately be called one of the founders of the movement that led to the Russian Revolution.

After his death the Diary continued as one of the underground texts that fuelled the revolutionary fire across Russia and in the various places of exile where Russian radicals congregated. Though it has to be said that Belinsky probably best understood the essence of the Diary, which is its permanent encouragement of the flowering of the individual human spirit, the expression of the whole of man's nature, unfettered by the shackles of tradition. Later generations of revolutionaries were to put it to far more prosaic use. For the rest of the 19th century the Diary passed from radical to radical. It is difficult to know its exact history during this period as its successive owners were understandably publicity-shy and left few traces of their whereabouts and activities. The Populist-turned-Marxist leader Plekhanov seems to have recuperated it sometime in the 1880s. He in turn entrusted it to his star pupil Lenin, who found its radical tone of great comfort during his lonely years abroad in Geneva and Paris. Indeed it played a direct part in the Russian Revolution. During the 1905 uprising, Lenin had decided to stay abroad, obeying his more prudent instincts. When it came to the February 1917 uprising though, he consulted the Diary on February 12, which urged him thus: »Today plan a surprise trip somewhere hot«. Immediately he resolved to set off for Moscow in the famous sealed train and changed the course of the revolution, ending with the Bolshevik takeover in October 1917.

More generally, it is clear that the nature of Lenin's rule was influenced by the Diary, as reflected both in his ruthless drive and in the speed of his decisions. By the time Lenin died in 1924, he had grown mistrustful of both his comrades Trotsky and Stalin, and so bequeathed the Diary to Nicholas Bukharin, whom he called in his testament »the greatest and most valuable theoretician of the party«. His theorizing was no real match for Stalin's peasant cunning though, and the Diary soon got Bukharin into trouble. To be fair, it was no easy task to Sovietize what was essentially an individualistic bible, no matter how glorious its part in the history of the Revolution. Whole schools were given special versions, with tasks such as »Today, work to achieve the goals of the Five-Year-Plan« or »Dispose of ten kulaks by lunchtime!« (at the height of the collectivisation hysteria in 1929). Yet this did not go far enough for Stalin. Unintentional lapses such as »How much do you love Comrade Stalin on a scale of 1 to 1000?« were seen as perilously close to inviting dissent, and undoubtedly contributed to the downfall and eventual execution of Bukharin. But there was worse to come for the Diary, or rather its bastardized Stalinist form. By the early 30s, such was Stalin's paranoia and fear of »Trotskyist contraband« that everything published (not just the Diary) was expected to be rewritten in his own personal style. Half the days in the 1934 »Correct edition« were about Stalin directly (»Compose a realist poem to the glory of the Revolution and its leader and nail it to an enemy of the working classes«). The other half were merely written in his plodding repetitious pseudo-scientific manner (»Today help organize your local communist associations with a view to undermining international capitalist superstructures«). Eventually fault was found with this edition too and its supervisor Sokolnikov was purged in the »Trial of the Seventeen« in 1937. Thus ended the sorry saga of the Soviet Diary.

Fortunately for us, the original emerged unscathed. Trotsky, who had seen which way the wind was blowing, managed to

procure Bukharin's copy and took it with him in exile in 1929. He wandered about for years, persecuted at a distance by Stalin who still feared his moral authority, until he eventually landed in Mexico. There he found a house in Coyoacan near Mexico City with his wife Natalia Sedova. The Mexican Communist Party was strong but deeply divided into Stalinist and anti-Stalinist factions. Trotsky soon settled in, making friends with local sympathizers. He was particularly close to revolutionary muralist Diego Rivera and even closer to his painter wife Frida

Kahlo. Rivera had helped Trotsky gain asylum in Mexico; they were comrades until 1938 when they split over ideological differences, and rumours of an affair between Trotsky and Kahlo.

Finally history caught up with him when Spanish communist and Stalinist agent Ramon Mercador smashed his head with an alpine pickaxe on August 20, 1940 while he was writing an accusatory biography of his nemesis. Rather gruesomely, he did not die from the blow but stood straight up, screamed, and started pelting his assassin with everything within reach, including his dictaphone. His eventual death the next night went relatively unnoticed, as the world was otherwise preoccupied at the time.

Trotsky's wife Natalia couldn't find the Diary after her husband's traumatic death. She suspected Stalin's agents had stolen it back, but the truth was closer to home. Frida Kahlo had indeed had an affair with Trotsky, in the course of which she'd borrowed the Diary. When the two of them broke up under suspicion from their spouses, she never returned it. Trotsky would not have been best pleased with her behaviour after his death: both her and Rivera showed little sympathy for him, seeking readmission to the Stalinist Mexican Communist Party and denouncing Trotskyism. Kahlo added insult to injury by slandering Trotsky as a thief and a coward. Her last painting was an unfinished portrait of Stalin, started

Communist sympathizers, and Trotsky's copy of the Diary, no doubt regarding it as some kind of timing masterplan for global insurrection.

The investigation into Kahlo's anti-American activities eventually petered out for want of firm evidence. No mention is made of the Diary, for the simple reason that Hoover kept it to himself. Like so many powerful men before him, he fell under its spell. Perhaps to those used to the hubris of arbitrary authority and unquestioning obedience, submitting to the Diary's straightforward orders represented something of a liberation.

At any event, its influence on Hoover was more tragicomic than machiavellic. The entry that particularly caught his eye was March 24, 1958: »Experiment with forbidden fantasies«. The result saw him attending at least two gay orgies at the New York Plaza Hotel in 1958, wearing »a fluffy black dress with flounces and lace stockings and high heels and a black curly wig« according to one witness. He was introduced as »Mary« and allegedly engaged in sex with boys as the Bible was read to him, throwing the Good Book down at climax. The latter claim is not considered reliable; but certainly the episode explains why the FBI had limited success against the Mafia during his tenure. With blackmail material such as this, underworld bosses Frank Costello and Meyer Lansky had little to fear from J. Edgar.

The Diary has lain in Hoover's classified files since his death in 1972. Under Exec. Order 11152 it was meant to be declassified 30 years

after the dictator's death in 1953, and interrupted by Kahlo's suicide in 1954. By one of those minor quirks of which history is fond, the Diary then ended up in the hands of the FBI. Kahlo had died at the height of the McCarthyite hysteria in the US. Under heavy political pressure, all government security agencies were looking for reds under the American bed, particularly writers and artists whom everyone knew were susceptible to communist leanings at the best of times. Mexico was America's backyard. Naturally the spotlight fell on Rivera and Kahlo, artists of international renown with documented links to one of the chief instigators of the Russian Revolution.

J. Edgar Hoover himself, head of the bureau since 1924 and vehement anti-commie, took an interest in their activities, so that immediately upon Kahlo's death FBI agents in Mexico raided her house and made off with addresses of supposed

later in May 2002. The FBI claim a clerical error prevented it from being found until November 2002, when it was finally made available to the public, and even then it languished at the bottom of a box in the FBI archive hall in Washington. It is only by amazing luck that the present authors, whilst engaged in a much larger authoritative study of the JFK Roswell cover-up, found it and decided to dust it off and update it for the benefit of the present generation. As with so much pertaining to this incredible artifact, it is impossible to tell whether the delay was deliberate.

One thing that history teaches us is certain: the Diary has always threatened various powerful groups by its very existence. May this new edition continue to do so.

Dr. Pedersen (1956–2003)

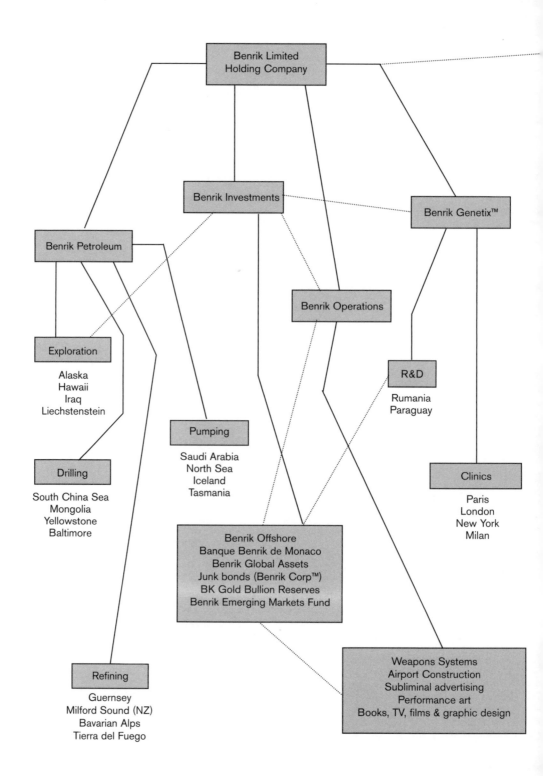

Chairman: Benrik
Chief Executive: Benrik
Vice-presidents: Ben Carey, Henrik Delehag
Executive directors: Simon Trewin, Claire Scott, Leo Hollis, Trena Keating,
Scott Waxman, Shailesh Gor, Chris Clarke, Jonas Jansson.
Non-executive directors: Richard Carey, Prue Carey, Kenneth Delehag, Anna-Lena Delehag.
Consultants: Lana Ivanyoukhina & Räkan, Kathy Peach, Katy Follain, Antony Topping, Stefanie and
Charlotte Drews, Jamie Colonna, Sophie Hewat, Mark Cole, Fiona Couper, Gaby Vinader, Joel Chovet,
Clelia Uhart, Sarah Woodruff, Charlotte Davies, Elizabeth & Alex Carey, Aunt, Eugene, Edwin Lee, Trevor Franklin,
Emily Haynes, John Hamilton, Chris Callard, Clare Pollock, Grainne Ashton, Hjalmar & Lovisa & Elin Delehag,
Jonas Delehag, Farmor & Farfar & Mormor & Morfar, Claes Kjellström, Marc Regan, TBWA STHLM,
Zoe Jaques, Åsa Fridh, Rasmus Nilsson, Lilja Ivanyukhina & Alexander Ivanyukhine, Alan Payne

Viking. Published by the Penguin Group
Penguin Books Ltd, 80, Strand, London, WC2R 0RL, England
Penguin Group US, 375 Hudson Street, New York, New York 10014, USA
Penguin Books Australia Ltd, 250 Camberwell Road, Camberwell, Victoria 3124, Australia
Penguin Books Canada Ltd, 10 Alcorn Avenue, Toronto, Ontario, Canada M4V 3B2
Penguin Books India (P) Ltd, 11 Community Centre, Panchseel Park, New Delhi – 110 017, India
Penguin Books (NZ) Ltd, Cnr Rosedale and Airborne Roads, Albany, Auckland, New Zealand
Penguin Books (South Africa) (Pty) Ltd, 24 Sturdee Avenue, Rosebank 2196, South Africa

Penguin Books Ltd, Registered Office: 80, Strand, London, WC2R 0RL, England

2

www.penguin.com
www.thiswebsitewillchangeyourlife.com

All illustrations, photography, design and
typography by Benrik, except as follows.

Where the work is not property and copyright of the authours, all attempts have been made by the
authors to contact correct copyright holders. The authors would like to gratefully thank for permission
to include the following within this edition: February 11 logo © Amnesty International; March 15 Gino's
photography layout and copy © Gino Marino (thanks again Gino!); April 24 photography © Johan Warden;
May 1 photography © Getty Images / Paul Weber; May 11 Thanx illustration © Rasmus Nilsson; May 14 text
© Prabhaker Mateti under open content license (modified slightly for purposes of humour, please excuse us
Prabhaker); May 17 illustration © Getty Images / Michele Warner; May 26 photography © Getty Images / Shuji
Kobayashi; July 7 photography © Charlotte Davies; July 26 photography © Getty Images / Ron Chapple;
September 29 thank you to HarperCollinsPublishers for the extract from The Diceman © George Cockcroft 1971;
October 25 photography © Getty Images / Laurence Monneret; November 9 photography © Robert Doisneau /
Rapho; November 20 photography © Jonas Delehag; December 19 photography © Lana Ivanyoukhina;
December 28 photography © Lana Ivanyoukhina. If there is further enquiry, please contact the authors c/o:
PFD, Drury House 34-43, Russell St, London WC2B 5HA, England

Printed in Great Britain by Butler and Tanner Ltd., Frome, Somerset
A CIP catalogue record for this book is available from the British Library

ISBN: 0-670-91462-2